12) 504

SEATTLE

Karl Lemay

D1395696

Travel better, enjoy more

ULYSSES

Travel Guides

Author	**Translation**	**Illustrations**
Karl Lemay	Danielle Gauthier	Lorette Pierson
	Suzanne Murray	Myriam Gagné
Editors		Marie-Annick Viatour
Daniel Desjardins	**Layout**	
Claude Morneau	Jenny Jasper	**Photographs**
		Cover Page
Project Director	**Cartography**	Sean O'Neill
André Duchesne	Patrick Thivierge	*Inside Pages*
	Yanik Landreville	Nick Gunderson
Project Coordinator		Seattle-King County
Jacqueline Grekin	**Computer Graphics**	Convention &
	Stéphanie Routhier	Visitors Bureau
English Editing		Camirique
Tara Salman	**Artistic Director**	
Jacqueline Grekin	Patrick Farei (Atoll)	

Distributors

AUSTRALIA: Little Hills Press, 11/37-43 Alexander St., Crows Nest NSW 2065, ☎ (612) 437-6995, Fax: (612) 438-5762

BELGIUM AND LUXEMBOURG: Vander, Vrijwilligerlaan 321, B-1150 Brussel, ☎ (02) 762 98 04, Fax: (02) 762 06 62

CANADA: Ulysses Books & Maps, 4176 Saint-Denis, Montréal, Québec, H2W 2M5, ☎ (514) 843-9882, ext.2232, 800-748-9171, Fax: 514-843-9448, www.ulysses.ca, info@ulysses.ca

GERMANY and **AUSTRIA**: Brettschneider, Fernreisebedarf, Feldfirchner Strasse 2, D-85551 Heimstetten, München, ☎ 89-99 02 03 30, Fax: 89-99 02 03 31, cf@brettschneider.de

GREAT BRITAIN and **IRELAND**: World Leisure Marketing, Unit 11, Newmarket Court, Newmarket Drive, Derby DE24 8NW, ☎ 1 332 57 37 37, Fax: 1 332 57 33 99, office@wlmsales.co.uk

ITALY: Centro Cartografico del Riccio, Via di Soffiano 164/A, 50143 Firenze, ☎ (055) 71 33 33, Fax: (055) 71 63 50

NETHERLANDS: Nilsson & Lamm, Pampuslaan 212-214, 1380 AD Weesp (NL), ☎ 0294-494949, Fax: 0294-494455, nilam@euronet.nl

PORTUGAL: Dinapress, Lg. Dr. Antonio de Sousa de Macedo, 2, Lisboa 1200, ☎ (1) 395 52 70, Fax: (1) 395 03 90

SCANDINAVIA: Scanvik, Esplanaden 8B, 1263 Copenhagen K, DK, ☎ (45) 33.12.77.66, Fax: (45) 33.91.28.82

SPAIN: Altaïr, Balmes 69, E-08007 Barcelona, ☎ 454 29 66, Fax: 451 25 59, altair@globalcom.es

SWITZERLAND: OLF, P.O. Box 1061, CH-1701 Fribourg, ☎ (026) 467.51.11, Fax: (026) 467.54.66

U.S.A.: The Globe Pequot Press, 264 Goose Lane, Guilford, CT 06437 - 0480, ☎ 1-800-243-0495, Fax: 800-820-2329, sales@globe-pequot.com

Other countries: Contact Ulysses Books & Maps (Montréal, Canada)

No part of this publication may be reproduced in any form or by any means, including photocopying, without the written permission of the publisher.

Canadian Cataloguing in Publication Data (see page 5)
© January 2000, Ulysses Travel Publications.
All rights reserved
Printed in Canada

If the Pope came to Seattle and went to Green Lake, and his hat blew off his head and went into the lake, and I walked on water, got the hat and slapped it back on his head, Seattle's headlines would read "Piniella Can't Swim".

Lou Piniella, manager of the Seattle Mariners, after his team lost the first game of the playoffs in 1995.

Table of Contents

Canadian Cataloguing in Publication Data

Lemay, Karl

       Seattle

       (Ulysses travel guide)
       Translation of: Seattle.
       Includes index.

       ISBN 2-89464-206-7

       1.Seattle (Wash.) -Guidebook. I. Title.
       II. Series

F899.S43L4613 199
917.97'7720443   C99-940868-2

Symbols

🏝	Ulysses' Favourite
☎	Telephone Number
≈	Fax Number
≡	Air Conditioning
ℜ	Restaurant
⊛	Whirlpool
ℝ	Refrigerator
K	Kitchenette
P	Parking
🐩	Pets
♿	Wheelchair Access
ℑ	Fireplace
△	Sauna
⊖	Exercise Room
pb	Private Bathroom
bkfst	Breakfast Included

ATTRACTION CLASSIFICATION

★	Interesting
★★	Worth a visit
★★★	Not to be missed

The prices listed in this guide are for the admission of one adult.

HOTEL CLASSIFICATION

The prices in the guide are for one room, double occupancy in high season.

RESTAURANT CLASSIFICATION

$	$10 or less
$$	$10 to $20 US
$$$	$20 to $30 US
$$$$	$30 and more

The prices in the guide are for a meal for one person, not including drinks and tip.

All prices in this guide are in U.S. dollars.

Write to Us

The information contained in this guide was correct at press time. However, mistakes can slip in, omissions are always possible, places can disappear, etc. The authors and publisher hereby disclaim any liability for loss or damage resulting from omissions or errors.

We value your comments, corrections and suggestions, as they allow us to keep each guide up to date. The best contributions will be rewarded with a free book from Ulysses Travel Publications. All you have to do is write us at the following address and indicate which title you would be interested in receiving (see the list at the end of guide).

Ulysses Travel Publications
4176 Rue Saint-Denis
Montréal, Québec
Canada H2W 2M5
www.ulysses.ca
E-mail: info@ulysses.ca

Thanks to:
Antonin and Gwladys; Amy, Madelaine and Eric; Jerry, Nick and Phil; Tina Beacher (Ned's); Kasey Brown, Hope Hayney, Alison McKeon and Kristine Richards (Mayflower Park Hotel); June Balli (Holiday Inn Express); David Blanford, Rochelle L. Adams and Margaret Monfort (Seattle-King County News Bureau); Brad Jones (Seattle-King County Convention & Visitors Bureau).

"We acknowledge the financial support of the Government of Canada through the Book Publishing Industry Development Program (BPIDP) for our publishing activities".

We would also like to thank SODEC (Québec) for their financial support.

List of Maps

Map Symbols

✈ **Airport**   🏌 **Golf**

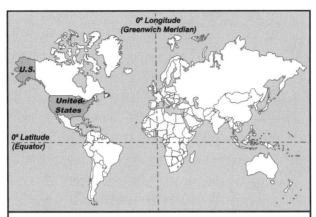

0° Longitude
(Greenwich Meridian)

U.S.

United States

0° Latitude
(Equator)

Where is Seattle?

Seattle
(47°N 122°O)

Washington State	
Population:	5 757 400 inhab.
Capital:	Olympia
Area:	176 617 km²
Currency:	U.S. Dollar

Population of Seattle	
Greater Seattle:	3 000 000 inhab.
Metropolitan Area:	534 700 inhab.

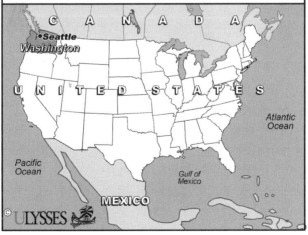

CANADA

•Seattle
Washington

UNITED STATES

Atlantic
Ocean

Pacific
Ocean

Gulf of
Mexico

MEXICO

© ULYSSES

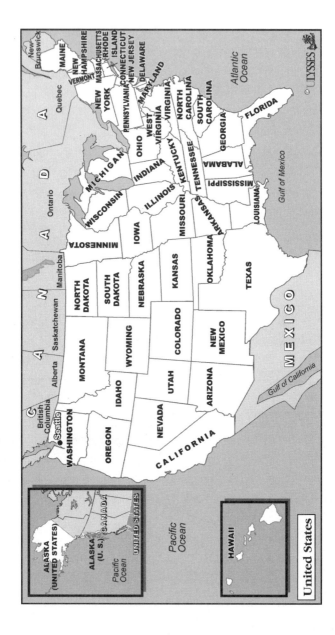

United States

Portrait

F or many, Seattle is synonymous with the good life. Myriad Starbucks cafés across town have turned it into the *caffè latte* capital of the West Coast. Others regard Seattle as a friendly and wholesome city.

T hen again, this "Princess of the Pacific Northwest" is also the birthplace of the Seattle Sound, which took off with notorious bands Nirvana and Pearl Jam.

B ut what is the true face of this city? Named after Native American chief Sealth, Seattle began modestly with a handful of American settlers and a lot of hard work. Over the years, with the coming of the railways, and thanks to the creative imagination of its citizens, Seattle matured into a much-loved city that has collected countless distinctions for its quality of life: "Best Big Place to Live in the US" (*Money Magazine*, 1995) and "Best City for Work and Family"

(*Fortune Magazine*, 1996). In short, it's good to live in Seattle.

S eattle rises on the shores of Puget Sound, a wide stretch of water flowing north to Vancouver Island and farther on to the city of Vancouver itself. In Seattle, nature is never more than a few short steps away. East of the University District, the vast Lake Washington spreads out; to the north, Lake Union flows into Puget Sound via the Chittenden Locks. And, in and around this impressive latticework of waterways, seven hills accentuate the city, bringing Rome to mind.

This western capital, however, has no excessive aspirations of grandeur, no great desire to overexpand. One word describes it best: simplicity. This longing for the simple life was embodied by Arthur Denny, one of the city's legendary founding fathers. Along with 20 others, he travelled aboard the Exact ferryboat from Portland to Seattle in 1851. Peering through his porthole at the infinite blanket of wilderness, he daydreamed of the whistle of trains pulling into his city. It was only much later that his vision became reality but it has been the dreams of the young, and not so young, that have made Seattle the city it is now.

Despite its humble beginnings, Seattle evolved into the Eldorado of the northwestern United States partly from the gold rush in 1896 and exhibitions such as the Alaska-Yukon-Pacific in 1909. Fifty-three years later, the Century 21 World's Fair exhibition portrayed Seattle as a peaceful city with an eye on the future. Today there is no doubt that the city has fulfilled this prediction: Boeing and Microsoft continuously define the cutting edge of technology, outclassing most of the competition; Starbucks cafés are a resounding success across the United States; and the chords of the Seattle Sound still reverberate and inspire rock bands despite the death of singer Kurt Cobain in April 1994.

Geography

Seattle lies in the northwest of Washington State, at latitude 47°39' N and longitude 122°17' W. All around, wherever one looks, there is water: to the east, Lake Washington extends over 22km; to the far west, a salty arm of sea called

Puget Sound flows into the Pacific Ocean, by way of the Juan de Fuca Canal; to the north, Lake Union connects with these two basins via canals like the Chittenden Locks; north of Lake Union three more lakes compose the waterscape of greater Seattle: Green, Haller and Bitter; finally, the Duwamish River flows south into Puget Sound.

The somewhat irregular layout of the streets in Seattle deserves a few words. A map of the city might lead you astray by giving you the impression that the "Emerald City" is set out like a checkerboard. Yet, nothing could be further from the truth! Considerable differences in levels – Queen Ann Hill reaches 140m whereas downtown is at sea level – cause unexpected detours; some streets in the old part of town, in the south, run for two blocks and come to a sudden stop; others zigzag up and down, from sea level to the highest point of the city, Queen Ann Hill.

All Roads Lead to – Seattle!

It is said that there are seven hills in Seattle. But, like the "100 steeples of Montreal," this was meant as a figure of speech. Indeed, east, north and south of downtown, Queen Ann Hill, First Hill, Capitol Hill and Beacon Hill provide challenges to urban planners. Yet mountains blanket the entire city, and sudden dips and jumps make you feel like you're riding on a roller coaster.

It seems that wherever you look, stunning landscapes surround you. And the minute you leave downtown Seattle, you are met from all directions by breathtaking wide-open spaces and lakes that seem as boundless as the sea.

History

Some 25,000 years ago, for reasons still unknown, tribes from northeast Asia – perhaps stalking their quarry – stepped off their continent and onto the American plateau, crossing what is now Bering Strait. Thus began the slow and very gradual peopling of this new territory. The nomads, in search of a milder climate, travelled through present-day Alaska and

Portrait

British Columbia before settling on sites which would later be known as Olympia, Everett, Snohomish and Bellevue. It is believed that the North American continent was devoid of human presence until these people arrived.

It was not until the 16th century that others began manifesting an interest in this far-off land. The Greek explorer known as Juan de Fuca was sent by the Spanish throne to "discover" this new country. His mission was to find the passageway linking the two great oceans, the Pacific and the Atlantic. Alas! Upon seeing the mouth of Puget Sound, he precipitately cried out "Eureka!" Unbeknownst to him, this passage was pure fantasy.

Naturally, others also turned their attention to this land which, from that moment on, became legendary. The Russians, in an attempt to annex these territories, twice sent Vitus Behring – the namesake of the strait – to discover the passageway that de Fuca had failed to locate. Meanwhile, the Russians established camps along the western coast of the present-day United States, between Alaska and northern California and, oblivious to the fact that others had staked a claim on this infinite territory, declared it theirs.

A diplomatic war erupted once the Russians and the Spaniards became aware of the territorial dispute in which they had become entangled. However, this political war failed to ignite any major conflict. They soon discovered that a third party, England, had joined the race to conquer this land of plenty. By sending James Cook (1778) and then George Vancouver (1792) to vanquish Vespucci's *Ameriga*, England signalled its presence to the two rivals already ensconced in the new territory. The successors to de Fuca and Behring were unable to withstand this formidable adversary for very long, as the English fleet – an undisputed killing machine – would have crushed the two adventurous nations effortlessly. Following in the footsteps of de Fuca two centuries before, Vancouver sought the passageway linking the two great oceans but, unable to find it, christened the towns, bays and other geographic sites encountered along the way using the names of his fellow crewmen.

And then the inevitable happened. After taking hold of the economy, the British had one last act to perform before declaring themselves kings and rulers of this pristine land: the spiritual conquest of the native inhabit

Fighting a Losing Battle Against the Europeans

Portrait

Clearly, the coming of Europeans disturbed the Native American communities in many ways. Diseases, such as chicken-pox, greatly affected the immune system of the Native Americans and decimated numerous tribes. Some also say that the original peoples of the modern-day State of Washington were not familiar with horses, supposedly introduced by the Spaniards. Truth or fiction? No one knows, as there exists no written document to prove, or disprove, this suggestion. Regardless, the fact remains that the Europeans considerably disrupted Native American lifestyles. The availability of various animals led to the development of the fur trade, and barter became a viable system, using alcohol as currency. The Native Americans never did recover, and alcoholism was the ruin of many Duwamish. Just the same, the firearms they received in exchange for their furs turned them into formidable hunters and allowed them to hold onto their territory for what amounted to a few meagre moments in the greater historical scheme of things.

ants. Several missionaries were sent to preach the word and evangelize the "savages". This was no easy task and many preachers lost their life in the attempt. This was the fate reserved to the Whitman clan in Walla Walla whose guinea-pigs, the Cayuse Indians, avenged themselves violently. Good doctor Whitman, convinced he was tending to the health of the atheists, accidentally took the wrong phial and poisoned the Cayuses with… laxatives and insecticides! The revenge of the Cayuse was terrible, and many clan members were scalped. And who could possibly blame the victimized Cayuses?

After Sealth Came Seattle

The cultural legacy of Seattle's first inhabitants, the Native Americans, will resound forever as the city is named after Chief Sealth, the Native American leader whose name was promptly distorted to better fit the Queen's English. And who better to represent this minority group than a man of Suquamish and Duwamish blood? This historic character was reminiscent of Louis Riel, the famous Métis leader of Manitoba, Canada, who was unjustifiably lynched to avoid a revolt amongst the Métis. Young Sealth witnessed the coming of George Vancouver in 1792 and later, in 1810, took command of both the Suquamish and Duwamish, from which point his authority remained unchallenged.

Although the chief's efforts were not in vain, we would be hard pressed to claim that the Native Americans gained much in this unfair battle over land. Despite Sealth's sustained efforts as diplomat and mediator between Native Americans and newcomers from across the Atlantic, the consequences remained dire: the Suquamish resigned themselves to inhabiting the Kitsap Peninsula while the Duwamish were forced to live where the Europeans could not follow them. The reserve "given" to the Suquamish is evidence of the European intolerance and hegemonic colonial mentality.

Chief Sealth suffered the same fate as Riel: he was submitted to a trumped-up trial and lynched soon after converting to the Anglican faith. He was buried on the Kitsap Peninsula, which overlooks the Seattle skyscrapers. And, like Riel, his likeness was immortalized in bronze after his death (corner of 5th Avenue and Denny Way). The most believed hypothesis as to how Seattle got its name suggests that the appellation Seattle is a corruption of Sealth - as the original name of New Duwamps was considered to be unattractive. Yet again, no written document exists to prove this and no hypothesis, no matter how plausible, can be considered seriously. One undisputed truth remains, however: Sealth lost his life for his peers while his enemies sought redemption by immortalizing his name in the heart of what his ancestors called the *Whulge*.

Natives and Pioneers

As mentioned above, the first people to inhabit the Seattle region were natives, namely the Duwamish and Suquamish. Scattered around a strait and a gulf extending over 560km², these nations attended to their daily tasks next to this stretch of water they called *Whulge* (in Suquamish), reaping the harvests of the sea and nourishing themselves with salmon. The *Whulge* was later renamed "Puget Sound" by Captain George Vancouver who, in a show of friendship, honoured galley mate Peter Puget. Thus began the slow but certain colonization of the region and the quick eradication of the ancestral ways of the forsaken nomadic people.

This dramatic historical backdrop did not prevent a handful of hardy souls from venturing out into the middle of nowhere in search of a better life. The spirit of New York and Boston already loomed over the heads of these men, undeterred by bitter cold or hard work. This is the story of David Denny and Lee Terry, two of the 21 adventurers who left Cherry Grove, Illinois in 1851 to try their luck at the other end of the United States. Their destination was Portland, Oregon, the limelight of the American West at the time. Travelling first by wagon, they sailed into Seattle aboard the Exact ferry. The Cherry Grove emigrants were considered to be the first men to have lived in Seattle; in reality, however, only the very bold actually settled down in the area, without forming any real community. Denny, Terry and the others set sail for Alki Point situated on the shores of actual Puget

Sound, more specifically in West Seattle. After rapidly exploring the surroundings, they chose this site as the location of their downtown: the deeper waters of Elliot Bay would facilitate the mooring of ships and ferry boats. But to survive, these men first had to find a way to make a living.

Their prayers were answered when the San Francisco *Leonesa* anchored near Seattle. The ship's captain immediately noticed the abundance of timber in the area and, concluding that he could conduct business with these high-spirited men, purchased 10,770m of lumber. In the year 1852, this was a very good omen.

Seattle's first businessman, Henri Yesler, made his fortune operating a sawmill. At the time, exporting lumber to San Francisco and Portland made up most of the town's commercial activities. A type of slide, called "Skid Road", not to be confused with "Skid Row" (a boom town full of saloons where cowboys, vagrants and drunks used to meet), was built to transport the blocks of wood to the port. New workers gladly set up house around Yesler's sawmill and the neighborhood became known as Yesler Wharf. Very soon, brothels, saloons, private residences and offices spread out over 300m^2 of muddy earth. This neighborhood actively contributed to Seattle's first economic boom and, for over 20 years, was the hub of all commercial and social activities to such an extent that Skid Road was re-christened Yesler Way in honour of this very unique tycoon.

Another of the fledging city's first heroes was Asa Mercer, also one of the 21 pioneers to set foot on the territory delimiting modern-day Seattle. He set out to accomplish a simple goal: find educated, refined and single women so that this citadel of the West might prosper and, more importantly, propagate. The difficult conditions, not to mention the poor infrastructure, certainly did not entice educated young women to venture out to the other end of a young continent whose history, like that of the American West, had no laurels to rest on. New England welcomed Mercer with open arms and provided him with 13 young women (a fateful number?) who agreed to follow him blindly to America's far west. It goes without saying that strength of character was required to survive in such primitive conditions; a girl would have to roll up her sleeves and accept her lot without complaint. Mercer's mission was a success: in less than a month all 13 maidens found a husband.

Fanning the Flames of the Great Seattle Fire

In the not so distant past, a single spark became the symbol of a disaster of titanic proportions. To make matters worse, the gods seemed determined to burden the fate of the proud and resourceful Seattle dwellers. Let us explain. As you may have guessed, a great fire raged through Seattle in 1889. All it took was a pot of glue set ablaze and a warehouse full of alcohol to cause this bastion built upon simple dreams go up in smoke. Nothing could have been more demoralizing.

It was 2pm when the drama erupted. Columns of smoke seen from kilometres away announced that a fire was raging in the area of Puget Sound. On June 6, 1889, 58 blocks of houses vanished, as if by magic. Citizens quickly took action to stop the destruction but the gods seemed bent on rattling the nerves of these adventurers cum residents when water reserves ran out! They did their best to stop this heaven-sent disaster but without success. Some even used slabs of sidewalk (!) to smoulder the flames but again this was to no avail.

The next day all that could be done was to take stock of the widespread damage. This bleak hour called for no half-measures. From that moment on, wooden structures were forbidden in the downtown area, and all buildings were to be rebuilt using stones and bricks. Then life resumed its normal course. Tents were set up and merchants continued as if nothing had happened – business as usual. The fire lasted six hours, and when it finally died down, the devil must have flown into a rage! By the same token, it was decided to remedy the embarrassing mud-flooded sidewalks. The Seattle Underground was born and from that moment on, the residents of Seattle would never so much as dirty the tips of their shoes.

The Railway: All Aboard!

From that moment on, Seattle and Tacoma began a rivalry over which city would obtain the next railway. The arrival of the Mercer "maidens" served to reinforce the frenzy provoked by word of a forthcoming railroad that would make everything so much easier. But destiny decided otherwise and the Northern Pacific Railroad, hoping to broaden its horizons, chose Tacoma, much to the chagrin of Seattle's denizens. But who could question this choice? Seattle's muddy earth was prone to landslides. Tacoma won the first inning if only by default. This disappointment shattered the hopes of these souls who ached for a simple life. But we now know that their happiness was merely postponed. The people of Seattle swallowed their pride and endured the rigours of travelling to and from their town...by boat.

A wind of hope swept through the entire city when a rumour spread that James J. Hill planned to extend his railway, the Great Northern Line, to the Emerald City, so called because of the numerous green spaces around it. Impatience peaked in record time and, in 1883, the small town was abuzz with excitement. People were increasingly dissatisfied with the train service provided at Tacoma, southwest of Seattle; they no longer cared to beg a generous neighbour for its railway, they wanted their own! Over the next 10 years, the rumour of a coming railway lead to an impressive demographic explosion in Seattle. However, it was only in 1893 that the gossip was confirmed and Seattle, thanks to James J. Hill, could finally boast of having its very own railway tracks.

To put it mildly, the mere talk of a railway was enormously beneficial to Seattle. In 10 years alone, its population skyrocketed from 3,500 in 1880 to 43,000 in 1890. This contributed to numerous success stories as many a brave soul found a job in the lumber exportation business or in the coal mines.

Clearly, such rapid demographic growth demanded that the city attend rapidly to the new needs of its citizens. First and foremost on the list of pressing problems to contend with was the draining of mud swamps: actual streets and sidewalks were built. Slow and outdated horsedrawn wagons were replaced by electric wagons. Finally, it had little choice but to install an efficient sewage system to dissipate the foul smells emanating from all corners of the city. Seattle blossomed rapidly and was ready to follow suit to the 20th century with its chin up and its heart filled with hope.

Seattle and Tacoma: A Relentless Rivalry

Let's step back in time and take a closer look at the rivalry between Seattle and Tacoma. The advent of the railway to Seattle removed any advantage Tacoma had over her northern neighbour and marked the beginning of a symbolic war between these two competitors of the State of Washington. The populations of the two cities grew by leaps and bounds at a comparable rate. As mentioned previously, Seattle went from 3,500 inhabitants in 1880 to 43,000 in 1890. During this time, south of the Emerald City, Tacoma's population increased from 1,000 inhabitants in 1880 to 36,000 in 1890. But Seattle's popularity won out and Tacoma's community failed to thrive over the next 20 years (from 1890 to 1910).

Strangely enough, the great fire of 1889 actually helped Seattle. From that moment until 1910, the city grew at a pace comparable to such metropolises as Los Angeles and Chicago. By pooling their efforts, local plumbers, blacksmiths, bricklayers and electricians provided Seattle with a workforce that was perfectly geared to the challenges brought forth by the 20th century. Tacoma, for its part, was unable to recover from the 1893 depression, and Seattle was crowned Princess of the American Northwest.

After a decade of competition with Tacoma, Seattle was invaded by the nouveau riche who wished to sweep away the simple lifestyle that had characterized the city until then. This new breed of wealthy urbanites advocated a more modern look as, money permitting, the rustic look was passé. And as the saying goes, "Money is no object."

The city hired Frederick Law Jr. and John C. Olmsted, sons of the famous landscape artist Frederick Law Olmsted who designed Central Park in New York City and Mont-Royal Park in Montréal. A new direction in the city seemed to be winding its way under the very noses of the less affluent citizens. The Olmsted brothers devised a series of avenues to join all the city's present and future parks. They advocated the segregation of neighborhoods, a first in the city's history. In reality, they

Portrait

wished to give a modern allure to the Emerald City by separating the rich from the poor neighborhoods. The city's simple, unadorned style was tossed aside to make way for open spaces devoid of natural scenery.

All these urban changes could not have taken place without Seattle supplanting another long-time rival: Portland, Oregon. The two cities grew at practically the same rate except that, in 1880, Portland was already home to 17,000 inhabitants. However, the economic and industrial factors mentioned above helped Seattle progress more rapidly than Portland and account for 237,000 souls by 1910, thus 30,000 more than Portland.

Gold Rush or Far-fetched Dream?

On August 16, 1896, George Washington Carmack and two Native American friends, Shookum Jim and Tagish Charley, discovered gold deep in the Yukon territory, Canada, right next to where the Klondike River flows into the Yukon River. The news spread like wildfire to Fortymile, a small village by the Yukon River. Over night, the hamlet turned into a mining town, as hordes of men hurried there in hopes of finding gold. A year later, the Klondike gold rush officially began when 68 rich prospectors returned to the 48th parallel with their pockets filled with gold.

The first ship to leave this land of milk and honey was the *Excelsior*. It dropped anchor in San Francisco on July 15, 1897 stirring a bit of excitement. However, Californians were no strangers to this kind of escapade and its often disastrous consequences, and the thought of digging the Alaskan soil for a few gold nuggets did little to whet their interest.

Two days later, the steamboat *Portland* docked in Seattle. Surprised by the quantity of gold on board, Beriah Brown, a journalist for the *Post-Intelligencer*, published an article raving about the ton of gold found by the foolhardy men. In truth, there were over two tons of gold nestled safely aboard the Portland. The article created a frenzy across Seattle. Even the mayor resigned in order to be part of this episode of American history!

However, the enthusiasm of these men on the road to riches (or so they hoped) was held in check by certain requirements: since the journey north to Alaska was very difficult, prospectors were required to bring enough food and clothing

The Klondike Craze

Seattle enjoyed its first boom thanks to Erastus Brainerd, a former journalist who headed a publicity campaign for the Seattle Chamber of Commerce inciting Klondike adventurers to buy their equipment in Seattle. Several towns vied for this "privilege," notably Vancouver, Portland and Tacoma but Brainerd made sure that Seattle obtained five times more publicity than other cities. He sent articles to all the major newspapers in the United States thus provoking a mass exodus to Seattle and sealing its fortune.

Brainerd won his bet: Seattle became known as *the* city to buy supplies and all types of articles, from warm clothes and condensed milk to dehydrated potatoes. Many merchants capitalized on this golden opportunity: the streets became busier than ever before and mounds of top-quality foodstuffs bearing the "Klondike" label proved to be such a success that stocks were virtually pillaged. But as in any kind of business, unscrupulous merchants played upon the naivete of customers by selling gophers and Siberian huskies supposedly trained to find gold. These dogs quickly became collectors' items and merchants sold them like hot cakes. However, at night, when all were asleep, brave souls kept watch for prowlers who sought to make off with these much sought-after animals.

to survive at least one year, hence the saying "A ton of gold, a ton of goods."

It is true that many gold diggers struck it rich be-cause of this daring expedi-tion. Obviously, most of the gold had already been panned before the thou-sands of opportunists flocked to Alaska from boom towns like Seattle, Vancouver, Portland and Tacoma. More than one man lost all his possessions in this foolhardy adventure. In spite of itself, Seattle prospered due to the raid on food supplies and clothes. Those who did strike gold returned to Seattle and opened lucrative businesses; yet many of those greedy for riches and glory were left penniless. It is rumoured that half of the $200 million of this Alaskan escapade were reinvested in Seattle. It is thanks to these riches reaped from the gold rush that Seattle secured its place as capital of the northwestern United States.

Prosperity and Glory: Easy Come, Easy Go

The Olmsted brothers remained at the centre of the reconstruction of Seattle by participating in a project called *City Beautiful* in 1903. This pompous project involved building sumptuous villas for the well-to-do of the region, which was done in no time at all, given the indisputable talent of the brothers.

Yet, had it not been for the 1896 gold rush, all these grandiose projects would never have seen the light of day. Besides, since the Olmsted brothers' original plan, Seattle had undergone

considerable changes. Firstly, the Pacific Northwest metropolis now included the town of Ballard, a large region south of Seattle as well as suburbs that extended west. Secondly, the suburbs were increasing at the speed of light to say nothing of breakaway entrepreneurs who ran their businesses on the outskirts of town. Consequently, means of transportation had to be provided to this sprawling new population. Tramways were introduced to service the vicinity of Lake Union, Capital Hill, First Hill and Queen Ann Hill. By the same token, new neighborhoods developed around Lake Washington as a consequence of the tramway route.

The wealthy continued to spend money like water and, in an effort to showcase their new home, organized the Alaska-Yukon-Pacific exhibit in 1909. Seattle prospered from this experience and became known across the United States. Afterwards, in 1911, the Union Pacific and Milwaukee Road became the fourth railway to lay its tracks across the city. Seattle looked more and more like a modern city, distancing itself from its age-old provincial roots.

The Olmsted brothers completed their lofty project. Be that as it may, Virgil Bogue, a talented engineer, architect and occasional Seattle resident, presented his own Plan of Seattle. He drew his inspiration from traditional fine arts: tree-lined boulevards, intersecting avenues branching off in all directions and leading to neo-classical buildings, as well as ample shopping centres. Put simply, Bogue wanted to turn Seattle into a Paris of the New World. Not to mention the masterpiece he planned to design, a grandiose civic centre, like those found in Denver, Cleveland and San Francisco.

However, the 1912 elections and the No vote cast by the people thwarted Bogue and his grand dreams. Paradoxically, another grandiose project was accepted and in 1914 the Smith Tower became the tallest building west of the Mississippi...In any event, all was not lost for Bogue who, with the help of well-informed and influential businessmen, sold the city on the idea of a seafront, eventually called the Waterfront.

Call to Arms

World War I gave a considerable boost to the economy as well as to the everyday life of most citizens. As the following numbers reveal, from 1909 to 1919, the number of industries,

number of workers, costs of materials and market value of products rose frenetically. In 1909, 753 companies employed 11,523 workers, at an average cost of $28 million, generating a revenue of $50 million; in 1919, these numbers increased sixfold: 1,229 businesses employed 40,000 workers at costs of $149 million and a generated revenue of $274 million. Yet, it was the construction of the Chittenden Locks in 1917. A canal connecting Laked Washington and Union to Puget Sound, that was the high point of the decade.

The city's growth was not limited by any means to this salient achievement. In 1918, Seattle also obtained the rights to the Stone & Webster tramways, which greatly facilitated commuting in this city in full expansion. In later years, other railways linked the Emerald City to Everett and Tacoma.

Changes continuously threatened the serenity that had always characterized this small city more concerned with stability than modernization. For instance, the downtown was moved from Pioneer Square, deemed unsuitable for daily commercial activities, to the former site of the University of Washington, affectionately nicknamed Metropolitan Tract.

This presented many local and national architects with an opportunity to put their talent to work. And what more could they ask for than such an idyllic canvas framed by boundless mountains and fields? Given Seattle's gorgeous backdrop, the immanent beauty of the sites waiting to be built was easily forgotten. Henry Bittman, Charles Bebb, Carl Gould, Abraham Albertson and numerous others spent many long hours mulling over the types of buildings that would define the face of Seattle as it turned steadfastly towards the year 1900.

We spoke earlier of Skid Row, a blighted area where swindlers and travelling bandits indulged in drinking and debauchery. This expression conveyed the decadence of the 1920s, when unemployment was on the rise and the 1929 stock-market crash impoverished unfortunate souls around the world. All the same, the 1920s began on the right foot and seemed to announce quite the contrary: the diversified economy and substantial rise in employment led all to believe that they were nearing the promised land. However, nothing was further from the truth. The years after World War One were synonymous with massive layoffs.

Stepping back further in time, we see how much the national strike of 1919 affected Seattle. Led by Dave Beck, teamsters protested against the despotic control of the Waterfront by a certain Harry Bridge. In short, it looked that the dream of Seattle was coming to an end and that a rude awakening was in store for all.

During this period, like today, politicians often served as scapegoats. President Hoover was particularly hit hard when a group of unemployed workers gathered outside Seattle and created Hooverville, a vast, dilapidated camp south of Pioneer Square. This area is now Safeco Field (see p 216) and is home to Seattle's baseball team, the Mariners.

However, hope always seemed to triumph in Seattle where, despite the bourgeois flights of fancy of the turn of the century, the firm belief in austerity remained anchored in its well-grounded citizens.

Private and public gardens continued to flourish, vegetables and other produce continued to grow, and everything seemed to be going beautifully. In fact, the suburbs and less popular neighborhoods of the Emerald City benefited from the Great Depression, an economic crisis unprecedented in the history of the United States. A return to a simpler lifestyle was advocated, and the capitalistic waves caused by the gold rush upstarts were quelled at last.

Not withstanding its small-town convictions, downtown Seattle did not recover its past momentum and developed but slightly. The city's sagging economy was somewhat revitalized with the formation of a new retail district. But, unlike the turn of the century, when ideas of grandeur were ubiquitous, Seattle could no longer compare itself to major U.S. cities like San Francisco, Los Angeles and Boston.

In the wake of this sombre period, Seattle slowly rekindled its joie de vivre and culture became its new focal point. A fresh, and perhaps more enthusiastic generation of architects carried on works began by the likes of Albertson, Bebb, Bittman and Gould. The new face of modern Seattle started to emerge after World War II. This generation of young architects, which included Fred Bassetti, Paul Hayden Kirk, Roland Terry and Victor Steinbrueck, added the final touches to their architectural works around 1946. They were particularly fond of Craftsman, Prairie and Shingle styles as well as the

Japanese models of Yeon and Belluschi (especially in the area around Portland). Paul Thirty, a graduate from the University of Washington, was lauded for the international-style residences he introduced to the State of Washington.

For the most part, proud Seattle citizens or residents of the State of Washington, these architects were praised for the local flavor they infused into their buildings. Their reputation was made, at least on the West Coast.

Like in California, the construction of theatres and concert halls revealed a tastelessness typical of western boom towns turned big cities. Tycoons and patrons made generous contributions to the arts for the common good of the townspeople, who tended to be more pragmatic than artistic.

This architectural extravaganza gave rise to a growing number of problems, such as the under-financing of the city's tramway system, which hadn't been profitable for a long time. Thus, the forerunner of the present-day Metro Bus System (see p 104) was ushered out.

Other than the Native Americans who lived peacefully on the shores of Puget

Portrait

Sound during the 19th century, we have yet to mention the various other ethnic groups that populate the city. Well let's talk about it.

Seattle unfortunately underwent some ugly racist episodes as its population became more and more diversified. World War II caused unprecedented waves of xenophobia towards Japanese residents, some of whom had been living in the city for several generations. They were imprisoned in Nazi-style concentration camps. Some managed to escape and, despite all the risks this entailed, return to their homeland.

Afro-Americans weren't much luckier although the racism they suffered was somewhat more discrete. For the most part, they came to Seattle to earn their living working in the factories. But, as the 1960s revealed, the Afro-American population was soon confined to a ghetto blandly referred to as Central Area, next to Highway 5.

"Fly Like an Eagle": The Advent of Boeing

A period of weak economic activity between the two World Wars was followed by a boom after the Second World War.

Without a doubt, the enterprise that distinguished itself most during this period was Boeing, enriched by the wars of the century. The company developed at such a rate in the field of aeronautics that it quickly ranked amongst the most important and innovative businesses in the United States. Over time, Boeing climbed to the top of the economic ladder in the Pacific Northwest.

However, it wasn't the only company to flourish to such a degree. Following in the successful footsteps of Boeing, the naval rearmament industry temporarily revitalized the naval industry in Puget Sound during the 1930s. In the public sector, Seattle City Light used the ubiquitous water sources, namely the Skagit River, to develop hydroelectric power.

World War II directly contributed to Seattle's prosperity. This economic growth – which continues today albeit somewhat unevenly – put marine and aeronautical construction at the forefront of development. In addition, a string of naval facilities (and the U.S. army) established themselves in the region, contributing to the success of Boeing. This also instigated mass immigration and the construction of simple homes for all the workers. Although the period between the two wars did not distinguish itself by noteworthy architectural developments, it did allow the people of Seattle to profit from the services offered by a city in full economic ferment. The expansion after World War II was only just beginning. In no time, the State of Washington saw its population double, as did the city of Seattle.

William Boeing founded his company in 1916 on the shores of Lake Union. Soon after, he claimed the land beside the Duwamish River, where he lay the foundations of an enterprise that still rules over Puget Sound. Because he initially had only one client, the federal government, in 1952, he decided to try his luck in the private sector. The construction of the Boeing 707 brought unimaginable dividends. This plane took off in 1959 and Boeing, both pioneer and ruler in the commercial aeronautics industry, swiftly secured a series of contracts around the world. In a few years, aviation became the centre of high technology in the United States; Boeing then launched the 727, a smaller plane, the 737 and, finally, the enormous 747.

Residential Decentralization: Welcome to the Suburbs!

Between 1950 and 1960, the inhabitants of Seattle spread north and east of Lake Washington, and the anti-urban mentality that characterized the beginning of the century reappeared. Paradoxically, critics loudly accused suburbanization of being nonsensical, provincial and anti-intellectual: ranches as far as the eye could see, the increase of unsightly commercial streets, in short, the profit and inertia that didn't dominate pioneers finally caught up with the young city. However, despite everything, this monotonous kind of urbanism spawned quaint residential neighborhoods reminiscent of Seattle at the beginning of the 20th century, except for the cars that replaced the trams.

This territorial expansion greatly worried the Native American population, who did not understand what was happening to their land and to the natural beauty of their surroundings. The growth of Boeing led to ecological problems, turning Lake Washington and Puget Sound into contaminated seas of pollution.

The bridges, such as the one spanning Lake Washington and connecting Seattle with the suburbs east of the lake, no longer sufficed as traffic reached monstrous proportions. Many proposals were studied. James Ellis undertook steps to unite several towns in and around Seattle to create one large Seattle metropolis, thus the name of his project, Metro. But the 1952 elections put a stop to Ellis's enthusiasm, and his vision was cast aside. Ellis then decided to exclude a number of towns he had originally included in his proposal; located south of Seattle, these towns cared little about cleaning up the waterways north of their homes... His proposal was finally accepted in 1958 when the suburbanites became favorable to such an endeavor, perhaps showing even more enthusiasm than city dwellers.

However, the Metro project underwent many changes: it now had to include the implementation of a sewage system in the city and the newly annexed additions to the metropolis. Soon after World War II, Seattle annexed Mercer Island, Lake Hills, Lake Forest Oak, Kenmore, Juanita, Medina, Hunt's Point, Clyde Hill, Bellevue, Newport and Bryn Mawr. Ten years after the start of this major urban renewal, the residents had a much greater appreciation of Lake Washington, and the beaches of Puget Sound were once again covered in fine sand instead of garbage.

Entrepreneurs and Celebrities at the End of the Millenium

It was feared for some time that the entrepreneurship and strong ideologies of the past would forever disappear. Yet a few events illustrate that Seattle was not content to ride the wave of its past exploits. A brief drop in air traffic sounded the alarm in Puget Sound and Boeing was forced to lay off employees, as it had done after World War II. As for the rest of the United States, it was deeply involved in the new war of the hour, Vietnam, and its economic activities continued to generate substantial profits.

Seattle slowly overcame this crisis and, in 1973 and 1974, as a full-blown recession hit the United States from coast to coast, the city had already begun its ascent and was ready to regain any lost ground. It was at this time that the Princess of the Pacific Northwest plunged into environmental causes. Its new generation, armed with a "greener" attitude, started to question many

Bill Gates

Bill Gates (1955-), child prodigy and founder of Microsoft, entered the world of software at the tender age of 13 when he created a computer program to play tic-tac-toe. He made his grand entrance into Harvard University in 1973 where he studied with Steve Ballmer and adapted the computer language BASIC (invented by John Kemeny and Thomas Kurtz in the 1960s) for the development of the first personal computer, the MITS Altair. Half-way through his university studies, he dropped everything and dedicated himself body and soul to the company he founded with childhood friend Paul Allen. In a flash, Gates took the lead in the computer industry by making his software fun and easy to use.

In 1980, while Microsoft was still a fledgling company, IBM offered Gates the opportunity to develop the DOS operating system as it was in a hurry to launch its personal computer. Gates accepted on condition that he reserve the right to sell his software to other manufacturers. IBM accepted, believing it was invincible... and, a few years later, Microsoft became even bigger than IBM!

In 1995, Gates and co-authors Nathan Myhrvold and Peter Rinearson published *The Road Ahead* in which they expanded upon the future of software and its impact on society. The next year Gates re-edited the book, adding computer network interactivity and new means of communication. Biotechnology was another theme that interested him, which is why he invested in the ICOS Corporation and bought stocks in the Chiroscience Group. Yet another of Gate's pet projects was the Corbis Corporation, which backed a business specialized in photo archives and visual art sourced from many private and public collections around the world.

A dramatic turn of events occurred in May 1998, the federal government and 20 U.S. states launched a lawsuit against Microsoft, accusing the mega-enterprise of violating the antitrust law. Netscape, a pioneer in Internet browsers, was having the carpet pulled from under its feet by Microsoft, which packaged its own browser, Internet Explorer, with its famous Windows operating system. Today, Internet Explorer runs on 90% of the personal computers around the world. In November 1999, more than a year after the hearings began, the court ruled that Microsoft is in a monopolistic situation. Microsoft is not, however, in immanent danger of crumbling – an appeal is pending.

anti-ecological precepts, turning Seattle into the cornerstone of social renewal. Having grown up in the suburbs, this younger crowd was determined to have a say in the urban planning of its city. This consciousness helped revitalize devastated districts and revive interest in historic quarters, such as Pike Place Market and Pioneer Square, thereby boosting the city's economy.

Anxiety over the lack of entrepreneurship was quickly shed when a consortium of businesspeople and politicians launched the Century 21 exhibit, or World's Fair, in 1962. As the previous exhibit had done in 1909, this major celebration opened many doors for Seattle and made its reputation around the globe. Over 9 million people visited the site, and many of the structures specially built for the exposition still stands today as Seattle's new "totem", including the Space Needle, and the Monorail. Events in the 1960s and 1970s instilled a climate in which cultural diversity, environmental awareness and economic dynamism lived in perfect harmony. However, it was mostly the international businesses, such as Microsoft, Weyerhaeuser, Nordstrom and Price Costco, and of course Starbucks, that put Seattle on the map, as did the virtual bookstore Amazon.com, a leader on the Internet. Even so, what kept Seattle in the headlines was the emergence of punk-rock bands like Nirvana and Pearl Jam who redefined music in the 1990s.

Economy

Since its early beginnings, Seattle's greatest strength has been its diversified economy. When the town was officially founded in 1869, the coal found in great abundance around Seattle was the first raw material to be exploited. Its exportation to cities like San Francisco and Portland ensured the viability of this industry in Seattle. Furthermore, the railway allowed businesses to ship their goods quickly to nearby cities. At the very beginning of Seattle's short history, timber was another major stronghold of the economy, as the region was densely forested. However, the forests were gradually depleted and today timber barely represents 1% of the city's economic production.

Coal and railways eventually gave way to more modern spheres of activity such as computer technology, biotechnology, medical equipment and environmental engineering. In fact, these various industries reduced the unemployment

rate to 9.5% in 1990. Biotechnology alone shows impressive numbers: a revenue of $1.6 billion and 10,000 jobs in the 100 companies in the region. The Boeing conglomerate, founded in 1916, employs the majority of Seattle residents. As for Bill Gates, he continues to cash in on the success of his world-renowned Microsoft company; however, in the Seattle region alone, there are about 1,500 other companies that develop software and personal computers.

Over the past few years, more and more companies have chosen Seattle as their stomping grounds due to its qualified labour force, its fields of education and research that respond to contemporary needs, as well as its infrastructures and modern transport system. In addition, the service sector wins first prize as "best employer" since 28% of the city's wage-earners work in this field. Second prize goes to the wholesale and retail industry (24%), whereas other principal fields of activity are the public sector (16%), non-perishable goods (11%) and transportation, including aviation (6.3%). Amongst the prosperous and respected companies based in Seattle, the largest businesses yield astronomical amounts of money every year: in 1995, the Boeing aerospatial engineering firm declared a revenue of $19 billion; Price Costco, a chain of warehouses selling products at discount prices and owner of Price Club, $18 billion; Weyerhaeuser, a pulp and paper company, $12 billion; and Microsoft, the software giant, $6 billion.

Tourism Infrastructure

The tourism industry in Seattle and the King County region generates a multitude of jobs and attracts some 24 million visitors every year. The metropolitan region is served by over 46,000 fervent travel specialists who counsel, lodge and feed, so to speak, all walks of nationalities from Japanese to Canadians. In fact, there are many services and sites for travelers such as the Meydenbauer Center and the Bell Harbor International Conference Center, which receives many speakers, and the Washington State Convention and Trade Center, which can accommodate up to 11,000 conference participants. Over 8,000 hotel rooms, 2,200 restaurants and a range of noteworthy tourist attractions, such as the famous Space Needle, make staying in Seattle an enjoyable experience.

International Trade

For several years now, Seattle hosted many international conferences and major events that have made this little-known city famous. In 1990, Seattle hosted the Goodwill Games; in 1993, the Asia Pacific Economic Cooperation (APEC) took place in the Emerald City; Russian president Boris Yeltsin toured the cultural capital of the Pacific Northwest in 1994; in 1995, a conference on technology even attracted King Harald V of Norway; and in 1996 Seattle hosted the conference of the Quadrilateral Trade Ministerial. In 1999, it also hosted the controversial UTO meetings.

The State of Washington, in spite of the fact that its low population represents only 2% of the total population of the United States (approximately 4.9 million inhabitants), is an American export leader. In fact, one out of every four jobs relies on this sector of activity. For the most part, the state exports transportation equipment, timber, paper and publishing equipment and electronics to principal international partners such as Japan, Canada, China, South Korea and Taiwan.

Population

According to the 1996 census, the population of Seattle has not increased in 30 years. In 1970 the population hovered at around 530,000 inhabitants but decreased in to 494,000 in 1980. Today, Seattle's population is 534,000, approximately the same as it was in 1970. What made the difference was the greater Seattle region: like most large U.S. cities, the suburbs have gained in numbers at the detriment of the city's centre. In 1970, the suburbs were home to nearly 2 million people. Yet, in less than 30 years, they have increased by one million people, which says a lot. Founded by American immigrants, Seattle is not what is commonly referred to as a multicultural city. There is, of course, the traditional Chinatown (also called the International District) but Seattle's ethnic diversity virtually stops there. Contrary to other American megalopolises, Seattle is made up of 75% Caucasians (Europeans and Americans combined) and only a small percentage of visible minorities. North of Seattle, however, a group of Scandinavians who emigrated to the U.S. between 1890 and 1910 form a small community.

Chinatown, or the International District, is situated southeast of downtown and is home to most of the Asians living in the Emerald City. The neighborhood has often changed names from Chinatown, to Japantown, to Manilatown and, recently, to the more politically correct International District. This neighborhood includes a medley of different nationalities from Asia and the Pacific Islands: Chinese, Filipinos, Japanese, Vietnamese, Koreans, etc. These varied ethnic groups represent 11% of the city's population.

Afro-Americans compose little more than 10% of Seattle's population. Most live in the Central Area district (South Seattle), birthplace of some of the big names in jazz, blues and rock 'n roll. Examples include Ray Charles, legendary pianist of rhythm and blues, jazz and popular melodies; Quincy Jones, singer-songwriter and, more illustriously, Michael Jackson's producer in the 1980s; and the enfant terrible of the 1960s, Jimi Hendrix, whose convolutions mixed with blues, abusive distortion and acid trips influenced a whole generation.

The Central Area dates back to the first years of the city when, in 1883, an entrepreneur by the name of William Grose bought 5ha east of First Hill, Seattle's first neighborhood. During the 1930s, music lovers flocked to neighborhood jazz and blues clubs to listen to the fresh new rhythms. Thanks to such nightclubs, as well as to institutions like the Langston Hugues Cultural Arts Center and Mount Zion Baptist Church, whose congregation is mostly Afro-American, the neighborhood has managed to keep its past very much alive. It is also here that the memory of Martin Luther King Jr., the late defender of Afro-American rights in the United States, is honoured by a park. A series of plaques recalls the significant events of his life in this 1.5ha park, and a 10m high sculpture stands proudly in the midst of a reflecting pool.

Let us conclude with a final word on the Native Americans who, as elsewhere in North America, represent a small fraction of the population. In the middle of the 19th century, before the arrival of people of European origin, the Duwamish and Suquamish ruled over the lands of the Pacific Northwest. Today, however, their descendents are few in number: a little over 7,000 Inuit, Aleutians and Native Americans, in other words less than 2% of the total population, live in the greater Seattle region.

Culture

Architecture

It is in what is presently known as the Pioneer Square Historic District that Seattle's first inhabitants settled down in 1853. Today, important personages such as Henry Yesler (who lent his name to Yesler Way, formerly Skid Road) and Doc Maynard are honoured with statues and buildings. And, although these structures are inanimate, one can still sense the exuberance that the early settlers might have felt as they went about their business in this neighborhood. Back then, the city was made up of a few basic wooden buildings, such as Henry Yesler's sawmill, a local business around which Seattle's very first neighborhood gradually evolved. From this point, the population increased by leaps and bounds, from a handful of souls, when the town was founded, to 12,000 inhabitants in 1885.

But this bright beginning was interrupted by an unprecedented tragedy in Seattle's history: the great fire of 1889. Following this disaster, wooden buildings were forbidden and the town was rebuilt using bricks and stones. The biggest changes to this downcast little city came over the next few years when major urban developments, such as the Denny Regrade, were undertaken. Sections of the city were raised over 6m, turning three-storey buildings into two-storey buildings. Stores were moved up from the ground to the second floor, and sidewalks were laid over the rubble. Today, it is possible to visit this early Seattle called the Seattle Underground.

One of Seattle's notable particularities was that it was built on a range of hills and mountains that rendered even the most simple activities, such as walking or driving, difficult. Several ideas were proposed to make the city more favorable to the daily activities of its inhabitants. However, only one of the urban proposals ever saw the light of day. R.H. Thompson, a city engineer since 1892, succeeded in creating the only truly flat section of the city: the Denny Regrade, formerly called Denny Hill. This began in 1902, when water from Lake Union was propelled with watering hoses onto the steep incline of Denny Hill. The mud and soil were then pushed down to Elliot Bay, creating what is now known as the Waterfront. This first stage ended in 1911, and the last part of Denny Hill was completely cleared away in 1929-1930.

In 1907, mayor Charles H. Burnett, in a bid to encourage local farmers, helped found Pike Place Market, a public market where cultivators could sell their produce. From 1907 to 1917, wagons were gradually replaced by buildings in which farmers displayed the fruits of their labour. In 1912, the Corner Market Building was also opened with the help of Thomas and Grainger, and in 1927 over 400 farmers sold their wares in this market. World War II, however, put a stop to the development of these thriving markets. Local authorities decided that they were no longer as profitable. Architect Victor Streinbrueck became the champion defender of the Pike Place Market and leader of the "Friends of the Market" group. However, it was only in 1971, during municipal elections, that the friends of the market were brought into consideration and that Pike Place Market – and eventually Pioneer Square – became a historic landmark, covering 3ha.

The end of World War I marked the beginning of a strong contrast in the city as the higher buildings of downtown, northwest of the Pioneer Square Historic District, clashed with the older surrounding buildings. In fact, between 1892 and 1911, houses and stores along Madison Street, James Street and Yesler Way rarely exceeded 8m in height.

Today, these dwellings have given way to skyscrapers of such metropolitan heights as 30m. Unfortunately, the downtown was forever separated from the Waterfront by the Alaskan Highway, built in the 1950s in the western part of the city. As for the Waterfront, it presents the usual array of restaurants, docks and fishing boats. Also noteworthy is the Public Aquarium, built in 1968. Finally, northwest of Pier 70, the dignified Myrtle Edwards Park, designed by engineers Kelly, Pitzelko, Fritz and Forsen, as well as architects Jongejan and Gerrard, revitalized the area alongside Elliot Bay. Built in 1963, Interstate 5 also dramatically altered the face of this city, dividing its simple neighborhoods in two. These two highways contributed to the urban sprawl of the city which, instead of centering itself around a business or commercial sector, stretches out like a spider's web from Pioneer Square north all the way to Lake Union. Despite Freeway Park, which links First Hill with the downtown area, the irreparable damage caused by Interstate 5 can but sadden more "classical" forms of urbanism.

Borrowing from international styles, buildings downtown show their real size when studied from a distance. Some are in locations that suit their contemporary look, however the city's commercial activities and nightlife do not thrive in this area.

In the 1950s and 1960s, construction projects were set in motion. At this time, an urban conservation group petitioned to turn Pioneer Square into a historic district, thereby preventing demolition of any kind. This led to the preservation of the non-linear aspect of the streets and to the creation of public spaces like Pioneer Square – triangular rather than square.

Some contemporary architects wanted to emphasize the quaint character of the neighborhood. For instance, the cobblestone paths of Occidental Park, created in 1972 by the architectural firm Jones & Jones, are in complete harmony with the Victorian architecture of the surroundings. Unfortunately, not all designers shared the same wisdom. Case in point, the costly and pompous Waterfall Park designed in 1978 by Sasaki, Dawson and Demay, basically a waterfall and a pile of rocks in a corner, which some

Portrait

Who will have the last laugh?

The totem pole depicting Chief Sealth is a popular landmark and convenient meeting place that was stolen in 1899 from Native Americans in Fort Tongass, Alaska. According to the story, when R.D. McGilivery, third lieutenant of an expedition to the north of the Pacific, landed in Fort Tongass, all of the inhabitants had gone fishing, deserting the village except for one frightened Native American. The lieutenant took this golden opportunity to cut down the grand totem pole and, with the help of a few sailors, saw it in half in order to carry it more easily to the ship City of Seattle and bring it to the city. The totem pole was again desecrated in 1937 when a petty thief deposited a pile of newspapers at its base and lit a match. Seattle then sent the totem pole back to Alaska to be restored by the descendants of the Fort Tongass people, a task for which they asked several thousands of dollars, thus avenging their long lost brothers and sisters.

what disfigured Pioneer Square.

Public Art

Unlike many other cities, where architecture often supersedes other forms of art, in Seattle it is public art that captivates tourists and locals alike. In 1973, a law stipulated that at least 1% of the funds dedicated to improving the city went towards the arts. Since then, contemporary artists have decorated and turned the city into an al fresco museum. And the best news is that it costs nothing to admire these works of art.

Creations range from traditional and postmodern to environmental works of art, some of which are so subtle that they are hard to distinguish in the surrounding Seattle "bush."

One publicly acclaimed sculpture is Richard Beyer's *Waiting for the Interurban (1978)* which represents a group of people waiting for the bus at the corner of Fremont Avenue N. and N. 34th Street.

Some socially motivated works of art impress by their gargantuan proportions. This is the case of the *Hammering Man (1992)*, Jonathan Borofsky's four-storey-high sculpture of a man raising a hammer in his hand every 15sec. The artist was trying to represent the workers of Seattle who, day in day out, earn their living by the sweat of their brow. Towering downtown, *Hammering Man* is admired by residents who see in this work not only a tribute to the common person but also an undeniable image of the efforts made by the first inhabitants to survive in this West Coast city.

Hammering Man

Electronic art also plays a role in Seattle's artistic environment. The Key Arena (formerly known as the Coliseum) houses two unusual contemporary creations. *Hydraulis* is an immense 20m high wall of water created by Trimpin and Clark Wiegman. *In the Event* is a video installation in which video monitors, controlled by a computer, move to the rhythm of superimposed images and a fascinating soundtrack.

Public art is not always fun and games. In 1991 Barbara Krueger protested against the demolition of a historic warehouse by painting graffiti-like messages on the walls of Piers 62 and 63: *Who is housed? Who is healed? Who decides?* Other creations use existing city monuments. Isamu Noguchi's *Black Sun*, for instance, is an immense black donut through which one can see the Space Needle off in the distance! Buster Simpson's interesting work, entitled *Seattle George*, erected at the Washington State Convention Center, depicts a symbiosis between two contradictory leaders of the past, namely George Washington and native leader Chief Sealth.

To create employment for artists, projects are conceived in association with architects and engineers. As such, these multi-disciplinary artists cover public buildings with their art such as police stations, fire halls, even prisons!

Professional Sports

Basketball

The Seattle Supersonics joined the NBA (National Basketball Association) in 1967-1968, the same year as the San Diego Rockets. Like most expansion teams, they lost more games than they won: the team scraped together a mere 23 victories in 82 games, and finished next to last, just ahead of the Rockets. The Supersonics were weak on defense, letting their adversary score over 150 points on four separate occasions. They improved slightly the following season, winning 30 games. Then, in 1969-1970, led by coach and player Lenny Wilkens, the team claimed 36 victories.

Fans had to wait until 1971-1972 to see the Supersonics finally crawl from the bottom of the standings, with 47 victories and 35 losses. With coach Spencer Haywood, they had a few hot streaks (eight out of 12 and 12 out of 13) before crumbling at the end of the season, losing eight of the final nine games. They nonetheless finished third in their division. However, when Lenny Wilkens was traded to Cleveland the following season, the Su-

personics fell to pieces and won only 26 games.

Led by the strategy of legendary Bill Russell (winner of 11 NBA titles in 13 seasons), the Supersonics made a comeback in 1973-1974, claiming 36 victories. The season was spiced with high points such as the night Fred "Downtown" Brown sunk a record 20 baskets, totaling 58 points, a record for the franchise. Haywood also distinguished himself by finishing 9th-place scorer of the league. In 1974-1975, the Supersonics joined the playoffs for the first time in their history, with a record of 43 victories and 39 losses. They won the first series against the Detroit Pistons, eliminating them in three consecutive games but then lost to the Golden State Warriors after six games. The next year, "Downtown" Brown ranked 5th scorer in the league and led his team to the same record as the previous year. However, the Supersonics lost to the Phoenix Suns in the first round of the playoffs.

In 1977-1978, coach Bill Russell was replaced by Bob Hopkins who did no better than 5 wins and 17 losses before he was fired. Lenny Wilkens returned to the bench and led his team to 42 victories and only 18 loses. To everyone's great surprise, they upset the Los

Angeles Lakers, who ranked first in their division. After defeating Denver and Portland, they came against the Washington Bullets. The six first games were neck to neck, each team winning three games. Yet this duel of underdogs saw the Bullets defeat Seattle, winning the last game 105 to 99.

The Supersonics prepared their revenge by winning a record 52 games in 1978-1979, a first for the franchise. Led by its water-tight defense, the best in the league, the Supersonics defeated the Los Angeles Lakers hands down. Then the Phoenix Suns gave Lenny Wilken's team a hard time during the seven games of the playoffs, at the end of which Seattle emerged as victor. The Washington Bullets repeated the feat of the previous year and reached the finals for a second year in a row. However, after losing the first game of the series to them, the Supersonics won the next four games and claimed the league championships.

The team continued its winning streak the following year, gathering 56 wins. "Downtown" Brown famous for his three-point shot. After a heated seven games, the Supersonics eliminated Milwaukee but were easily eliminated from the series by the Los Angeles Lakers

headed by new recruit Ervin "Magic" Johnson. Following their best season ever, the Supersonics yet again went to the dogs and, as they say in the business, prepared themselves to reconstruct the team. The 1980s, despite average seasons, discouraged Seattle partisans who wanted the efforts of their favorite team rewarded by significant wins. Hope was rekindled in 1986 when rookie Xavier McDaniel set a new mark on the courts. The Supersonics made it to the semifinals but were knocked down by the mighty Lakers in four quick games.

In 1991-1992, new coach George Karl helped the Supersonics reach fourth place in the division and qualify by the skin of their teeth for the playoffs. They surprised the Golden State Warriors by beating them three games to one but were then defeated by the Utah Jazz in five games. The next year, they finished second behind the Phoenix Suns, losing against them after seven games in the semi-finals.

Led by Shawn Kemp, Gary Payton, Hersey Hawkins and Detlef Schrempf, the 1993-1995 teams of the Supersonics showed impressive statistics (120 victories and only 44 losses) but were unable to win any of the important games. In

1993-1994, they were eliminated during the first round of the playoffs by the Denver Nuggets and lost to the Los Angeles Lakers the following year. However, they finally woke up in 1995 and unseated the reigning champions, the Phoenix Suns, before confronting the "winning machine", the Chicago Bulls, who, with 72 victories and 10 losses in the regular season, had the best record in the history of basketball. The Bulls easily won the first three games while the Sonics won the next two. But it was too little too late and the Seattle team lost the sixth and final game of the series.

The Supersonics did not make the playoffs in the 1998-1999 season, which was interrupted by a strike. Nonetheless, the mass popularity of basketball in the United States will undoubtedly ensure a good future for this franchise.

Baseball

Seattle has shown strong support for its Mariners, who have competed in the American Baseball League since 1977. The Mariners underwent many adjustments during their first year and finished the season with a bad record, 68 victories against 98 losses. Lee Stanton was the team's first

big star, leading most of the offensive categories. The following year, the Mariners disappointed fans with an even lower record than the first year: a measly 56 wins! Leon Roberts was the best Mariners hitter but failed to help the team out of its losing streak. Bruce Bochte, Willie Horton, Leon Roberts and Tom Paciorek formed the core of this young team. Bochte led in hits, and Horton, scoring 106 points, had his name printed in the Mariners' record book.

The next years were pretty much the same for the Mariners. In 1980, they failed to win 60 games for the second time in three years and 1981, interrupted by a strike, was no better for these landlubbers. In 1982, the team managed to climb out of the bottom of the standings to finish fourth in its division but still could not rival the best teams. Bill Caudill was an excellent relief pitcher.

The year 1984 marked the gradual end of mediocrity for the Mariners. The outstanding performances of two of its rookies, Alvin Davis and Mark Langston, impressed both managers and fans. Davis was named Rookie of the Year by outshining the record number of runs scored by his team and scoring 116 RBIs. Langston, a left-handed pitcher, struck out over 200 hitters and was the best pitcher in the league. But, in spite of these two new stars, the Mariners failed to win more games than they lost.

From 1985 to 1989, Davis, Gorman Thomas, Phil Bradley and pitchers Langston and Mike Moore tried to accumulate victories without success. In 1989, things finally started to change for the Mariners. They traded star pitcher Langston to the Montréal Expos for Brian Holman, Greg Harris and Randy Johnson. Ken Griffey Jr. and Edgar Martinez got good results in the starting lineup. Yet the real changing of the guard occurred in 1990 when Griffey and Martinez dominated in most of the outield positions of the team. Eric Hanson carried off 18 victories while Randy Johnson slowly got used to his new teammates before throwing a no-hitter. Expos managers must surely have kicked themselves...

The first triumphant season for the Mariners was in 1991 with their record-breaking 83 wins. They repeated this feat in 1993 by capturing 82 games, but it was the performances of Chris Bosio, threw and Johnson that caught most of the attention. Bosio led the second no-hitter in the history of the Mariners; Griffey hit 45 homeruns, putting

the former team record (29) to shame; and Johnson struck out over 308 hitters, a feat accomplished by only a handful of pitchers.

The Mariners won their first division series in 1995. Hot-headed Jay Buhner headed up the Mariner hitters by batting 40 home runs driving in 121 runs; Johnson won the Cy Young award for the best pitcher in the league; and the Mariners upset the New York Yankees but lost out to the Cleveland Indians. The year 1997 closely resembled 1995: Ken Griffey Jr. hit 56 home runs and drove in 147 runs, rewriting the Mariners' record book; Johnson became the first Mariner pitcher to win 20 games. But the Mariners were defeated by the Baltimore Orioles during the first round of the playoffs.

In 1998, the Mariners were forced to trade Randy Johnson to the Houston Astros as team owners no longer had the financial means to offer a "reasonable" contract to the left-handed wonder. Furthermore, ever since the construction of the new stadium, Safeco Field, many predict that the owners will have no other choice but to trade either Griffey Jr. or Alex Rodriguez, a 24-year-old superstar, since the future of this franchise, and of baseball in general, depends on one thing: money. That having been said, if the Mariners do not make it to the playoffs, the team stands to lose substantial amounts.

American Football

Every Sunday afternoon (or Monday night) since 1976 football fans in Seattle have been flocking to the **Kingdome** (*201 South King St.*, ☎ *206-682-2800*) which seats over 66,000 people. The Seahawks, however, have yet to win the crowning glory of the NFL (National Football League), the Super Bowl. In reality, the Seahawks have never distinguished themselves on the field, as their poor record of 156 victories and 188 loses reveals. Their first year in the league often saw them take a hard licking, putting them at the bottom of the standings: two wins and 12 losses. Over the years, gaining more experience, the franchise became more and more solid and even made it to the playoffs on a few occasions without causing any big surprises. After a few tumultuous seasons, the Mariners presented a record of 12 victories and only four losses in 1984. Yet, despite the efforts of Steve Largent, best wide receiver in the team's history and holder of numerous franchise records,

and quarterback Dave Krieg, all-time leader in touchdowns and number of yards passed, the Seahawks came home empty-handed. They unseated the reigning champions, the Los Angeles Raiders, but then lost to the Miami Dolphins 31 to 10 the following week. Ever since that dream season was cut short, the Seahawks have only been able to scrape up 98 wins out of 207 games, and they reached the height of absurdity in 1992 with a pitiful record of two wins and 14 losses.

Following the 1998-1999 season, the Seahawks hired Mike Holmgren, who led the Green Bay Packers to the top during the 1996-1997 season but lost the Super Bowl the following year to the Denver Broncos led by John Elway. Dare we make the following prediction: the Seahawks should have a very good team in 1999-2000 and subsequent years.

Hockey

Seattle unfortunately does not enjoy the pleasures brought by the endless action of games in the National Hockey League (NHL). However, it is in a more intimate – yet occasionally very noisy – environment that the Seattle

Have You Ever Heard of the Metropolitans?

Before 1926, the prestigious Stanley Cup was awarded every year to the best professional hockey team competing in the National Hockey Association (NHA), the Pacific Coast Hockey League (PCHL) or the National Hockey League (NHL). The Seattle Metropolitans played their first PCHL game in 1915 wearing red-, green- and white-striped sweaters emblazoned with a big S. In 1916-1917, they won top honours by becoming the first American team to win the cup, beating the celebrated Montreal Canadians. The Metropolitans again won the PCHL championship in the 1918-1919 season, and the rematch between the Canadians and the Metropolitans promised to be full of excitement. After five games, fans were on the edge of their seats: two victories on each side and a tie. Unfortunately, the series had to be cancelled due to an outbreak of influenza. In 1919-1920, the Metropolitans had one last chance to win the Stanley Cup but were defeated by the Ottawa Senators who won three out of the five games in the series. The Metropolitans were disbanded before the start of the 1924-1925 season. Five of their players were elected to the Hockey Hall of Fame in Toronto: Frank C. Foyston, Harry (Hap) Holmes, Lester Patrick, Gordon Roberts and John Phillip (Jack)

Thunderbirds, members of the Western Canadian Junior Hockey League, hit the ice.

In junior hockey, franchises are often forced to move because of poor revenues.

Thus began the story of the Vancouver Nats' franchise in 1971, which moved to Kamloops in 1973 and played as the Chiefs for four seasons (1973-1977). In 1977, they headed to Seattle where the club became known as the Breakers until 1985. It was in 1986 that the team adopted its current name, and it was as the Thunderbirds that they won top honours in 1989, with a record of 52 wins, 17 defeats and three ties. The Thunderbirds seemed poised to win the prestigious Memorial Cup, awarded to the winner of a round-robin tournament between junior league champions of Western Canada, Ontario and Québec.

Alas, despite the efforts of Glen Goodall, Victor Gervais and Corey Schwab, the Thunderbirds were defeated by the Swift Current Broncos. Nonetheless, good year or bad year, the Thunderbirds push themselves to the limit and give a very good show every night.

Portrait

Table of Distances (km/mi)

Via the shortest route

© ULYSSES

1 mile = 1.62 kilometres
1 kilometre = 0.62 miles

Row ↓ / Column →	Calgary (AB)	Denver (CO)	Los Angeles (CA)	Montréal (QC)	New York (NY)	Portland (OR)	Salt Lake City (UT)	San Diego (CA)	San Francisco (CA)	Seattle (WA)	Tacoma (WA)	Toronto (ON)
Denver (CO)	1806/1115											
Los Angeles (CA)	2569/1586	1680/1037										
Montréal (QC)	3668/2264	2978/1838	4636/2862									
New York (NY)	3948/2437	2952/1822	4598/2838	624/385								
Portland (OR)	1283/792	2017/1245	1581/976	4816/2973	4755/2935							
Salt Lake City (UT)	1440/889	841/519	1124/694	3635/2244	3582/2211	1291/766						
San Diego (CA)	2658/1641	1779/1098	204/126	4750/2932	4612/2847	1789/1101	1221/754					
San Francisco (CA)	2151/1328	2057/1270	624/385	4844/2990	4792/2958	1037/640	1212/748	823/508				
Seattle (WA)	1103/681	2125/1312	1876/1158	4427/2733	4717/2912	289/175	1349/833	2080/1284	1338/826			
Tacoma (WA)	1142/709	1873/1156	2595/1602	4739/2925	4020/2781	1370/846	1481/914	2400/1481	1092/674	51/32		
Toronto (ON)	3437/2122	2446/1510	4093/2527	548/338	828/511	4240/2617	3079/1901	4190/2643	4282/2643	4181/2581	4212/2600	
Vancouver (BC)	975/602	2344/1447	2075/1281	4632/2859	4842/2989	509/319	1546/954	2272/1402	1537/949	226/140	280/173	4400/2716

Example: The distance between Seattle and Montréal is 4,427 km/2,733 mi.

Practical Information

I nformation in this chapter will help visitors better plan their trip to Seattle and its surrounding area.

Please note that the area code for Seattle is 206.

Entrance Formalities

Passports and Visas

Travellers from Canada, the majority of Western European countries, Australia and New Zealand do not need visas to enter the United States. A valid passport is sufficient for stays of up to three months. A return ticket and proof of sufficient funds to cover your stay may be required. For stays of more than three months, all travellers, except Canadians and citizens of the British Commonwealth, must obtain a visa (*$120*) from the U.S. embassy in their country.

Caution: as medical expenses can be very high in the United States, travel health insurance is highly

recommended. For more information, see the section entitled "Health" on p 65.

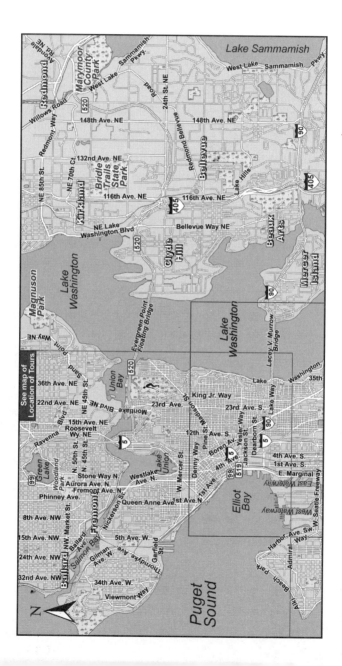

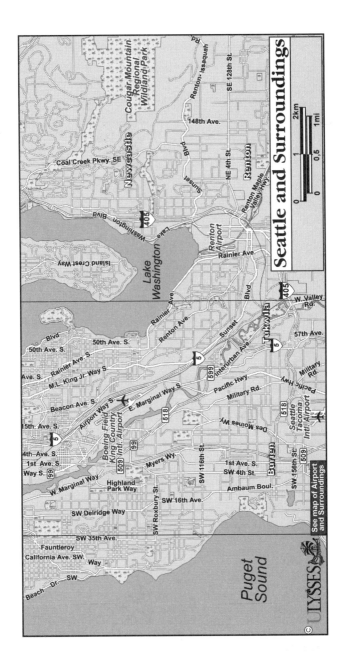

Seattle and Surroundings

Customs

Foreigners may enter the United States with 200 cigarettes (or 100 cigars) and duty-free purchases not exceeding $400, including personal gifts and 1 litre of alcohol (you must be 21 years of age to drink alcohol). There is no limit on the amount of cash you are carrying, though you must fill out a special form if you are carrying the equivalent of more than $10,000. Prescription medication must be placed in containers clearly marked to that effect (you may have to produce a prescription or a written statement from your doctor to customs officials). Meat and its by-products, all kinds of food, grains, plants, fruits and narcotics can not be brought into the United States.

For more information, contact:

United States Customs Service
1301 Constitution Avenue NW
Washington, DC 20229
☎ *(202) 566-8195*

Embassies and Consulates

U.S. Embassies Abroad

Australia
Moonah Place, Canberra, ACT 2600
☎ *(6) 214-5600*

Belgium
27 Boulevard du Régent,
1000 Brussels
☎ *(02) 508-2111*
⇔ *(02) 511-2725*

Canada
2 Wellington Street, Ottawa, Ontario
K1P 5T1
☎ *(613) 238-5335*
⇔ *(613) 238-5720*

Consulate:
Place Félix-Martin, 1155 Rue Saint-Alexandre, Montréal, Québec, H2Z 1Z2
☎ *(514) 398-9695*
⇔ *(514) 398-9748*

Consulate:
360 University Avenue, Toronto
Ontario, M5G 1S4
☎ *(416) 595-1700*
⇔ *(416) 595-0051*

Consulate:
1095 West Pender, Vancouver, British
Columbia, V6E 2M6
☎ *(604) 685-4311*

Denmark
Dag Hammarskjölds Allé 24,
2100 Copenhagen Ø
☎ *(35) 55 31 44*
⇔ *(35) 43 02 23*

Germany
Clayallee 170, 14195 Berlin
☎*(030) 832-2933*
⇌*(030) 8305-1215*

Great Britain
24 Grosvenor Square, London
W1A 1AE
☎*(171) 499-9000*
⇌*(171) 491-2485*

Italy
Via Veneto 119-a, 00187 Roma
☎*(06) 46741*
⇌*(06) 467-42217*

Netherlands
Lange Voorhout 102, 2514 EJ, Den
Haag
☎*(70) 310-9209*
⇌*(70) 361-4688*

Spain
C. Serrano 75, Madrid, 28006
☎*(1) 577-4000*
⇌*(1) 587-2239*

Switzerland
93 Jubilam Strasse, 3005 Berne
☎*31-357-72-34*
⇌*31-357-73-98*

Foreign Consulates and Delegations in Seattle

Australia
There is no Australian
Consulate in Seattle; contact
the one in San Francisco or
Los Angeles.

Australian Consulate General
1 Bush Street, 7th floor
San Francisco CA 94104-4413
☎ *(415) 362-6160*
⇌ *(415) 986-5440*

Australian Consulate General
Century Plaza Towers, Level 19
2049 Century Park East, Los Angeles
CA 90067
☎*(310) 229-4800*
⇌*(310) 277-2258*

Belgium
World Trade Center
2200 Alaskan Way, Suite 470
Seattle, WA 98121
☎*728-5145*
⇌*728-9399*

Canada
412 Plaza 600
corner 6th Avenue and Stewart Street
Seattle, WA 98101-1286
☎*443-1777*
⇌*443-9662*

Denmark
1400 Tower Bldg.
1809 Seventh Avenue
Seattle, WA 98101
☎*(206) 622-1320*
⇌*(206) 623-5694*

Finland
Carl L. Helgren, C.E.
900 University Street, #19Q
Seattle, WA 98101
☎*(206) 382-3703*

Germany
2500 One Union Square
600 University St
Seattle, WA 98101
☎*(206) 682-4312*
⇌*(206) 682-3724*

Practical Information

Great Britain
820 First Interstate Center
999 Third Ave
Seattle, WA 98104
☎*(206) 622-9255*
⇌*(206) 622-4728*

Italy
23732 Bothell - Everett Highway
Suite L
Bothell, WA 98021
☎/⇌*(425) 485-8626*

Netherlands
Two Union Square, Suite 5100
Seattle, WA 98101-2346
☎*(206) 682-5151*
⇌*(206) 621-2660*

New Zealand
6810 51st Ave NE
Seattle, WA 98115
☎*(206) 525-9881*
⇌*(206) 525-0271*

Norway
806 Joseph Vance Bldg.
1402 Third Avenue
Seattle, WA 98101-2118
☎*(206) 623-3957*
⇌*(206) 622-9552*

Spain
There is no Spanish consulate in Seattle; contact either
the one in Los Angeles or
San Francisco.

***Consulate General of Spain in Los
Angeles***
5055 Wilshire Blvd, Suite 960
Los Angeles, CA 90036
☎*(213) 938-0158*
☎*(213) 938-0166*
⇌*(213) 938-2502*

***Consulate General of Spain in San
Francisco***
1405 Sutter Street
San Francisco, CA 94109
☎*(415) 922-2995*
☎*(415) 922-2996*
⇌*(415) 931-9706*

Sweden
1215 4th Avenue, Suite 1019
Seattle, WA 98161
☎*(206) 622-5640*
⇌*(206) 622-1756*

Switzerland
There is no Swiss consulate
in Seattle, the one in San
Franciso represents California, Oregon and Washing-
ton:

456 Montgomery Street
Suite 1500
San Francisco, CA 94104
☎*(415) 788-2272*
⇌*(415) 788-1402*

Tourist Information

Tourist Information Offices

For tourist information,
brochures or maps, contact
the **Seattle-King County Convention and Visitors Bureau**
(*Mon to Fri 8:30am to 5pm;
520 Pike St., Suite 1300, Seattle, WA 98101,* ☎*461-5800,*
☎*461-5840,* ⇌*461-5855*). You
can receive their free information package by contact-
ing them by fax, telephone
or E-mail.

Excursions and Guided Tours

Many different guided tours of the city and cruises are offered. The following are the names of several companies. It is best to contact each one for more detailed information about their programs, schedules and rates, which are not listed here as they are subject to change.

Argosy Cruises
Pier 55, Suite 201
Seattle, WA 98101
☎623-4252
www.argosycruises.com

Discover Seattle's Chinatown
P.O. Box 3406
Seattle, WA 98114
☎236-0657
≈583-0460

Sightseeing of Seattle
☎526-1444

Spirit of Washington Dinner Train
625 South 4th Street
P.O. Box 835
Renton, WA 98057
☎(425) 227-RAIL
☎800-876-RAIL
www.seattle.sidewalk.com/

Victoria Clipper
☎448-5000
☎(250) 382-8100
☎800-888-2535
www.victoriaclipper.com

Uncommon Tours
☎768-1234
www.uncommon-tours.com

Underground Tours
☎682-4646
☎888-608-6337
www.undergroundtours.com

Getting to Seattle

By Plane

From Canada

Seattle is such a popular destination for Canadians, that all airlines offer regular flights. Air Canada, for example, flies to Seattle three times a week from Montreal, Toronto and Vancouver. The trip takes one hour from Vancouver and between 6 and 9hrs from Toronto and Montreal, depending on the length of your stopover from the latter. During the low tourist season, Air Canada flies to Seattle at least once a day from the cities mentioned above. Charter flights are cheaper, but it's better to reserve in advance whichever way you fly because seats may not be available, especially during peak season. Remember that all passengers leaving Canada must pay a departure tax of $10 CAN.

From Europe

Unlike Canada, most European countries do not offer regular flights to Seattle. The only daily direct flights are from Amsterdam aboard Northwestern Airlines (affiliated with KLM) and London with British Airways. The flight from London to Seattle takes about 9hrs and from Amsterdam to Seattle about 11.

Sea-Tac International Airport

Seattle's International Airport is located 21km away from downtown, west of the International Boulevard, between South 136th Street and South 210 Street. It is a modern, 1000ha airport with many airlines, foreign-exchange offices, as well as several modest little restaurants and five Starbucks cafés. There are also a few ATM machines, two of which are in the luggage pick-up area. To get downtown, there are several options: limousines, taxis and buses can take you just about anywhere in the metropolitan area.

For information concerning flight arrivals and departures, traffic, parking, and transportation to Seattle:
☎*(206) 431-4444*
☎*(800) 544-1965*
www.seatac.org

From the Airport

Renting a car is the easiest way to get to downtown Seattle. Once you leave the airport, just take Highway 509 north, which becomes Highway 99 (Alaska Highway) until you get to a huge stadium, which is none other than Safeco Field (see p 216) where the Mariners play.

SuperShuttle
$25/2 people; reservations required
☎*622-1424*
☎*425-981-7053*
The SuperShuttle connects the airport with Seattle's metropolitan area.

Grayline Express
$7.50 one way
$13 round trip
☎*626-6088*
Grayline Express runs between the airport and downtown twice an hour.

Metro
$1.10
821 2nd Ave.
☎*553-3000*
☎*800-562-1375*
Metro has three bus lines servicing Seattle's downtown: the 194, 174 and 184. They are located at door 6, next to the luggage claim, on the ground floor of the airport.

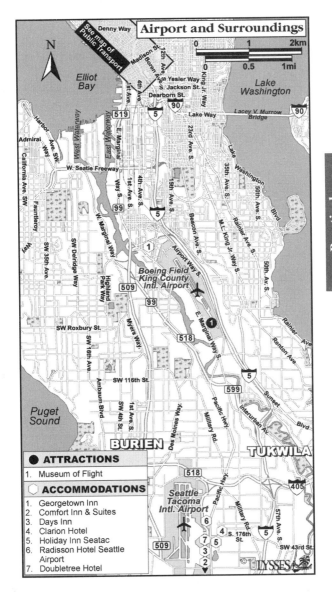

Airport and Surroundings

N

Elliot Bay

Lake Washington

Denny Way
Madison St.
12th Ave.
Boren Ave.
4th Ave.
1st Ave.
Yesler Way
S. Jackson St.
Dearborn St.
King Jr. Way
Lacey V. Murrow Bridge

Lake Way

Harbor Ave. SW
West Seaway
East Seaway
E. Marginal Way
Admiral Way
California Ave. SW
W. Seattle Freeway
Fauntleroy Way
1st Ave. S.
4th Ave. S.
15th Ave. S.
23rd Ave. S.
Beacon Ave. S.
35th Ave. S.
50th Ave. S.
Lake Washington Blvd.
M.L. King Jr. Way S.
Rainier Ave. S.

W. Marginal Way
SW 35th Ave.
SW Delridge Way
Highland Park Way
Airport Way S.

Boeing Field King County Intl. Airport

Myers Way
SW Roxbury St.
SW 16th Ave.
SW 116th St.
Des Moines Way S.
1st Ave. S.
SW 4th St.
Ambaum Blvd.

Puget Sound

BURIEN

TUKWILA

Pacific Hwy.
Military Rd.
Sunset Blvd.
Interurban Av.
Renton Ave.
50th Ave. S.
57th Ave. S.

Seattle Tacoma Intl. Airport

SW 43rd St.
S. 176th St.

● ATTRACTIONS
1. Museum of Flight

○ ACCOMMODATIONS
1. Georgetown Inn
2. Comfort Inn & Suites
3. Days Inn
4. Clarion Hotel
5. Holiday Inn Seatac
6. Radisson Hotel Seattle Airport
7. Doubletree Hotel

© ULYSSES

0   1   2km
0   0.5   1mi

See map of Public Transport

Practical Information

There are many taxis from different companies at the airport. A taxi to downtown costs about $30 for one person.

Finally, if you want to take a limo (☎*431-5904*), just go to door 6 in the airport, near the luggage claim, and a limousine will bring you to the heart of the Emerald City for $30.

Airline Companies

Air Canada
☎*467-7928*

Alaska
☎*433-3100*

American
☎*800-433-7300*

Continenta
☎*624-1740*

Delta
☎*800-221-1212*

Horizon
☎*800-547-9308*

North West
☎*800-225-2525*

South West
☎*800-435-9792*

TWA
☎*447-9400*

US Air
☎*800-438-4322*

United
☎*800-241-6522*

Car-Rental Agencies

Most of the major international or North American car-rental companies, such as Budget and Hertz, have offices at the airport.

Advantage
☎*824-0161*

Alamo
☎*433-0182*

Avis
☎*433-5231*

Budget
☎*682-2277*
☎*243-2400*

Century/Rent Rite
☎*246-5039*

Dollar
☎*433-5825*
☎*682-1316*

E-Z Rental
☎*241-4688*

Enterprise
☎*248-9013*

Hertz
☎*682-5050*
☎*248-1300*

Holiday Rent-A-Car
☎*248-3452*

National
☎*433-5501*

Reliable Auto Rental
☎*243-3211*

Rent-A-Wreck
☎*246-8486*

Thrifty
☎*246-7565*
☎*625-1133*

U Save
☎*242-9778*

Xtracar
☎*248-3452*

The trip through the U.S. to Seattle takes about the same time as through Canada and passes by some major cities, as well as some gorgeous scenery. In particular, Wyoming and South Dakota are known for beautiful landscapes with spectacular valleys. Heading west in Canada, just before Vancouver, you'll drive th482rough Rainbow County, British Columbia, which borders beautiful Washington State.

By Car

From Canada

Seattle is accessible from anywhere in Canada via the TransCanada Highway, but it can take several days to get there from Eastern or Atlantic Canada. The TransCanada starts in St. John's Newfoundland and ends in Vancouver, British Columbia. From there, you have to drive south along Highway 99 until the U.S. border, then drive farther south for 2.5hrs until Seattle.

You can skip Canada, and drive through the States on Highway 20 to Detroit, where it becomes the 401, and then take Highway 94 to Chicago and Highway 90 to Seattle. You can also take the more scenic little roads that follow the 90 if you have more time.

By Bus

Efficient and inexpensive, the bus is the best way to and around Seattle.

For schedules and destinations contact Greyhound (☎ *800-231-2222*).

The **Voyageur** bus company is affiliated with **Greyhound** in Canada:
Toronto (☎ *416-393-7911*),
Montréal (☎ *514-842-2281*)
Vancouver (☎ *604-482-8747*)

Smoking is prohibited on most lines. In general, children under five travel free. Travellers over 60 are eligible for special discounts. Animals are not permitted on board.

By Train

In the United States, the train is not always the least

Practical
Information

expensive way to travel, and it is certainly not the fastest. It can be interesting, however, for long distances as it is very comfortable (try to get a seat in a panoramic car to take advantage of the scenery). For schedules and destinations contact: **AMTRAK** (☎ *800-872-7245*), the only passenger rail company in the United States. The **King Street Station** is located at the corner of Jackson Street and 3rd Avenue (☎ *382-4120*).

Getting Around Seattle

General Orientation

It is best to rent a car to get around Seattle because public transportation is not very efficient and taxis, after a while, are no bargain. However, it is even better to explore the downtown on foot because parking lots are virtually non-existent and traffic is heavy. In any case, you will appreciate a walking tour of the city more than one on wheels, since most tourist attractions are quite close to each other.

Public Transportation

METRO Bus System

In Seattle, when you will often hear people talking about taking the "METRO", they are not referring to a subway like in New York, Toronto or London. The METRO is an above-ground monorail that runs around the city starting in the International District and ending near the Washington State Convention Center (see p 121) on 9th Avenue between Pine Street and Olive Way. The five stations (International District Station, Pioneer Square Station, University Street Station, Westlake Station and Convention Place Station) on the line make getting around the city much easier. The METRO operates between 5am and 11pm during the week and from 10am to 6pm on Saturday. No service on Sundays.

The area between South Jackson Street, 6th Avenue South, Alaskan Way and Battery street is called the ride free zone: from 6am to 7pm, all passengers travel for free on the METRO and the buses within this area.

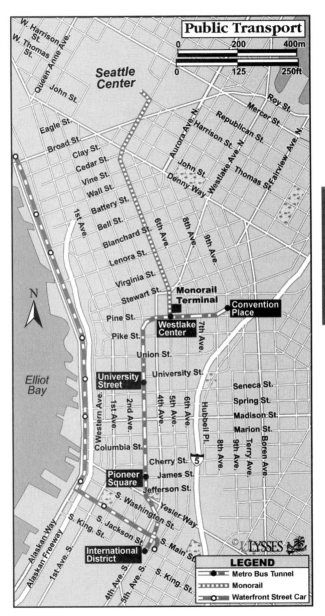

Outside this area, the fare is $1, $1.25 during rush hour, and the fare for seniors is $0.25 at all times. If you are planning to stay in Seattle for an extended period of time, you can also buy a bus pass for $36 (only valid during normal hours) or $45 (also valid during rush hour).

The bus system in Seattle leaves much to be desired. It is actually much quicker to walk than to take a bus.

By Car

Driving is undoubtedly a pleasant and efficient way of getting around Seattle, thanks in part to good road conditions and lower gas prices than in Europe or Canada. Excellent maps are available in travel bookstores and gas stations.

Car Rentals

To rent a car in Seattle, like most places in North America, you have to be 25 years of age and payment must be made by credit card. The only problem with renting a car in Seattle is finding a place to park it. Count on spending $10 to $15 a day for valet parking.

Driver's License

As a general rule, foreign drivers' licenses are valid in the United States. Take note that certain states are linked by computer to provincial police services in Canada and that a ticket issued in the United States is automatically transfered to your file in Canada.

Driving and the Highway Code

Signs marked "Stop" in white against a red background must always be respected. Some stop signs are accompanied by a small sign indicating "4-way". This means that all vehicles must stop at the intersection. Come to a complete stop even if there is no apparent danger. If two vehicles arrive at the same time, the one to the right has right of way. Otherwise the first car at the intersection has the right of way.

Traffic lights are often located on the opposite side of the intersection, so be careful to stop at the stop line, a white line on the pavement before the intersection.

Turning right on a red light after a full stop is permitted, unless otherwise indicated.

When a school bus (usually yellow) has stopped and has its signals flashing, you must come to a complete stop, no matter what direction you are travelling in. Failing to stop at the flashing signals is considered a serious offense, and carries a heavy penalty.

Seat belts must be worn at all times.

There are no tolls on the highways, except on most Interstate highways, indicated by the letter I, followed by a number. Interstate highways are indicated by a blue crest on a white background. The highway number and the state are written on the sign. "Interstate" is written on a red background at the top of the sign.

The speed limit is 55mph (88kph) on most highways. These signs are rectangular with a black border, white background and black writing.

The speed limit on Interstate highways is 65 mph (104 Kph).

Red and white triangular signs with the word "Yield" under them indicate that vehicles crossing your path have the right of way.

A round, yellow sign with a black X and two Rs indicates a railroad crossing.

Gas

Because the United States produces its own crude oil, gasoline prices are less expensive than in Europe; gas is also less expensive than in Canada, due to hidden taxes north of the border. Self-serve stations will often ask for payment in advance as a security measure

Car Theft

Car theft can be a serious problem in Seattle, and tourists are most often the targets. What car robbers do is run into your vehicle from behind, whether or not it is moving. Be alert and, above all, do not stop to talk with the other driver.

Picking up Hitchhikers

Do not pick up hitchhikers. Always lock your doors and be on your guard if suspicious-looking characters approach your vehicle.

By Taxi

Taxis are easy to spot and can be an affordable means of transportation if you are in a group, because they can accommodate up to four passengers. Seattle taxi drivers are generally very friendly and will tell you right away whether or not

Practical Information

they know how to get where you are going. Just in case, make sure you have detailed information about your final destination. Here are a few cab companies that roam the streets of Seattle:

Grey Top
☎282-8222

Orange Cab
☎522-8800

Yellow Cab
☎622-4000

By Ferry

Washington State Ferry Terminal
Pier 52
☎464-6400
☎888-808-7977
☎800-84-FERRY
www.usdot.wa.gov/ferries
If you want to visit Bainbridge and Vashon Islands or go cycling outside Seattle, the ferry is the best way to get there. All ferries depart from the Washington State Ferry Terminal. Many people living on the islands work in Seattle, making this city's port one of the busiest on the Pacific Coast of North America for ferry traffic. Call the Washington State Ferry Terminal for ferry schedules.

Insurance

Cancellation

Your travel agent will usually offer you cancellation insurance when you buy your airline ticket or vacation package. This insurance allows you to be reimbursed for the ticket or package deal if your trip must be cancelled due to serious illness or death.

Theft

Most residential insurance policies protect some of your goods from theft, even if the theft occurs in a foreign country. To make a claim, you must fill out a police report. It may not be necessary to take out further insurance, depending on the amount covered by your current home policy. As policies vary considerably, you are advised to check with your insurance company. European visitors should take out baggage insurance.

Health

This is the most useful kind of insurance for travellers, and should be purchased before your departure.

Your insurance plan should be as complete as possible because health care costs add up quickly. When buying insurance, make sure it covers all types of medical costs, such as hospitalization, nursing services and doctor's fees. Make sure your limit is high enough, as these expenses can be costly. A repatriation clause is also vital in case the required care is not available on site. Furthermore, since you may have to pay immediately, check your policy to see what provisions it includes for such a situation. To avoid any problems during your vacation, always keep proof of your insurance policy with you.

Health

Vaccinations are not necessary for people coming from Europe or Canada. On the other hand, it is strongly suggested, particularly for medium or long-term stays, that visitors take out health and accident insurance (see above). There are different types, so it is best to shop around. Bring along all medication, especially prescription medicine. Unless otherwise stated, the water is potable throughout Seattle.·

Safety and Security

Seattle is far from being a dangerous city; however, you should still take the necessary precautions, such as being careful not to reveal the contents of your wallet when paying for something, to avoid attracting any undesired attention. If you run into problems, however, remember that the number to dial for all emergencies is **911**, or **0** through the operator.

Downtown Seattle becomes a virtual ghost town after sundown. Wandering the deserted streets and alleys after dark is therefore not recommended. At night, gangs of young people roam the streets, but shouldn't approach you. There are many homeless people in Pioneer Square, but the most they will do is politely ask you for money.

Women

Women travelling alone in Seattle should not encounter any problems. Even whistling and catcalls are uncommon. Should you be verbally harassed, the best thing to do is ignore it and continue on your way.

Practical Information

Climate

Seattle has a temperate climate, which makes it pleasant year-round. Summers are not too hot and winters are not too cold. In fact, the temperature rarely exceeds 24°C in summer, thanks to winds blowing in from the Pacific. In spring and autumn, the temperature ranges between 15°C and 20°C, and in winter rarely drops below the freezing point. Seattle is known for being a very cloudy city, but it doesn't rain more here than in Chicago or New York. The average annual rainfall is 92cm, and the rainier months are between November and March.

Packing

Light, casual clothing is suitable for Seattle's clement climate. Unless you plan on spending most of your time in fancy restaurants, you don't need to dress up too much: Seattle is a relaxed laid-back city, and casual clothing, such as jeans, sweat pants, comfortable skirts and dresses, as well as light sweaters and some woolens, should suffice. Bring shorts and T-shirts if you are visiting in summer.

If you're the type that likes to sit in cafés and read,

you'll be in heaven here – Seattle is a city of coffee shops.

Also bring sunglasses to watch the sunsets, because they are particularly spectacular in Seattle.

Since Seattle is a cloudy city, bring a raincoat and an umbrella. In case you prefer not to lug such items around with you, there are plenty of places to buy these items in Seattle.

Bringing a camera and binoculars is also a good idea because the "Princess of the Pacific Northwest" has some magnificent scenery.

Mail and Telecommunications

Mail

Post offices are open from Monday to Friday from 8am to 5:30pm (sometimes until 6pm) and Saturdays from 8am until noon.

US Post Office
5706 17th Avenue NW
☎467-7289

101 Broadway East
☎283-5973

2010 15th Avenue West
☎762-9310

17233 15th Avenue NE
☎ *(425) 486-1555*

415 1st Avenue North
☎ *246-7483*

Telephone

Throughout this guide, you may notice phone numbers preceded by *800* or *888*. These are toll-free numbers, generally accessible from all over North America.

To call Seattle from elsewhere in North America, dial *1-206* and then the seven-digit number you are trying to reach.

When calling other places in North America from Seattle, dial *1* then the area code followed by the seven-digit number you are trying to reach.

For long-distance calls outside of North America, dial *011* + the country code + the area code + the local number.

Country Codes

Australia	**61**
Belguim	**32**
Germany	**49**
Great Britain	**44**
Holland	**31**
Italy	**39**
New Zealand	**64**
Spain	**34**
Switzerland	**41**

It is generally less expensive to use your own telephone company's direct service access number.

Canada Direct
☎ *(800) 555-1111*

AT&T
☎ *(800) CALL-ATT*

MCI
☎ *(800) 888-8000*

British Telecom Direct
☎ *(800) 408-6420*
☎ *(800) 363-4144*

Australia Telstra Direct
☎ *(800) 663-0683*

Most hotel rooms are equipped with phones as well as fax machines, but it is more expensive to call out from your hotel room than from a payphone.

Money and Banking

Currency

The monetary unit is the dollar (*$*), which is divided into cents (*¢*). One dollar=100 cents.

Bills come in one, five, 10, 20, 50 and 100 dollar denominations; and coins come in one- (penny), five- (nickel), 10- (dime) and 25-cent (quarter) pieces.

Practical Information

Exchange Rates

$1 CAN	=	$0.67 US	$1 US = $1.47 CAN
1 £	=	$1.60 US	$1 US = 0.62 £
$1 Aust	=	$0.64 US	$1 US = $1.55 Aust
$1 NZ	=	$0.51 US	$1 US = $1.97 NZ
1 guilder	=	$0.46 US	$1 US = 2.18 guilders
1 SF	=	$0.62 US	$1 US = 1.59 SF
10 BF	=	$0.25 US	$1 US = 37.76 BF
1 DM	=	$0.51 US	$1 US = 1.94 DM
100 PTA	=	$0.61 US	$1 US = 164.9 pesetas
1000 lire	=	$0.52 US	$1 US = 1,919 lire
1 Euro	=	$1.00 US	$1 US = 0.99 euro

Dollar and fifty-cent coins exist, as does a two-dollar bill, but they are very rarely used. Virtually all purchases must be paid in U.S. currency in the United States. Be sure to get your travellers' cheques in U.S. dollars. You can also use any credit card affiliated with an American institution like Visa, MasterCard, American Express, Interbank, Barclay Bank, Diners' Club and Discovery. **Please note that all prices in this guide are in U.S. dollars.**

Banks

Banks are open Monday to Friday from 9am to 5pm, Saturday from 9am to 3pm and Sunday from 11am to 3pm.

Banks can be found almost everywhere, and most offer the standard services to tourists. Most automatic teller machines (ATMs) accept foreign bank cards so that you can withdraw directly from your account (check before to make sure you have access) and avoid the potentially high charges of using a real teller. Most machines are open at all times. Cash advances on your credit card are another option, although interest charges accumulate quickly. Money orders are a final alternative for which no commission is charged. This option does, however, take more time. The easiest and safest way to carry money is by traveller's cheque.

Take note, however, that **non-residents** of the United

States cannot open bank accounts. If you are a resident (permanent or not, i.e. students or immigrants) of the United States, you can open a bank account by presenting your passport or U.S. citizenship card.

Exchange

Several banks readily exchange foreign currency, but almost all charge a **commission**. There are exchange offices, on the other hand, that do not charge commission, but their rates are sometimes less competitive. These offices often have longer opening hours. It is a good idea to **shop around**.

Banks and Exchange Offices

Thomas Cook
Westlake Centre
400 Pine Street, Level 1
Seattle, WA 98101
☎ **682-4525**

Thomas Cook
Sea-Tac International Airport
Main Terminal, B Concourse
Seattle, WA 98158
☎ **248-6960**
☎ **248-7250**
☎ **248-7380**

AAA Washington
330 6th Avenue North
Seattle, WA 98109
☎ **443-5692**

Credit Cards

Most credit cards are accepted at stores, restaurants and hotels. While the main advantage of credit cards is that they allow visitors to avoid carrying large sums of money, using a credit card also makes leaving a deposit for car rental much easier and some cards, gold cards for example, automatically insure you when you rent a car. In addition, the exchange rate with a credit card is generally better. The most commonly accepted credit cards are Visa, MasterCard, and American Express.

Business Hours

Stores are generally open from Monday to Saturday from 9:30am to 5:30pm (sometimes until 6pm). Supermarkets are usually open later; in some places they are open 24 hours a day, seven days a week.

Practical Information

Public Holidays

The following is a list of
public holidays in the
United States. Most stores,
administrative offices and
banks are closed on these
days.

New Year's Day
January 1

**Martin Luther King, Jr.'s
Birthday**
third Monday in January

President's Day
third Monday in February

Memorial Day
last Monday in May

Independence Day
July 4

Labor Day
first Monday in September

Columbus Day
second Monday in October

Veterans' Day
November 11

Thanksgiving
fourth Thursday in November

Christmas
December 25

Accommodations

Seattle certainly does not
lack in accommodation
options. However, the city's

strong economy and clean
environment attract many
travellers, especially business people, and it may be
hard to get a room of your
choice in a hotel. Three
words of advice: reserve in
advance. During Christmas
and Canadian and U.S. na-
tional holidays, many people come down from Van-
couver or up from California. Now you know! Many
of the hotels suggested in
this guide (see p 149) are
strategically located and
thus offer magnificent views
of Mount Rainier, Puget
Sound and various areas of
the city.

Most of the luxury hotels
are located downtown and
have indoor pools, whirl-
pools and restaurants. The
area around Seattle Center
offers basic accommoda-
tions, with the main advantage being their proximity
to the Space Needle and
Seattle Center. Young travellers can stay at the youth
hostel in Pike Place Market.
This area also has a luxurious "boutique-hotel" (see
p 161) that will satisfy the
most demanding of travel-
lers. And the oldest hotel in
Seattle is in First Hill, the
prestigious Sorrento Hotel
(see p 169).

Prices mentioned in this
guide are for one room
double occupancy during
peak season. During this
period, rates are more expensive and vacancies are

scarce. During low tourist season, from November to March, rates are lower, but Seattle's weather is not very pleasant, so your stay might not be as pleasant as in high season.

Many different hotel-room wholesalers can make reservations for you. Here are a few:

Seattle Hotel Hotline
Apr to Oct, Mon to Fri
8:30am to 5pm
520 Pike Street, Suite 1325
☎*461-5882*
☎*800-535-7071*
The Seattle Hotel Hotline can provide you with information about Seattle hotels free of charge. They also specialize in all-inclusive packages.

Seattle Super Saver package
Nov to Mar
520 Pike Street, Suite 1325
☎*461-5882*
☎*800-535-7071*
The Seattle Super Saver Package offers rooms that are discounted, sometimes up to 50% off. This is a great way to save some greenbacks!

Pacific Reservation Service
P.O. Box 46894, Seattle, WA 98146
☎*439-7677*
☎*800-684-2932*
⇌*431-0932*
www.seattlebedandbreakfast.com

Those who want to stay in a bed and breakfast, in a loft, a chalet or even aboard a yacht, the Pacific Reservation Service can help them find the establishment of their choice. This organization represents more than 200 properties in the Seattle metropolitan area.

Restaurants

This chapter contains descriptions of restaurants in each part of Seattle in order of price, from the least to the most expensive. Prices indicated apply to a full meal for one person, not including drinks and tips. At the least expensive places (*$*), where the bill should come to no more than $10, the atmosphere is informal, the service quick and the clientele local. In mid-range restaurants (*$$*), where a meal will still only cost you between $11 and $20 the ambiance is more relaxed, the menu more varied and the service slower. In fine dining establishments (*$$$*), where the price of a meal varies from $21 to $30, the cuisine ranges from simple to refined, but the décor is more attractive and the service more personal. Finally, there are the luxury restaurants (*$$$$*), where prices start at $31. At these places, which often cater to gourmets, the cuisine is an art and the service is always impeccable.

Bars and Nightclubs

Some establishments charge an entrance fee, especially when there is a band. Tipping is not obligatory, but it is appreciated. A 10% to 15% tip on drinks is the norm. The legal drinking age in the United States is 21. Bars and nightclubs are required by law to check your age, so be sure to bring along I.D. (Passport, driver's license, medicare card) with your birthdate even if you are over 30, because carding is common.

Tipping

Tipping applies to all table services, that is in restaurants or other places in which customers are served at their tables (fast food service is therefore not included in this category). Tipping is also compulsory in bars, nightclubs and taxis.

The tip is usally about 15% of the bill before tax, but varies, of course, depending on the quality of service. The tip is not included in the bill; you must calculate it yourself and leave it on the table for the server.

Media

Seattle has many publications. The two most popular dailies are the **Seattle Times** (*www.seattletimes.com*) and the **Seattle Post-Intelligencer** (*www.seattle-pi.com*). These two newspapers have a good section on Arts and Entertainment in their weekend edition. To get around Pike Place Market, pick up a **Pike Place Market News**, which is distributed all over this historic market. The very useful **Discovering Pioneer Square Map & Guide** is distributed all over town and is available at the Elliott Bay Book Company (see p 231).

The Seattle Weekly
www.seattleweekly.com

The Stranger
www.thestranger.com

The two weeklies above are excellent sources for information on what's happening in town. Published every Thursday, they offer a whole range of information on the best restaurants and nightclubs and upcoming concerts. Free of charge, they are distributed all over town, in magazine stands, shopping centres and in some stores.

Radio

Seattle has many radio stations, but unlike those of other big North American cities that all seem to play the same music over and over, Seattle's radio stations play a surprisingly original mix. On the FM dial you can listen to everything from classic rock to jazz, R&B, hip-hop and classical music. Those who enjoy listening to pop rock should tune into **KSLY 92.5** , **KCMS 105.3** or **KISS 106.1**. For R&B, soul and hip-hop music, turn your dial to **90.5** or **Q93**. Hard-rock fans should adjust their dial to **KCOC 102.5** to hear Led Zeppelin and Alice Cooper. For light jazz, **KWJZ 98.9** will please Pat Metheny fans. Younger travellers will definitely want to listen to **Buzz 100.7** or **KCMU 90.3**. The latter is run by students from the University of Washington. **KMPS 94.4** is the station for country-music fans and **KING 98.1** is for classical-music lovers.

Gays and lesbians will want to check out **The Lesbian & Gay Pink Pages**, published bi-annually, one covering winter and fall events, and another (you guessed it!) covering spring and summer. Gay and lesbian Internet users can find a whole range of information on the **Seattle Gay News Online** (*www.sgn.org*) web site. To find out what's going on in the Queen Anne district, get a copy of the **Queen Anne News**, a monthly that is more for city residents than for travellers, but visitors might find it useful, nonetheless.

This paper is available in local shops and restaurants.

You can find out more about Seattle's street life in **The Real Change** (*www.realchangeneus.org/StreetWrites/*). This paper spawned a writers' club called the Street Writers, and won an award from the Distinguished Writers Series, based in Tacoma, Washington. The two club publications are Bedless Bards, a collection of essays, and Out of the Margins, which, with 1,000 copies published three times a month, became an instant success.

Children

All sorts of family adventures await you in Seatle. Here is some advice to help you make the most of it.

Make your reservations early and make sure that children are welcome where you plan on staying. If you need a crib or extra cot be sure to request it when reserving. A good travel agent can be indispensable when it comes to this, and also for planning your various excursions.

If you are travelling by plane, ask for seats facing a partition, as you will have more room. Bring diapers, extra clothes, snacks, toys and small games in your carry-on luggage. If you are travelling by car, the same articles will be equally indispensable. Also be sure to bring enough water and juice to avoid dehydration.

Never travel without a first-aid kit. Besides adhesive bandages, antiseptic cream and diaper rash ointment, don't forget doctor-recommended allergy, cold and diarrhea medication.

When its time for a night out, many hotels can provide you with a list of reliable babysitters. You can also use the services of a daycare; check the phone book and make sure that it is a licensed establishment.

Several parks and tourist attractions have special activities for children. These are listed throughout this guide, or check the local newspapers for more information.

Senior Citizens

American Association of Retired Persons (AARP)
9750 3rd Ave. NE, Suite 400
Seattle, WA 98115
☎*526-7918*
AARP members, aged 50 and older, have several benefits including reductions on trips organized by various travel agencies and airlines.

When it comes to your health, be particularly careful. Besides your regular medications, also bring along your prescription in case you need to renew it. You might also consider bringing along your medical file, along with the name, address and telephone number of your doctor. Finally, make sure that your health insurance covers you while abroad.

Disabled Travellers

Seattle is trying to make most attractions, hotels and restaurants more easily accessible to disabled travellers. For more information, contact the mayor of Seattle's office:

Mayor's Office
618 2nd Ave., Suite 250
Seattle, WA 98104
☎*684-0500*
≈*684-0494*

Canadian travellers might want to contact the following organization:

Keroul
4545 Av. Pierre-de-Coubertin, C.P. 1000, succursale M, Montréal H1V 3R2
☎*(514) 252-3104*

Miscellaneous

Time Zone

Seattle is on Pacific Standard Time. It is three hours behind Montreal, Toronto and New York City, eight hours behind Great Britain, and nine hours behind continental Europe. Daylight Savings Time (+ 1 hr) begins on the first Sunday in April and ends on the last Sunday in October.

Drugs

Recreational drugs are against the law and not tolerated (even "soft drugs"). Anyone caught with drugs in their possession risks severe consequences.

Internet

Since Seattle is the computer capital of the world, there are a multitude of Web sites on the city to browse. Here are the best ones:

www.travelseattle.com
www.seattle.sidewalk.com
www.seeseattle.org
www.seattlesquare.com

Electricity

Voltage is 110 volts or 60 cycles (Europe: 50 cycles) throughout the United States, as in Canada. Electrical plugs are two-pinned and flat. Visitors from outside North America will need a transformer and a plug adapter, available here or at a travel boutique or bookshop before your departure.

Practical Information

The United States Uses the Imperial System:

Weights
1 pound (lb) = 454 grams (g)

Linear Measure
1 kilogram (kg) = 2.2 pounds (lbs)
1 inch = 2.2 centimetres (cm)
1 foot (ft) = 30 centimetres (cm)
1 mile = 1.6 kilometres (km)
1 kilometres (km) = 0.63 miles (mi)
1 metre (m) = 39.37 inches (in)

Land Measure
1 acre = 0.4 hectares (ha)
1 hectare (ha) = 2.471 acres

Volume Measure
1 U.S. gallon (gal) = 3.79 litres
1 U.S. gallon (gal) = 0.83 imperial gallon

Temperature
To convert °F into °C:
subtract 32, divide by 9, multiply by 5

To convert °C into °F:
multiply by 9, divide by 5, add 32

Outdoors

As mentioned throughout this guide, Seattle is known as the Emerald City for very good reason.

Indeed, everywhere you turn are various shades of green that will leave you spellbound, making the greater Seattle area, and all of Washington State, a veritable smorgasbord for the eyes and for fans of the great outdoors. Whether you're in search of parks or sandy beaches, hiking trails or bicycle paths, you will be spoiled for choice, as Seattle has done its utmost to facilitate access to these activities so prized by residents and visitors alike.

Parks

Magnuson Park
6500 Sand Point Way NE
☎ **684-4075**
If there's a park that lends itself to all kinds of outdoor activities, it's Magnuson Park. Indeed, it's not unusual to see several kites dotting the sky or encounter leisurely walkers admiring its 200-odd ha of broadleaved trees where birds chirp gaily. Named after former U.S. senator Warren G. Magnuson, the park, which lies just south of the

NOAA (National Oceanic and Atmospheric Administration), is great for walking, running or in-line skating as you take in the maritime activity on Lake Washington.

Gas Works Park
300 Meridian Ave. N.
☎ **684-4075**
Seattle even displays originality in its parks! Gas

Works Park is, at first sight, mostly a family park, laid out on a former industrial piece of land where folks can have a picnic or play with the children in sandboxes. But what draws walkers, cyclists and in-line skaters taking the Burke-Gilman Trail (see p 83) are the remains of industrial buildings such as the spooky towers that make for downright strange and incongruous, yet somehow appealing, public works of art.

Seward Park

5900 Lake Washington Blvd. S.
☎ *684-4075*

A few kilometres farther south, Lake Washington Boulevard East turns into Lake Washington Boulevard South and leads to Seward Park, which lies on a peninsula jutting into – you guessed it – Lake Washington. The park offers the opportunity to stroll through a fabulous forest studded with conifers standing majestically against the Seattle sky.

A looping trail just over 1km long allows you to circle the park, where you'll often encounter cyclists, hikers, walkers and other outdoor enthusiasts. While admiring the flora and fauna that abound in Seward Park, you can entertain yourself by observing the marine and winged species that criss-cross or fly over Lake Washington, as boats sail by in the distance.

Carkeek Park

950 NW Carkeek Park Rd.
☎ *684-4085*

While venturing into northwest Seattle, where the stunning view of Puget Sound alone makes it worth the trip, you'll discover Carkeek Park, which has hiking trails swamped with walkers or families in search of peace and quiet. The park offers an enchanting view of the Olympic Peninsula, which gradually changes colours in the distance as the sun sets: shades of orange, red and green blend into one another, creating a tableau. A railway criss-crosses the park, so watch out for trains as you cross the tracks.

Covering about 90ha, Carkeek Park has a beach perfect for a pleasant stroll. It is a wonderful spot for a picnic, as tables are provided for visitors who also come here to fly kites or simply to take a break from the hustle and bustle of the city.

To reach the park, take Interstate 5 to the Northgate Way Exit, then westbound N. 105th Street to Greenwood Avenue N. Proceed along the latter until N. 110th Street: the park lies right nearby, at the corner of Carkeek Park Road.

Discovery Park
every day 4am to 11pm
3801 W. Government Way
☎ *386-4236*
After many years of uncertainty, Discovery Park finally saw the light of day in 1972. In the early 20th century, this grand park, which sprawls over 250ha, was the site of a military fortress known as **Fort Lawton**. Several traces of the fort remain, including officers' houses and a cemetery where the memory of soldiers and immigrants are buried. Established in 1900, the fort was originally built to defend the United States from an Asian invasion, which never came to pass.

The park is the most "natural" of its kind in Seattle: practically no human-made developments clutter the wild landscape, which disappears into strange labyrinths that harbour extraordinary flora and fauna; you might even catch sight of a raccoon or a bald-headed eagle. A cougar was even seen here once!

Unlike other Seattle parks, Discovery Park, which occupies the whole western part of the city, is not regularly swamped with walkers and hikers. Quiet and serenity reign supreme here, but do not hesitate to roam its 5km of trails as, other than exposing you to an unparalleled environment, they will leave you in awe of the beauty of Puget Sound and Elliot Bay. Moreover, the view from the bluffs overlooking these stretches of water is breathtaking, the Olympic Peninsula magnificently extendly across the Seattle horizon.

Outdoor Activities

Cycling

Cycling buffs are often frustrated by the dearth of decent bike paths. And sometimes, even if such paths exist, cyclists must share them with avid joggers or adept in-line skaters. The city has remedied this problem by instituting **Bicycle Saturdays and Sundays** (☎ *684-7583*), a 2km-long stretch of Lake Washington Highway South, between Colman Park and Seward Park, is reserved for cyclists. From 10am to 6pm, this path draws a multitude of solo cyclists or families pumping their legs in the hopes of shedding a few extra pounds, or simply to stay in shape. This activity is nothing new, as Bicycle Saturdays and Sundays have been going strong for the last 30 summers. Unfortunately, most of the loveliest bike paths in the region are located outside the city

Outdoors

limits. But taking a ferry or strapping your bike to the roof of your car will allow you to reach these idyllic spots and peddle at your leisure.

In Snohomish Valley, a little outside of town, you can take a 12km-long bike path that, soars 315m above sea level at its highest point. To get there, take Exit 194 off Interstate 5 to Monroe, then Route 203 to Monroe Riverside Park. The bike path starts in front of the park, on the south side of the Skykomish River.

Also located outside of town, the **Lopez Island** bike path stretches over 13.5km. To get there, take the Anacortes ferry, which leaves the Washington State Ferry Terminal at Pier 52, and enjoy the leisurely sail to Lopez Island.

The bike path, which soars about 500m above Puget Sound, starts at the port. You'll have to scale a hill from the very outset, but take heart, for the next one isn't for another 4km or so. The ride can last all day and, if you feel like it, you can also visit the San Juan Islands on the way.

One of the most pleasant bike paths on the outskirts of Seattle is the one that skirts the south side of Lake Washington. Take Renton-bound Interstate 405 to Exit 5, which leads to Coulon Beach Park, where the bike path starts. This path, along which you can see a few ducks paddling in the waters of Lake Washington, stretches over 9km. Experienced cyclists and novices alike will appreciate the view as well as the ease of the bike path.

If you enjoy riding your bike on an island or want to give it a try, head to the Washington State Ferry Terminal at Pier 52 and take the ferry to **Bainbridge Island** (☎ *464-6400*). A 15km-long bicycle path skirts the island 1km above Puget Sound, treating you to the beauty of the Kitsap Peninsula. On the way, you'll cross the **Fort Ward** and **Battle Point** parks, where you can stop for a picnic.

Terrene Tours
117 32nd Ave. E.
☎ *325-5569*
⇒ *328-1937*
Those interested in touring with the services of a company that specializes in cycling, hiking and skiing can contact Terrene Tours.

The company offers guided tours of Puget Sound; equipment is available for rent at Pier 54 on the Waterfront.

Golf

Green being the predominant colour of the Seattle area, it comes as no surprise to find many golf courses that are a pleasure for both amateurs and professionals to roam, with putter in hand.

Jackson Park Golf Course
$22
1000 NE 135th St.
☎ *363-4747*
Open since 1930, the Jackson Park Golf Course, which was designed by Englishmen William Henry Tucker Sr. and Frank James, is spread over some 5,600m. Here golfers can practice their putts on a green course laid out for that purpose, and those with the unfortunate habit of sending their balls into sand traps can even practice these difficult shots on the chipping green. Jackson Park has a par-68 18-hole course as well as a par-27 9-hole course. Proper golfing attire is mandatory. You must reserve your tee time six days in advance by telephone or seven days in advance in person.

To get there, take northbound Interstate 5 to Exit 175, then head east along NE 145th Street, south along 15th Avenue NE and west along NE 135th Street, which leads to the golf course.

Jefferson Park Golf Course
$22
4101 Beacon Ave. S.
☎ *762-4513*
The Jefferson Park Golf Course is conveniently located in the centre of town, stretching just south of the downtown area in the Beacon Hill district. Measuring a little over 5,400m in length, the golf course features a practice range, allowing golfers to work on their tee shots. The course was designed in 1917 by Scotsman Thomas Bendelow, the mastermind behind several other beautiful golf courses in the United States.

Like the Jackson Park Golf Course, Jefferson Park features both a 9-hole course and an 18-hole course, the latter with a par of 67. It is, however, generally more crowded than Jackson Park. You must reserve your tee time six days in advance by telephone or seven days in advance in person.

West Seattle Municipal Golf Course
$21
4470 35th Ave. SW
☎ *935-5187*
Designed in 1928 by H. Chandler Egan, the West Seattle Municipal Golf Course is probably the most difficult of Seattle's three

Outdoors

public golf courses. Reserving a tee time on this 6,000m course of narrow fairways is a bit of a challenge: you must do so six days in advance by telephone or seven days in advance in person. But, even if your score card proves to be disappointing, you'll get your money's worth as the course boasts a magnificent view of Mount Rainier and the downtown-Seattle skyline, with the towering Space Needle shining in the distance.

To get to the course, take Interstate 5, then Exit 163 to the West Seattle Freeway. Continue for 1km to Fautleroy Way and turn left on 35th Street SW, at which point you'll be just a stone's throw from the golf course.

Ultimate Golf
every day 9am to midnight
11200 Kirkland Way
Kirkland, WA 98033
☎ *(425) 827-3641*

The passion for golf has sometimes taken on wild proportions, considering it is now possible to play a full round indoors or a "virtual" game on a cathodic screen that indicates where the ball ends up after a shot. At Ultimate Golf, you will feel as if you were playing a real game, without having to drag a golf cart along a course's 18 (or 9) holes in the full heat of the sun. This course was

created by entrepreneurs with definite flair who have successfully combined computer science and realism, a concept sure to be appreciated by Tiger Woods wannabes.

Flying

Open Cockpit Biplane Tours
7001 Perimeter Rd., Boeing Field
☎ *763-9706*

Those who want to soar above the city of Seattle and get a bird's eye view of the region can climb aboard an Open Cockpit Biplane Tours aircraft with a friend. To get there, take Exit 161 off southbound Interstate 5 to Galvin Flying Service; Perimeter Road will lead you to the white-and-green Flight Training Building, whence the flights leave. You can fly over the downtown area ($79 to $99/2 people), Vashon and Blake Islands as well as the downtown area ($149/2 people), or Snoqualmie Falls ($249/2 people). The pilots fly restored planes: a Travel Air (1927) and two WACO-UPF-7s (1940).

Fishing

Sport Fishing
$65
Pier 54
☎ **423-6364**
Why not take advantage of
the countless bodies of
water surrounding Seattle
by treating yourself to an
afternoon of sport fishing
with the pros at Sport Fishing? You can enjoy a worry-
free trip, as they provide
on-board assistance on
boats that can only accommodate three to four fishers
at a time. They will even
send you your catch
through the mail! This
company can also arrange
to have local restaurants
prepare your hard-earned
fish for you.

Possession Point Fishing Charters
*Port of Everett, Interstate 5 S.,
Exit 193 or 194; turn right
onto Marine View Drive and
continue to the port*
☎ **652-3797**
☎ **800-433-FISH**
If you get the urge to go all
the way down to Everett,
south of Seattle, and to
hang out with Captain
David "King David"
Morgison for a while, head
to the Port of Everett and
meet the Possession Point
Fishing Charters team,
whose specialty is salmon

fishing. The boats can accommodate two to six
fishers.

Hiking

Seattle abounds in hiking
trails that look out onto
Lake Washington, Lake
Union or Elliot Bay. Needless to say that the wonderful vistas provided from
these trails alone is worth
the trip.

The very popular **Burke-
Gilman Trail** extends over
22km and links the Fremont
and Kenmore districts. A
chaotic medley of cyclists,
in-line skaters, joggers and
hikers sometimes congre-
gates here, especially on
weekends. If you prefer
peace and quiet and "real"
nature, take the Waterfront
Trail, which skirts the
Washington Park Arbore-
tum (see p 132) and Lake
Washington. From this
1.5km trail, you'll also get
the chance to observe birds
resting in Montlake Cut, a
bay just south of the University District. Along Lake
Washington, a trail known
as the **Seward Park Loop**
winds through the park of
the same name (*at S. Juneau
Street and Lake Washington
Boulevard S.*).

Outdoors

In North Seattle, in the vicinity of Green Lake, are the **Green Lake Trails**, namely two 5km-long trails along which, oddly enough, people walk to see and be seen... What's more, hikers can even enjoy trout fishing right nearby! Those who are crazy about outdoor activities flock here, be they hard-core skateboarders, joggers, hikers or families.

Finally, if you plan on visiting Discovery Park (see p 79), why not hike along its 4.5km of trails? Here is a chance to sunbathe on North or South Beach or admire the conifers of the forest.

Whale Watching

San Juan Safaris Marine Activity Center
$40
P.O. Box 2749, Friday Harbor, WA 98250
☎ *(360) 378-2155 Ext. 505*
    800-451-8910 Ext. 505
www.sanjuansafaris.com
The Marine Activity Center at the San Juan Islands' Roche Harbor Resort offers a 3hr cruise on which you can behold impressive marine mammals such as orcas. During your cruise, you might also get the chance to see bald eagles, blue herons, dolphins and seals.

Snug Harbor
2371 Mitchell Bay Rd., Friday Harbor, WA 98250
☎ *(360) 378-4762*
⇌ *(360) 378-8859*
The Snug Harbor company also offers whale-watching sea excursions.

Sea Kayaking

Kayak Port Townsend
*$28/2hrs, $39/3hrs,
$68/6hrs, 30min*
435 Water St., Port Townsend
WA 98368
☎ *(360) 385-6240*
⇌ *(360) 385-6062*
www.olympus.net/kayakpt
Fans of sea kayaking are
sure to want to make the
trip to Port Townsend,
north of Seattle. The Kayak
Port Townsend firm offers
guided excursions and rents
out kayaks (*$15/hr per
kayak*) and all the necessary
equipment.

Crystal Seas Kayaking
$39/person
P.O. Box 3135, Friday Harbor
WA 98250
☎ *(360) 378-7899*
www.pacificrim.net/tildkayaking
Located on the San Juan
Islands, Crystal Seas
Kayaking offers a 3hr
guided excursion. This
gives you the chance to
paddle safely through the
waters of Puget Sound,
where you may be fortu-
nate enough to encounter a
whale or a seal.

Rafting

Alpine Adventures
P.O. Box 253, 894 Hwy 2,
Clocktower Building
Leavenworth, WA 98826
☎ *(509) 782-7042*
☎ *in Seattle (253) 838-2505*
A few companies offer
rafting excursions. Operating out of Leavenworth,
east of Seattle, the Alpine
Adventures team will take
you paddling in the tumultuous waters of the region.

**North Cascades River Expedi-
tion**
$45
P.O. Box 116, Arlington
WA 98223
☎ *800-634-8433*
☎ *(360) 435-9568*
⇌ *(360) 435-0796*
www.cftinet.com/tildrafting
In Arlington, a little north of
Seattle, the North Cascades
River Expedition company
has been offering different
expeditions of varying
levels of difficulty since
1980.

Outdoors

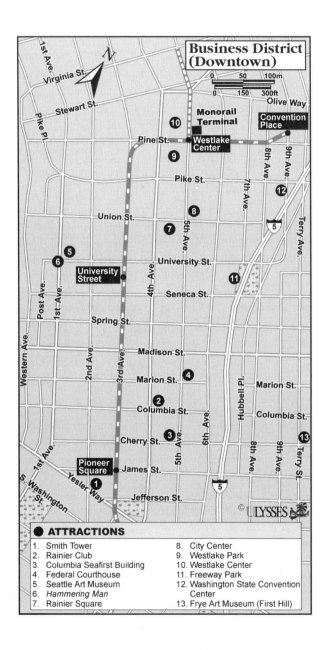

Business District (Downtown)

Virginia St.

Stewart St.

1st Ave.

Pike Pl.

Olive Way

Monorail Terminal

⑩

Convention Place

Pine St. ●**Westlake Center**

⑨

Pike St.

⑧

Union St.

8th Ave.

7th Ave.

I-5

Terry Ave.

⑦

5th Ave.

⑤
⑥
University Street●

University St.

4th Ave.

Seneca St.

⑪

Post Ave.

1st Ave.

Western Ave.

Spring St.

2nd Ave.

Madison St.

3rd Ave.

Marion St.

④

②
Columbia St.

Hubbell Pl.

Marion St.

Columbia St.

Cherry St.
③

5th Ave.

6th Ave.

8th Ave.

9th Ave.

Terry St.

⑬

Pioneer Square●

James St.

1st Ave.

Yesler Way

①

S. Washington St.

Jefferson St.

I-5

⑫

© ULYSSES

0   50   100m
0   150   300ft

● ATTRACTIONS

1. Smith Tower
2. Rainier Club
3. Columbia Seafirst Building
4. Federal Courthouse
5. Seattle Art Museum
6. *Hammering Man*
7. Rainier Square
8. City Center
9. Westlake Park
10. Westlake Center
11. Freeway Park
12. Washington State Convention Center
13. Frye Art Museum (First Hill)

S eattle, a city where tradition and modern times go hand in hand, has recently stepped into the spotlight after having long been overshadowed by sister cities Los Angeles and San Francisco.

The grunge phenomenon, also called the Seattle Sound, took the musical world by storm in the early 1990s, reviving the punk rage that took over radio stations around the world at the end of the 1970s when the Sex Pistols sang the virtues of anarchy. But the new lords of rock 'n roll, Kurt Cobain (Nirvana) and Eddie Vedder (Pearl Jam), soon had their rhythms copied and popularized, and hardcore once again took a back seat to more civil tempos.

To speak of grunge now in Seattle is anachronous: the Seattle Sound is *passé*, locals will tell you. Case in point, you will not find the least trace of the not-so-far-off times when Seattle was the epitome of living on the edge. Be that as it may, this musical epic heralded a new gilded age for the Princess of the American Northwest.

The expansion of Microsoft, the software

giant, and the ongoing growth of Boeing have turned Seattle into the economic hub par excellence of the State of Washington. Specialized publications galore extol the quality of life its citizens enjoy – not to mention the lush greenery that surrounds their humble city.

It is hard to picture Seattle without having been there. Other than the Space Needle, seen in movies like *Sleepless in Seattle* and *It Happened at the World Fair*, what is this city known for? Sports fans will immediately yell: Ken Griffey Jr.! Indeed, this young baseball player is on the verge of setting new records, as he chalks up homeruns, RBIs and spectacular catches.

This travel guide will help you discover the bountiful sights of this "green" city bestowed with gem-like parks and interesting museums. Idle your way through the historic district of Pioneer Square and admire the totem poles created by Duane Pasco; stroll along the Waterfront and watch

the coming and going of ferry boats as you bite into your halibut hamburger; visit Pike Place Market, the oldest public market in the United States; and let the skyscrapers downtown inspire the photographer in you. Furthermore, in the Capitol Hill neighborhood, you can shop for fashionable clothes and CDs on Broadway Street; in the university neighbourhood, you can visit two fascinating museums, the Burke Museum and the Henry Art Gallery; and, at this point, you still have not visited the artsy Fremont neighbourhood, the Museum of Flight south of Pioneer Square or the Baillard Locks north of the city!

Pioneer Square

Many of the city's historic buildings are concentrated in Pioneer Square. These buildings, some of which date back to the end of the 19th century, others to the turn of the 20th century, have survived years of economic prosperity - and decline - as well as ever-recur

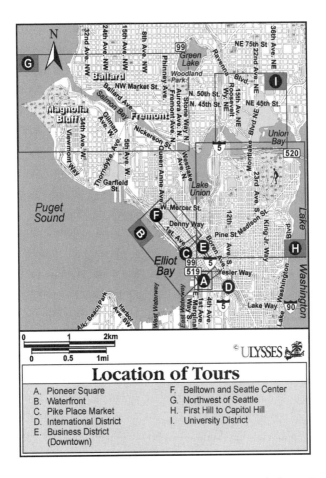

Location of Tours

A. Pioneer Square
B. Waterfront
C. Pike Place Market
D. International District
E. Business District
(Downtown)

F. Belltown and Seattle Center
G. Northwest of Seattle
H. First Hill to Capitol Hill
I. University District

ring renovations. However, these buildings of olden days are more attractive from the outside than the inside, which, except for some antique elevators and native engravings, is more likely to interest architecture lovers than anyone else.

The expression "Skid Row" originated in Pioneer Square at a time when construction lumber was transported (or "skidded") to the seafront and shipped to San Francisco or Portland. Today, the brick-inlaid roads, exuding warmth and character, the numerous works of public art and the fashionable restaurants have attracted yuppies, architects, artists and media celebrities to the neighbourhood.

Bordered to the south by **Safeco Field**, new home of the Mariners baseball team, Pioneer Square is not very large. It extends north to Yesler Way and is bordered by 1st and 4th Avenues South to the west and east.

This historic neighbourhood south of downtown has undergone many urban face-lifts over the years. Once a Native American village, little is known of the nations who lived here prior to 1852 when the Exact schooner dropped anchor in the Seattle port.

The Great Seattle Fire (see p 19) destroyed Pioneer Square back in 1889. Stone and brick buildings replaced the former wooden structures, thereby infusing new life into this part of town which was Seattle's business centre. But, when the downtown area moved north in the 1920s, the neighbourhood was more or less abandoned. It was only in the 1960s that interest was rekindled, thanks to the efforts of several "green" residents, notably architect Ralph Anderson's (who took out a mortgage on his house to buy one of

the buildings in the neighbourhood for $30,000). Desolation prevailed in this neighbourhood before Anderson's initiative to re-establish Pioneer Square's status. His efforts to revitalize Pioneer Square were backed by architect and landscape designer Victor Steinbrueck, architect Ibsen Nelsen, furniture designer Ben Masin, Seattle mayor Wes Uhlman and art gallery owner Richard White. As a result, Pioneer Square was declared a historic site in 1970.

Even today, the spirit of the 1960s still floats in the air, thanks to art galleries founded by the peace and love generation, which have weathered the passage of time and encouraged artists to show their work in this quaint neighbourhood of another era.

It is very enjoyable to walk in this neighbourhood, especially as it is relatively quiet during the day. You can pop into one of the many bookstores, such as the famous **Elliot Bay Book Company** (see p 231), or pay a visit to one of the several antique dealers, some of whom ask exorbitant prices for rather mundane-looking objects whereas other less opportunistic and more professional dealers will be most obliged to help you to choose a special gift for a friend. Toy stores, sports

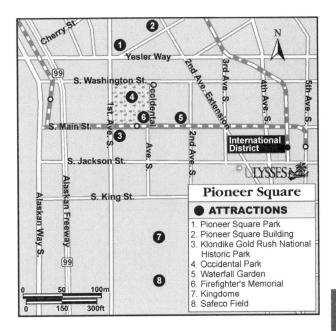

boutiques, small publishing houses and avant-garde record dealers also abound.

However, Pioneer Square's main attraction is certainly its nightlife. Today's perpetual youth hangs out in the sports, rock and blues bars or in the more romantic nightclubs crowded into this quickly visited block (see p 207).

Unfortunately, it is also in this part of town that poverty is most felt, especially in Occidental Park, a favorite hangout for many vagrants who, despite their

appearance, rarely bother passers-by. Still, it is best to be wary of this area at night. Several homeless shelters occupy this historic square in perfect harmony with other establishments in the neighbourhood, and the homeless share their "home" with tourists, art-gallery owners and artists.

This tour begins in the very heart of this historic centre, **Pioneer Square Park** ★★ (*every day 6am to 11:30pm; 100 Yesler Way, corner of 1st Ave.*, ☎ **684-4075**), an excellent rendezvous for residents and visitors alike. On

Exploring

the eastern side of the park, **Doc Maynard's Pub** (see p 208) marks the starting point of the **Underground Tour** (see below). To the south is the original Skid Road, where blocks of wood were transported to the oceanfront in the early times. This square, rich in history also features a bust of Chief Sealth, the Native American after whom the Emerald City is named.

How Pioneer Square Park became a triangle can only be explained by the twists of fate and conflicts that resulted from its construction. Indeed, two of the town's pioneers, Doc Maynard and Arthur Denny, argued repeatedly over how the streets in the downtown of yore should be laid out. The first preferred diagonal roads; the second, straight north-south arteries. The result? A geometric compromise. From that moment on, the park came to symbolize the meeting of two diametric opinions. On the positive side, it is virtually impossible to miss as it separates the neighbourhood from the present-day downtown area.

Recorded in the national register of historic places, the park's **Pergola Shelter** ★ was built in 1909 on the site of what used to be immense public latrines, nothing of which remains today. It is the perfect place to sit

down on one of the park s benches and people-watch or admire the architecture of surrounding buildings such as the Grand Central, Merrill Place, Maynard, Mutual Life or Pioneer Square Building. Grab a seat fast or someone might take your place in a hurry, forcing you to postpone your leisurely contemplation for another time.

The **Pioneer Square Building** ★ (*606 1*st* Ave.*) flanks the eastern side of the park. The construction of this Victorian-style building designed by Elmer Fisher began shortly after the great fire in 1889 and ended in 1892. Upon its completion, the American Institute of Architects declared it the most beautiful building west of Chicago. Architecture aficionados will no doubt admire the antique elevator and gate, the first of its kind in Seattle. A tower even crowned the building until an earthquake toppled it to the ground in 1949.

This building rises above the remains of old Seattle, which you can visit on the **Underground Tour** ★★ (*$6.50; every day 10am to 6pm, variable schedule; 610 1*st* Ave.,* ☎ *682-4646*). The name of this guided tour can be misleading, as some tourists have remarked. No, it is not a tour of punk-rock relics! The starting point of this guided tour, a little difficult to locate, is via Doc Maynard's Pub. This underground odyssey allows you to descend into pre-fire Seattle, when 30 or so blocks of houses made up its downtown. This 1.5 visit allows you to explore only three blocks of houses, which will nonetheless give you a good idea of the customs and manners of the city's original residents. Who knows? You might even cross paths with a rat...

Head west on Yesler Way to 1st Avenue South. Then go south and turn left on Main Street.

If you are interested in the Gold Rush, visit the **Klondike Gold Rush National Historic Park** ★★ (*free; every day 9am to 5pm, closed on holidays, 117 S. Main St.,* ☎ **553-7220**). Open to the public since June 5, 1979, this museum has gathered an impressive collection of historical records documenting Seattle's part in the Gold Rush. The city was chosen as the location of this museum because of its role in this unprecedented episode of American history, linked to the birth of San Francisco in 1849. In fact, after only eight months of crazy expeditions, city merchants made over $25 million selling equipment and supplies to the hardy souls who set out to northern British Columbia, leading to an economic boom that helped forge the Seattle we know today.

The museum is called a "park" because of the rangers in full uniform who passionately recount the trials and tribulations of the gold rush. The staff certainly knows its history! For hours on end, they can regale you with stories of isolated events that took place during this turning point for Seattle, which, before the Gold Rush, depended heavily on the exportation of timber to fill the stomachs of its citizens.

Short films are also shown, notably *The Gold Rush*, directed by Charlie Chaplin (1925) at a time when his appeal was beginning to decline because he was distancing himself from the zaniness that had made audiences around the world laugh. Another 30min film does a better job at depicting the misery and swindling going on behind the Gold Rush. In short, many of those who travelled to northern Canada returned disillusioned, not rich (see p 23). A series of photos and written accounts top off this compelling visit.

Exploring

Upon exiting the Klondike Gold Rush National Historic Park head east to **Occidental Park ★★** (*every day 6am to 11:30pm; 200 S. Main St., ☎ 684-4075*), which was moved from Pioneer Square when the area was restored in 1971. Those who have been to Paris might see this 0.5ha park lined with trees and cobblestones as a northwestern pastiche of a Parisian park. Some of the city's less affluent residents can be seen gabbing away on benches or under the rotunda in the northwest section of the park, while others beg more or less

politely. Don't be surprised if someone even hails you from afar. There is no need to be frightened as these people are unlikely to cause you any problems. The eastern side of the Grand Central Building towers over the rotunda built in 1972 and serving as a stage for blues and jazz bands during spring and summer.

This park gives you the opportunity to see some lovely public art, such as Tom Askman's metallic **Firefighter Silhouettes ★** which commemorates the 1889 fire.

Mythical Tall Tales

Donated by Richard White, the spectacular totem poles that grace the northern section of Occidental Park were created by Duane Pasco. These Aboriginal monuments have guarded the park since the late 1980s, lending a dramatic note to the setting and conjuring the Native American legacy of the region. In 1971, Duane Pasco created *Killer Whale,* which represents a man standing on the tail

of a whale. The most evocative and frightening of the totem poles, *Tsonqua,* facing the more benign *Bear,* represents the "provoker of nightmares" that Native American mothers spoke of to frighten their children. The masterpiece of the park, and the largest of the totem poles, is called *Sun and Raven* and was exposed for the first time during the Expo '74 World's Fair in Spokane, Washington..

The Waterfall Garden ★ *(219 2ⁿᵈ Ave. S.,* ☎ **684-4075** or **624-6096**) features a 7m fountain created in 1977 by Masao Kinoshita and sponsored by the Annie E. Casey Foundation. Cascading over large rocks, this fountain also marks the birthplace of the United Parcel Service. The park features exotic plants, gingkoes as well as some tables and benches often occupied by local workers during their lunch break. Although a fence surrounds the park, it is easy to miss. Keep your eyes open wide: it is at the corner of South Main Street.

Continue east on South Main Street until you come across **Fire Station No. 10 ★**. At the corner of 2ⁿᵈ Avenue, Ellen Ziegler's bronze mosaic, **Firefighter's Memorial ★**, is another tribute to the firemen who skillfully battled the fire of 1889.

Now take Occidental Avenue South which runs perpendicular to the park and is crowded with art galleries, antique dealers and cafés. This avenue has been closed to cars since 1972, and many of its buildings date back to the last decade

of the 19ᵗʰ century. You will undoubtedly notice Elmer Fisher's State Building on the southeast corner of South Main and Occidental Avenue South. Every first Thursday of the month from 6pm to 8pm, the very enjoyable **Gallery Walk** (see p 224) invites one and all to visit the many art galleries in the area, maybe even sip a complementary glass of wine.

Situated south of Pioneer Square, the **Kingdome** *(corner of 4ᵗʰ Ave. and King St.,* ☎ **296-3128**) is located where "Hooverville" was at the turn of the century (see p 26). However, this former home of the local baseball team, the Mariners, and football team, the Seahawks, might already have been demolished by the time you visit. The close results of a referendum gave the city the green light to build a new stadium right next to the Kingdome as "the house that Ken Griffey Jr. built." was unable to generate the substantial revenues needed to keep hosting baseball and football games.

On July 15, 1999, **Safeco Park ★** (☎ *326-4001*) opened its doors to some 47,000 spectators for a game pitting the Seattle Mariners against the San Diego Padres. For the first time ever, Seattle baseball fans had the chance to attend an open-air ball game since the Kingdome, like the Houston Astrodome and Montreal's Olympic Stadium, was a covered stadium with artificial turf instead of natural grass. Note: The Seahawks will play at Husley Stadium for the next two years in the University District starting in the year 2000.

From now on, Mariner games will be played at Safeco Field. It is recommended to reserve seats for Seahawk games ahead of time before new coach Mike Holmgren spruces up this under-funded team of the National Football League (NFL) by dishing out the kind of salaries that will certainly make ticket prices go up. As for the Mariners, judging by their performance on the field, you should have no trouble getting same-day tickets although, with the new stadium, who knows? Seats might sell like hot cakes!

Waterfront

The Waterfront, a long promenade lining Elliot Bay where the many piers of the port of Seattle are located, is full of souvenir shops and a hotel. In the bay, you can see small boats being gently rocked by the waves as well as large shipping vessels.

To visit the Waterfront in comfort, take the **Waterfront Streetcar ★** (*$0.85, $1.10 at rush hour; Mon to Fri 7am to 6pm, Sat to Sun 10am to 6:30pm, during the summer every day until 10pm; 821 2nd Ave. S., ☎ 553-3000*). Its route begins on South Jackson Street at the corner of 5th Avenue South (see p 96) and makes its final stop at Pier 70 at the corner of Broad Street. This old means of transportation is often crammed with tourists who go from one attraction to the next. Departures are every 20min. The tramway along the Waterfront was created in 1980, yet the wagons were built in 1927 in Melbourne, Australia. Because streetcars travel relatively slowly, you might as well walk if you are in a hurry: you will walk as fast (if not faster!) as this old albeit charming tramway of yesteryear. The price of a

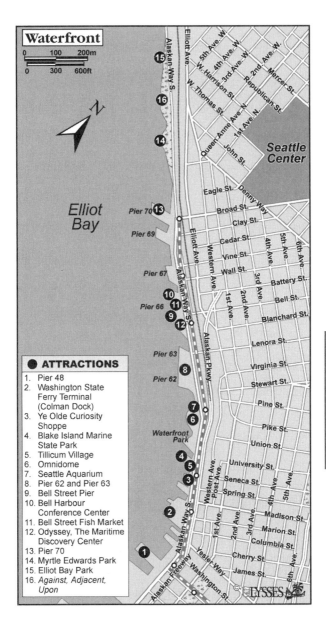

Waterfront

| 0 | 100 | 200m |
| 0 | 300 | 600ft |

Elliot Bay

Pier 70 **13**
Pier 69

Pier 67

10
Pier 66 **11**
9
12

Pier 63 **8**
Pier 62

7
6
Waterfront Park

4
5

3

2

1

15

16

14

Seattle Center

5th Ave. W.
4th Ave. W.
3rd Ave. W.
2nd Ave. W.
Mercer St.
W. Harrison St.
Republican St.
Queen Anne Ave. N.
1st Ave. N.
W. Thomas St.
John St.

Eagle St.
Denny Way
Broad St.
Clay St.
Cedar St.
4th Ave.
6th Ave.
Vine St.
Wall St.
3rd Ave.
Battery St.
2nd Ave.
1st Ave.
Bell St.
Blanchard St.
Lenora St.
Virginia St.
Stewart St.
Pine St.
Pike St.
Union St.
University St.
Seneca St.
Spring St.
Madison St.
Marion St.
Columbia St.
Cherry St.
James St.

Western Ave.
Post Ave.
1st Ave.
2nd Ave.
3rd Ave.
4th Ave.
5th Ave.
6th Ave.

Elliot Ave.
Alaskan Way S.
Alaskan Pkwy.
Yesler Way
Washington St.
Alaskan Freeway

● ATTRACTIONS

1. Pier 48
2. Washington State Ferry Terminal (Colman Dock)
3. Ye Olde Curiosity Shoppe
4. Blake Island Marine State Park
5. Tillicum Village
6. Omnidome
7. Seattle Aquarium
8. Pier 62 and Pier 63
9. Bell Street Pier
10. Bell Harbour Conference Center
11. Bell Street Fish Market
12. Odyssey, The Maritime Discovery Center
13. Pier 70
14. Myrtle Edwards Park
15. Elliot Bay Park
16. *Against, Adjacent, Upon*

ULYSSES

Exploring

ticket increases slightly at rush hour. Tickets can be purchased in Bartell Drugs pharmacies or at the head offices of the **METRO** (*821 2nd Ave. S., ☎ 553-3000*).

You should be aware, however, be forewarned that the waterfront of today is first and foremost a tourist trap. Indeed, most of the shops carry very tacky souvenirs. Yet this is place to hop aboard one of the many ferries or shuttles that sail to Bainbridge Island, Vashon Island, Whidbey Island, the San Juan Islands or even to Victoria and Vancouver, Canada. This neighbourhood has recently been invaded by new tenants who, from their new condominiums, enjoy the local exoticism as well as an unimpeded view of the Sound. The waterfront is also an ideal vantage point for watching seamen at work or contemplating containerships and small fishing boats floating in Elliot Bay with the everpresent Puget Sound as a backdrop.

The **Waterfront Tour** begins at the southern-most edge of the waterfront, **Pier 48**, more specifically at the **Washington Street Public Boat Landing**. Plaques displayed here and there along the Waterfront tell the history of the port, and telescopes provide a closer look at Puget Sound and the is-

lands off Elliot Bay. Keep your eyes wide open and you will see an outdoor art exhibit in the form of potent social messages painted as graffiti on the walls of the various piers.

A little farther north, ferries depart from the **Colman Dock**, also called the **Washington State Ferry Terminal**, (*801 Alaskan Way, Pier 52, ☎ 464-6400 or 800-843-3779*) and sail to Bainbridge, Bremerton and the Vashon Islands in Puget Sound, as well as to the Olympic Peninsula. If you plan on visiting any of these islands on foot, leave your car in downtown Seattle as there is no parking at the pier. However, cars are allowed on the various ferries, except on the one to Vashon Island, for $7; additional passengers, foot passengers and cyclists must pay $3.50.

In 1889, Joe Standley founded **Ye Olde Curiosity Shop** ★★ (*free; Mon to Thu 9:30am to 6pm, Fri and Sat 9am to 9pm, Sun 9am to 6pm, closed on Thanksgiving, Christmas and New Year's Day; Pier 54, ☎ 682-5844*), which features a vast array of strange objects, from giant clams to shrunken wooded heads. This store did not get off to a successful start; apparently, during its first three days of business, it made only $0.25! "Daddy" Standley, as he was affectionately called, soon befriended sailors and Native Americans who passed on all sorts of handcrafted objects such as Inuit engravings, ivory horns, tools and instruments used in the Gold Rush, filling the store with considerable ethnological lore. Standley presented this eclectic collection at the Alaska-Yukon-Pacific exhibit in 1909 before selling it to George Heye, founder and curator of the New York Museum of the American Indian, for the tidy sum of $5,000, a small fortune in those days.

This little store has provided objects as bizarre as they are unusual to numerous museums such as the Royal Ontario Museum, the Seattle Burke Museum and the prestigious Smithsonian Institute in Washington D.C.. This store cum museum showcases, amongst other eccentricities, a mummy, Siamese twins as well as walrus and whale genitalia. In short, this store is a haven of the kitsch and the abnormal.

At **Pier 56** you can hop on a ferry that sails to the **Blake Island Marine Park ★**, a 215ha island named after George Smith Blake who sailed along its coastline between 1837 and 1848. You can also visit **Tillicum Village ★★** *($55; every day during the summer from May to Oct; weekends only during the winter; also possible to reserve visits; ☎443-1244)* and sample typical Native American dishes, such as smoked salmon, and watch masked dancers perform tribal dances. Revisit childhood dreams as you gaze up at the impressive totem poles scattered around the island and admire the work of local craftsmen as they carve wooden masks or produce paintings of various animals with strong spiritual connotations.

For an extraordinary movie experience, go to the **Omnidome ★** *($6.95, extra $3 per additional film, $12.95 for the Seattle Aquarium and film, $15.95 for the Seattle Aquarium and two films; every day from 10am to 5pm; Pier 59, corner of the Alaskan Hwy; ☎ 622-1868 or 622-1869, ⇰622-5837)*, which projects grandiose wilderness adventures on a 30m, 180 IMAX screen. The soundtrack is emitted from the front and back, basically from everywhere, giving the audience an extra thrill. One of the films, ***Eruption of Mount St. Helen*** *(every day 10am, 11:35am, 1:05pm, 2:35pm, 5:35;m, 7:05pm, 7:45pm)*, recounts the events of May 18, 1980 when 75 million tons of volcanic ash fell onto the region of Spirit Lake and instantly modified its ecosystem. The volcanic blast was heard 700km away and its force was equal to that

Exploring

of 27,000 atomic bombs, causing a column of smoke to rise 10km above the mountain.

Other movies with ecological themes, including a short movie on storm chasers and another on mountain gorillas, are also presented. If you dream of Alaskan landscapes, see *Alaska: Spirit of the Wild* (*every day 1:45pm, 4:45pm*), which was nominated for an Academy Award in 1998. The director, George Casey, also the director of *Eruption of Mount St. Helen* and producer of *Africa*, pulled out all the stops to impress the audience with breathtaking shots, notably the IMAX signature; high-angle aerial shots. *Spirit of the Wild* features a group of polar bears fishing, frolicking and fighting. Small children might be frightened by images of the bears tearing their prey to pieces. Casey brings to the big screen the first frost of winter to the rebirth of the tundra in the springtime as well as an impressive assortment of marine mammals, such as humpback whales, which reside in the Great North. None other than Charlton Heston narrates this film.

Faithful to its name, Roger Payne's film, *Whales* (*every day 4:45pm*), features whales whose titanic size, for many, makes them almost as fascinating as dinosaurs. Close-ups of the whales and of the rainbows created by the sudden bursts of water from the top of their heads, will render many speechless. This short 40min film also features killer whales and blue whales. Payne also follows the annual migratory journey of the humpback whales from south of Argentina to Alaska, where they stuff themselves with plankton and other minute sea creatures.

Waterfront Park, which extends from Pier 57 to Pier 59, is another attraction by the water. However, this little park would largely go unnoticed were it not for the **Seattle Aquarium** ★★★ (*$6.50, aquarium and Omnidome $12.25; from Memorial Day to Labour Day 10am to 7pm, from Labour Day to Memorial Day 10am to 5pm; 1483 Alaskan Way or Pier 59; ☎386-4300*), one of the main reasons for visiting this part of town. The aquarium is home to an impressive range of animals: over 400 species of birds, plants and marine mammals. Furthermore, since February 1999, it also includes 60,000 salmons, two red octopuses, several species of sea stars, as well as river otters named *Skykomish*, *Sammamish* and *Skookumchuck* (all Native American names) who have all but stolen the show from the sea otters. Formerly the aquarium's big stars, Kenai, Lootas and Kodiak put on a show every day at 11:30am, 2pm and 5pm when they swallow large quantities of crabs and oysters and cavort about to the great delight of youngsters and adults. Jellyfish and other invisible creatures can be examined using microscopes, and the **Discovery Lab** provides close contact with starfish, baby barnacles and hermit crabs.

Get a close look at the black-tipped reef sharks - not man-eating - and electric eels swimming in the **Pacific Coral Reef Basin**. The aquarium is also fortunate to have amongst its "residents" the first octopus ever born in captivity. The park's two red octopuses mated, and the female began to lay her eggs in March 1982 and the hatching took place from October to December. Although only one offspring survived, the aquarium nonetheless earned the Edward H. Bean prize from the American Association of Zoological Parks and Aquariums for the first octopus ever born in captivity.

After 15 months in captivity, the octopus now weighs approximately 30kg and, with its arms extended, measures 3m! The reconstitution of the underwater kingdom of Puget Sound,

called *State of the Sound*, in a dome containing 400,000 gallons of water (approximately 1,500,000 litres), has recently been replaced by a new exhibit called *Sound to Mountains*.

Today the only remaining part of the first exhibit is the Underwater Dome in which scuba divers feed the animals every day at 1:30pm.

Sound to Mountains features the river otters mentioned above. These mammals distinguish themselves from their cousins, the sea otters, by the many physical habitats in which they can survive, from rivers and lakes to freshwater ponds. Occasionally, river otters are even spotted swimming in Puget Sound or lounging on the beach. The aquarium is ideal for families, especially for small children who can play in the amusement park or dress up in animal costumes. A 40ft (10m) interactive freshwater mural, an old log that kids can climb (or hide in!), a forest as well as information panels explaining the reproduction cycle of salmons in the region are also part of the attractions.

Exploring

Social Art

Make no mistake: the graffiti on the walls of **Pier 62** ★ and **Pier 63** ★ is a form of public art, not a random act of vandalism. Depending on the light, and your position, you may – or may not – see some of the potent social messages. Marking the spot where Native Americans berthed their boats in the 19th century, these two piers were given a make-over in 1989 when architects Henry Smith Miller and Laurie Hawkinson, landscape artist Nicholas Quennel, historian Gail Dubrow and engineer Guy Nordenson, erected a galvanized iron gate onto which artist Barbara Kruger painted in red short questions with social significance. *Who Salutes Longest? Who Is Free to Choose? Who Follows Orders? Who Dies First? Who Laughs Last? Who Is Housed? Who Is Healed? Who Is Born to Lose? Who Makes History? Who Is Bought and Sold? What Disappears? What Remains? Who Decides? Who Does the Crime? Who Does the Time? Who Is Beyond the Law? Who Speaks? Who Is Silent? Who Controls Who?* The least that can be said of this work is that it makes you stop and think…

Finally, aquarium employees will be more than pleased to answer any questions.

Continue north until you reach **Pier 66**, location of the **Bell Street Pier ★**, south of the Edgewater Hotel (see p 151). Extending over 5ha, it includes a marina, public spaces, restaurants and a spectacular view of Puget Sound and its islands. The **Bell Harbour Conference Center ★** occupies 16,000 m² and can accommodate up to 1,000 guests. It is the only conference centre in the United States to offer simultaneous translation in six languages. The marina welcomes boats ranging from 8 to 35m, for up to one week. However, reserve your berth ahead of time (☎ **615-3952**) if you plan on staying more than 24 hours.

You can stroll along the docks for hours and discover the pier's many restaurants, in particular Anthony's Pier 66. You can also grab a snack at The Fishin' Place or at the Bell Street Deli. Hop over to the **Bell Street Fish Market ★** and, like at Pike Place Market, choose the fish that you will fry or bake later that evening. At the Polare store, you can equip yourself with warm seafaring ware made by Highliner (clothing line of the Seattle Ship Supply) as well as

more recognizable brands like Champion, Stormy Seas and Regatta.

Occupying the same pier, **Odyssey, The Maritime Discovery Center ★★★** (*$6.50; every day 10am to 5pm; 2205 Alaskan Way or Pier 66, ☎374-4000, ≈374-4002*), a 10,000m² area built at a cost of $15 million, is a cultural and educational exhibit on Puget Sound. Indeed, the State of Washington's economy is so maritime dependent that one out of every four individuals works in this sector. The exhibit at the Maritime Discovery Center focuses on local activities in Puget Sound and the northern part of the Pacific Ocean, such as commercial fishing, protection of the marine environment and commercial trade. The centre also explains the consequences of human acts on marine life. The exhibit is divided into three themes: *Ocean Trade* stresses the importance of the Pacific Ocean for the local economy; *Harvesting the Sea* explores the dangers of commercial fishing and *Sharing the Sound* explains how to benefit from the virtues of this interior sea while protecting it from pollution. All three exhibits feature high-tech interactive stations: you can steer a container-ship safely into port as a captain tells you how to get to the dock safely in time (you only

Exploring

have two minutes!) or you can kayak down a waterway while watching your progress on a monitor. Furthermore, this maritime centre provides answers to questions you never thought of asking on subjects like the construction of ferryboats, the secrets of an Alaskan cruise or the design of baseball gloves. You will surely learn something new! In all, over 40 interactive stations guide you through this most interesting museum.

Pier 66 used to house the head offices of the Port of Seattle, which has moved to Pier 69. The **Victoria Clipper** ferryboat sails from this pier to its namesake city on Vancouver Island, in British Columbia, Canada. **Pier 70** is the tramway terminal; you can take the tram from here and get off at Pier 48 or continue along the waterfront to Pier 90. Pier 66 also includes the **Myrtle Edwards Park ★** *(3130 Alaskan Way, between W. Bay St. and W. Thomas St.,* ☎*684-4075),* which covers 1.5ha between Pier 70 and the grain elevators to the north.

The grain elevators also feature an exhibit on their operation. Head north and follow the **Elliot Bay Bikeway** to Pier 86. This haven of greenery provides a breathtaking panorama of the **Olympic Peninsula** on the horizon, ferries languidly making their way to the various islands in Puget Sound, like Bainbridge Island, parcels of the Magnolia and West Seattle neighbourhoods, the port of Seattle and ferryboats returning from more or less short journeys. In the far off distance, the well-informed eye can make out Mt. Rainier. Closer still, the **Kingdome**, home of the Mariners and Seahawks, looms like a spaceship and, last but not least, the **Space Needle** watches over the city.

This park is a favorite spot for jogging or taking a romantic walk as you watch dogs playfully chase their tails in this endless green expanse crossed by old train tracks. This park borders the Elliot Bay Park, and together they form an extensive grassland facing Elliot Bay.

Victoria Clipper

A Matter of Taste

Seattle residents are very attached to their "natural" art, as demonstrated by the Seafirst Bank episode. Strong objections were raised when the financial institution decided to sell the work entitled *Three Pieces Vertebrae* (1968) by Henry Moore to a Japanese investor in 1987. The protests were so strong that the sale was blocked, and today Moore's work still graces 1001 Fourth Avenue Plaza.

Other artists did not enjoy the same support. In 1976, creator Michael Heizer presented his *Adjacent, Against, Upon* which stirred up the ire of scribes and residents alike. The three blocks of granite, more or less leaning against one another, have suffered countless attacks by indignant citizens who felt that their tax money should have been used more wisely. This art work stands at the centre of Myrtle Edwards Park.

You will also notice the rose garden and the park's fishing port as well as the controversial sculpture entitled *Against, Adjacent, Upon* ★. Artist Michael Heizer, who starred in a movie by film-maker and art historian Rainier Crone, stirred up the anger of Seattle citizens when he presented his extremely minimalist work of art: three blocks of granite extracted from the Cascade Range arranged, as the title indicates, against, besides and on top of one another.

With time, this piece of art transcended the initial frustration of taxpayers who couldn't understand what was perfectly clear to children: one simply had to climb or sit on this work of art to fully appreciate its artistic worth! Finally, if you want to develop your muscles, go to the extreme north of the park where various pieces of equipment allow you to work on your biceps and triceps.

Exploring

Pike Place Market

Whatever may be thought or said, Seattle is definitely a modern city complete with skyscrapers that reach vertiginous heights, professional sports teams and shopping centres galore – mass consumerism at its best. However, Pike Place Market tips the scale in favour of the old days and counterbalances the constantly evolving modernity cultivated by the Princess of the Pacific Northwest. Indeed, as you stroll through this market, you might feel as if you were in Seattle at the beginning of the 20th century.

This marketplace, which has a tumultuous past, was founded on August 17, 1907. Its purpose was to provide an area where farmers could sell their products at reasonable prices, thereby lowering the exorbitant prices of food supplies, which it has continued to do until now. The Pike Place market was an overnight success. Market activities peaked during the

Pike Place Market

0   25   50m
0   75   150ft

Waterfront Park

ATTRACTIONS
1. Sanitary Building
2. Corner Market
3. Main Arcade
4. Economy Market
5. Economy Atrium
6. The Clock
7. Bronze Pig
8. Victor Steinbrueck Park

ACCOMMODATIONS
1. Green Tortoise Hostel
2. Inn at the Market

Stewart St.
Pike Pl.
Post Alley
Pine St.
Western Ave.
Pike St.
1st Ave.
2nd Ave.
Pike St.
Union St.
Alaskan Way S.
Alaskan Freeway
99

© ULYSSES

1930s when more than 600 farmers sold fresh produce at low prices to citizens and travellers. It is no coincidence that during this period the market was glorified since, by helping people to cope with the financial troubles caused by the 1929 depression, it became the nerve centre of a vital economic activity that gave jobs to many unemployed and provided a pleasant meeting place where people could spend the whole day. By the 1930s the market was a flurry of activity, unimaginable today, with approximately 55,000 people visiting it daily.

In the 1950s, when many city dwellers moved to the suburbs to save on housing costs, the *raison d être* of the market came under fire. Market activities collapsed, and numerous urban conversion projects eyed this unique space. However, during the 1960s, ecologists and other activists gathered to oppose the demolition of this area. At the head of this movement, landscape artist and architect Victor Steinbeck firmly believed that the cultural and historic worth of this marketplace deserved to be protected. This was accomplished in 1971 when, through a referendum, the citizens supported his vision and triumphed over the selfish designs of Seattle's business community. A few years later, Pike Place Market was declared Market Historic District. And this is how the Friends of the Market saved it from a sad fate. With its fish stalls, seafood restaurants (expensive and mediocre), curiosity shops, bookstores and marginal record dealers, the Pike Place Market has everything to please food lovers as well as amateurs of unique objects. This market definitely has a special aura about it. Rain or shine merchants yell at the top of their lungs to attract you to their stalls full of provisions. This market is geared to locals who refuse to pay full price at the supermarket and prefer to be served by "pros" who take the time to educate their customers.

Sculpture of Worker and Seagulls

Exploring

It is a pleasure to explore this vast market at your leisure because it is virtually impossible to follow a specific itinerary, given the many shops and stores here. Venture into the **Sanitary Market** and discover international fast-food (no junk food however), such as Asian and Greek, as well as other types of sandwich counters. Cafés don't limit themselves to the ubiquitous Starbucks - although this chain's first coffee shop was in Pike Place Market.

The Corner Market ★ includes **Left Bank Books** (see p 231), a bookstore that brings marginality to new heights; should you be looking for poetry, feminist essays or Angolan literature, chances are you will find the book you have been dreaming of here. The fragrance of fresh fish and freshly picked produce in the **Main Arcade ★★** will surely challenge your senses, and the merchants of the **Pike Place Fish Market** will try to squeeze a few dollars out of you with their friendly calls and smiles. Then, as you wander through the northwest section of the market, you might be tempted to buy a handmade Native American artwork. The **Sanitary Market Building ★**, located north of the Corner Market, welcomes merchants with a delightful assortment of fresh fruits and vegetables as well as shops crammed with all sorts of mementos, notably religious objects, postcards, toys and wallets, etc. Accessed on the south by Pike Street, the **Economy Market ★** includes a gamut of small restaurants where, for instance, you can buy a French crepe and savour it as you continue exploring. The **Read All About It** newsstand (**☎ 624-0140**) has newspapers from all over the world in addition to an information centre *(corner of 1st Ave. and Pike St., ☎ 628-7453)*. In the **Economy Atrium**, located beneath the Economy Market, you will find the **No Boundaries Café** (see p 180) and a smoke-free area where you can eat and rest. Continue east and you will end up back in the **Main Arcade** (under the **immemorial clock ★**), location of romantic restaurants like **Il Bistro** and the **Alibi Room**, two very charming establishments (see p 184 and 210).

But the market's main attraction, if you can call it that, is without a doubt its *Bronze Pig ★★★* which has become the ultimate emblem of the Pike Place Market. Rachel the pig was created in 1986 by Georgia Gerber, a resident of Whidbey Island, an island in Puget Sound. Georgia was inspired by a real pig named Rachel who won first prize at an annual fair in 1985 thanks to her weight of approximately 340kg! Rachel is no fat-looking bronze statue, however. She is, in fact, a huge piggy bank whose contents are donated annually to organizations such as the Pike Market Medical Clinic, the Downtown Food Bank, the Pike Place Market Senior Center and the Pike Market Child Care & Pre-school and to other associations that extend a helping hand to the destitute and the children of the city.

This pretty much sums up the ground floor. However, beneath this armada of merchants, there are five more floors of stores, record dealers and halls of fame. All you need to do is find your way in this indescribable maze of shops and alleys and discover the nooks and crannies of this market of another era!

North of Pike Place Market, the **Victor Steinbrueck Park** ★ *(2000 Western Ave.,* ☎ *684-4075*) commemorates the architect-landscape artist of the same name who helped resuscitate Pike Place Market as well as Pioneer Square. It is populated by street musicians who sometimes get the crowd dancing, market goers and, more particularly, seagulls and other flying species that steal sandwich crumbs left by

kindred spirits having lunch. From this park, you have a somewhat obstructed view (by two totem poles) of the Waterfront and Puget Sound; its 20-odd tables make it an ideal picnic spot for both Seattleites and tourists. With a couple of coins, you can use one of the powerful telescopes to get a closer view of Bainbridge Island and the other islands that spangle Puget Sound. Unfortunately, the proximity of the Alaskan Highway viaduct makes the park rather noisy during rush hour.

International District

Named in 1964 by mayor, Wes Uhlman, International District is the politically correct title given to Seattle's Chinatown. This appellation has proven to be quite accurate as a multitude of Asian peoples, more particularly Vietnamese, Japanese, Laotians, Filipinos, Koreans and Chinese, live side by side in this neighbourhood. This district is bordered from the west to the east by 2nd and 12th Avenues South, and from the north to the south by Washington and S. Weller Streets.

Exploring

Misery and Racism

Life hasn't been very easy for residents of the International District. During WWII, many Japanese Americans living there were incarcerated, forced from their homes, or killed. Living conditions started to deteriorate rapidly in the 1950s. In the 1960s, many southeast Asians came to live in the International District, nicknamed "Little Vietnam". The quality of life hit its lowest point in 1970, when the Ozark Hotel burned down, killing 20 people. Then, many homes were levelled to construct Highway 5, which divides the city in two.

Since the end of the 19th century, it has welcomed Asian immigrants who came to join family members or to find work in this economic capital of the American Northwest. Moreover, this neighbourhood includes a variety of ethnic restaurants that feature original, if not somewhat disconcerting, menus. However, the bleak history of this district is even more disconcerting than certain types of the food it serves.

The first wave of immigration coincided with the construction of the railroad in the 1880s; subsequently, various tycoons vied for the Chinese workforce that rushed to the American West Coast. The first anti-Chinese protests occurred in 1886 but, when the economy reached its lowest point in 1893, many immigrants were forced to return to their homeland. The Japanese began arriving in Seattle in 1879 and soon formed the largest ethnic minority in the city. They built the Toyo Club gambling house, which quickly became the second largest in the United States. The Japanese also established the Japanese American Citizens League in 1930, which saw to the well being of its fellow Japanese citizens until the start of War World II.

By 1920, many immigrants had saved enough money to bring their families over to this American dreamland. Japanese, Chinese and Filipinos have lived in harmony in this neighbourhood since the 1920s; Seattle being the only city where these three ethnic groups lived together.

However, numerous problems beset this community.

Even today, most of the residents in the International District are poor, and the community must address sensitive issues such as public security and increasing housing costs. It is desperately trying to find land on which to build apartments for the less wealthy, but the problem of "modernization" could not be no more present than in this neighbourhood: the face of Seattle is slowly changing and many luxurious apartments have been built here over the past few years, which worries many of the lower income residents. And, up until very recently, the federal government had even talked about building a prison! Despite these social problems, the animosity between White Americans and Asians is nowhere to be seen in the dark alleyways that house restaurants and shops, and the International District is one of the most visited neighbourhoods as much by Seattleites and visitors who enjoy its exoticism.

We recommend you start the tour by climbing aboard the tramway on South Jackson Street that runs along the waterfront to **Pier 70** (see p 104). It is hard to believe that, between the 1920s and the 1950s, this street was lined with smoky jazz clubs where the likes of Quincy Jones and Ray Charles made their musical debuts in the 1940s. Nothing remains of the swing, bop and cool jazz periods, and the dilapidated industrial buildings that have replaced the former bars do not reflect in any form or manner this effervescent musical period.

At the corner of South Jackson Street and 4th Avenue South, **Union Station ★**, adorned with a clock that measures the passage of time, is the starting point of the underground bus network (METRO), which runs along 3rd Avenue all the way to Pine Street. It then heads east to the terminus, at the corner of 9th Avenue.

To see a large-scale Japanese supermarket, visit **Uwajinaya ★ ★** *(every day 9am to 8pm; 519 6th Ave. S., ☎624-6248 or 800-889-1928, ≠624-6915)*, south of South Jackson Street. The founder of this gigantic emporium, Fujimatsu Moriguchi, named his store in honour of his native village: he originally opened his store in Tacoma in 1928, and then moved with it to Seattle after World War II. Today, his son Tomio is president of the company and has since opened a second store in Bellevue, east of Seattle.

Continue your visit on S. Weller Street by heading east to 8th Avenue S. Then continue north all the way to S. King Street.

Exploring

Taste-bud Titillation

It's one-stop shopping for every Asian victual under the sun at Uwajimaya, whether you're looking for ingredients for a particular recipe or simply wish to sink your teeth into a juicy mango. It is best to visit the place on an empty stomach and let yourself be tempted by its many fish markets and restaurants. You'll be unable to resist the oysters, crabs, and other bounties from the sea, which you can select from the very tanks that contain them (however briefly). This International District landmark has long known that sushi would eventually become all the rage: this delicacy has appeared on the takeout menus of various restaurants for 70 years! Strolling through the warren of passages is sure to make you ravenous, at which point you can treat yourself to *wasabis.* On climbing the stairs, you will come upon florists selling bonsai and *ikebana.* Those fascinated by kimonos and calligraphy materials are also sure to find what they're looking for. This vast emporium is also home to Kinokuniya, an outlet of the largest Japanese bookstore chain in the United States.

In addition to the **Seattle Asian Art Museum** (see p 139), Seattle has another shrine to Asian culture, the **Wing Luke Asian Museum** ★★ (*$2.50, free on Thursdays; guided tours for groups of 10 persons or more Oct to Jun; Tue to Fri 11am to 4:30pm; Sat to Sun 12pm to 4pm; 407 7ᵗʰ Ave. S.* ☎ *623-5124,* ⚏ *623-4559*).

Built in an old car garage next to the Theatre Off Jackson, this is the only museum in the United States that is dedicated to the Pan-Asian community. It was named after Wing Luke, the first Asian politician elected in the State of Washington who won a seat in the Seattle City Council in 1962.

Tragically, this pioneer died in a plane crash in 1965 and the community erected this museum in 1967 to honour his memory.The Wing Luke Asian Museum presents the culture, art and history of the various peoples of Asia and the Pacific Islands, such as Hawaii. For Americans, Asians and people from the Pacific Islands, it provides the opportunity to gain a better understanding of themselves. The museum prides itself on being the only one in the United States to present a critical view of the mass Asian immigration to the American West Coast.

The largest of the two exhibits recounts the 200-year-old history of Asian immigration, starting with the first Hawaiians who chose to reside in the State of Washington; then come the numerous Asians who left their country to establish themselves in the New World, such as the Vietnamese, Laotians, Koreans, Japanese, Filipinos, Chinese and Cambodians, as well as the people from southern Asia and the nomadic mountain tribes. Called *One Song, Many Voices*, this exhibit describes early Asian life in the Evergreen State as well as a few anecdotes on Asian businesses, social clubs, barber and, sports teams.

It takes a few hours to tour the second exhibit, which includes photos, rare objects, hand-painted kites, as well as a series of video interviews that describe the challenges involved in adapting to a new country. You will also gain deeper historical knowledge as you learn about the racism inflicted upon the first immigrants and the Japanese during World War II.

Head west on King St. again all the way to Maynard Street.

To really soak up the atmosphere of the International District, head to the **Hing Hay Park ★** (*corner of S. King St. and Maynard Ave. S.*), built in 1975 and paved with red bricks. Although there is rarely anyone in the park, its location makes it one of the central points of the neighbourhood. Indeed, during special events like the International District Summer Festival, lively crowds gather in this park to celebrate. The big pagoda, built in Taiwan and given to Seattle by the city of Taipei, is typical of the traditional architecture of

Exploring

this small island, with its large fresco and dragon. The memory of the Chinese-Americans killed in World War II is honoured with a memorial decorated with flowers left by families, friends and kindhearted passers-by.

Take S. Maynard Street north to Main Street.

After hiking up Maynard Street, you will spot a little haven of greenery called **Kobe Terrace Park** ★ (*every day 6am to 11:30pm; 700 S. Washington St., between Main St. and S. Washington St., next to Highway 5*) ☎ *684-4075*) This park, known as Yesler Terrace Park until 1975, spreads over 0.5ha and is criss-crossed with footpaths that lead to a 200-year-old stone lantern that weighs 3,600kg. This lantern was graciously offered by one of Seattle s twin cities, Kobe, Japan (hence, the name of the park). Maintained with care, this elegant park clearly distinguishes itself from the rest of the neighbourhood, composed of warehouses, markets paved with red bricks, restaurants and herbalists. Local residents take special care of the cherry trees, going so far as to cut off the dead branches.

On cloudless days, this park affords a wonderful view of Mt. Rainier, Pioneer Square

and the **Danny Woo International District Community Gardens** (*corner of S. Maynard St. and S. Main St., ☎ 624-1802*), named after the donor of the land, the late Danny Woo, pioneer of and restaurant owner in the International District. Gardeners of the older proudly tend to the plants and vegetables they grow on these miniature parcels of land.

Created in 1975 by volunteers, the Danny Woo gardens are reminiscent of the compact size and design preferred by Asian landscape artists. Unfortunately, this park, which *a priori* seems like a lost paradise, does not always provide a peaceful setting: the noise of nearby Highway 5, which borders the park on the east, sometimes makes silence and serenity impossible. Nevertheless, you will generally find peace and tranquility here.

Financial District

Bordered from west to east by 1st Avenue and Highway 5, and from south to north by Yesler Way and Olive Way, the business sector has witnessed, over the past five years, a new trend of architecture in which new buildings are more or less

International District

ATTRACTIONS
1. Union Station
2. Uwajimaya
3. Wing Luke Asian Art Museum
4. Hing Hay Park
5. Kobe Terrace
6. Danny Woo International District Community Gardens

RESTAURANTS
1. Four Seas Restaurant

Exploring

identical. One wonders if there is such a thing as a typical Northwestern American style of architecture or whether this is simply the unimaginative reproduction of existing trends. You be the judge! The postmodern look of the newer buildings is somewhat surprising as classical shapes and lines have seemingly been abandoned and replaced by sinuous curves.

This avant-garde look, coupled with the inhuman traffic in greater Seattle, generated the mass migration of Seattleites to this neighbourhood. There's certainly plenty to do here, with art galleries and theatres galore and a decent nightlife.

Contrary to what might be expected, Seattle's prominent companies, such as Boeing and Microsoft, have their head offices outside the financial district, which is cramped and difficult to drive in (many one-way streets make driving downtown nerve-racking). Other smaller local companies, like Nordstrom, however, have opened major stores in the downtown area.

In addition to the ubiquitous skyscrapers, you will see a range of well-known shops, such as the famous Niketown, which has stores in major American cities such as New York and Chicago, in addition to Planet

Hollywood, owned by Sylvester Stallone, Bruce Willis, Demi Moore and Arnold Schwarzenegger. But like New York's Wall Street, this district becomes lifeless after business hours, which makes it less attractive to visitors during the evening. Yet this is where you will find the city s finest restaurants, luxury hotels, youth hostel and shopping malls, the epicentre of the downtown's economic activity.

You will enjoy walking along 5th Avenue past the **Westlake Park** in front of the Westlake Center. The **Washington State Convention and Trade Center** (the tourist information office is located here) is a mountainous edifice that straddles University and Pike Streets from the south to the north, and 7th and Terry Avenues from the west to the east, thus separating the downtown area from First Hill. Highway 5 also passes beneath this strangely shaped giant. It is also in this neighbourhood that you can travel on the METRO Bus System, an underground transport network allowing you to get around downtown free of charge from 9am to 5pm.

Rising to a height of 42 stories and built in 1914, the **Smith Tower** ★★ *($2; every day 10am to 5pm; 506 2nd Avenue, corner of Yesler Way, ☎682-9393 or 622-4004),* torn between Pioneer Square and downtown, is the work of the Gaggin & Gaggin architecture firm from Syracuse, New York. Entrepreneur L.C. Smith, the Smith-Corona typewriter baron who lent his name to the building, invested a hefty amount of money in his tower, going as far as adorning the window frames with bronze. He also had the building's interior decorated with Alaskan marble and Mexican onyx. Leaving nothing to chance, he made sure that the foundation (made of some 300,000kg of concrete) was fireproof and able to resist earthquakes.

At the request of his son Burns Lyman, L.C. Smith added another 24 stories to the modest proposal of 18 floors that he submitted to the City of Seattle. His son had heard of the praise lavished upon the designers of the Eiffel tower in 1889 and convinced his father to erect a monument that would go down in the history books. For a long time this tower was considered to be the tallest building west of the Mississippi: only three buildings in New York City surpassed its height

when it was built at the beginning of the century. Since then, however, it has been supplanted by another Seattle high-rise, the **Columbian Seafirst Tower** (see p 118), and its size of yesteryear seems lilliputian when compared to the other mammoth buildings that grace the Seattle skyline. Nowadays, the Smith Tower, which figures in the national register of historic sites, is mostly visited for its **Chinese Room ★**. This architectural gem has ornately carved wood paneling and is often used for wedding receptions. You can sit in the Wishing Chair, a chair bequeathed by the empress of China of the day. According to the legend, a single woman who sits on the chair and makes a wish to be married will see her dream come true in the coming year...

From the observation deck on the 35th floor, you get an almost panoramic view (300°) of Seattle's surroundings and of Mt. Rainier. The eccentric Ivar Haglund, creator of the Ivar's Acres of Clams restaurant (see p 178), owned the building in the 1970s and caused a frenzy when

Exploring

Smith Tower

he announced that he planned to replace the old elevators with new ones. Fortunately, a consortium of well-informed people came to the defense of the building and stopped the Norwegian in his tracks: he then sold the building.

Between Rainier Tower and the Columbia Seafirst Center (see below) you will probably notice a building that stands out from all the others, the **Rainier Club** ★ *(corner of Columbia St. and 4th Ave.)*. Unfortunately, this is all you will see of the building as it is reserved for members only. Founded in 1988 by a group of businesspeople, the building was completed in 1904 in the Dutch-Gable style of architecture. The architect of this prestigious club, Kirtland Cutter, drew his inspiration from Englishman Aston Hall. In 1929, as the club enjoyed unprecedented success, a new wing was added on by architect Carl Gould whose Georgian portal now serves as the building's main entranceway.

The Columbia Seafirst Center ★★ *($3.50; Mon to Fri 8:30am to 4:30; 701 5th Ave., between Cherry St. and Columbia St.,* ☎*386-5151,*⇌ *386-5119)* is a 76-story structure with a futuristic black mirror effect built in 1984

during a decade when numerous titanic buildings went up. The Columbia Seafirst Center towered over the Smith Tower and became the tallest building west of the Mississippi. Less elegant than Smith Tower, and less corny than the Space Needle, it dominates the Seattle skyline. From the observation deck on the 73rd floor, you will get the best view of the city, the Cascade Mountains, Mt. Rainier, the Olympic Peninsula and Puget Sound.

Hell, no! We won't go!

Hippie protestors demonstrated against the Vietnam War on the lawn of the Federal Courthouse.

The Federal Courthouse ★*(corner of 5th Ave. and Madison St.)* was designed by architect Louis A. Simon and completed at the end of the 1930s. Like many other federal buildings, its austerity is prevalent, reflecting the glum times after the 1929 depression. Notice the magnificent stairs designed to welcome the great political figures of the State of Washington.

The Seattle Art Museum ★★ *($7; Tue to Sun 10am to 5pm, Thu 10am to 9pm; 100 University St., corner of 1st Ave., ☎ 654-3100)*, whose elegant postmodern building was designed by architect Robert Venturi, features oriental art, a major part of the museum's permanent collection. However, one of most popular attractions stands outside the museum to greet visitors: the ***Hammering Man*** ★★★ is a wonderful example of the public art that Seattle is famous for. This 15m silhouette represents the proletarian strength that has built the past and present Seattle. The motorized structure raises a hammer four times every minute. Artist Joseph Borofsky said of his work: "At its heart, society reveres the worker. The Hammering Man is the worker in all of us".

The five-storey Seattle Art Museum is a skilful mixture of granite, clay and marble, that was completed in 1991 at a cost of $62 million. The museum harbours art works from many peoples from Asia, Africa and the South Sea Islands, as well as Native American and pre-Columbian pieces. Unfortunately, although the collection features a vast assortment of Native American artifacts, they are all too familiar and somewhat stereotypical. However, the African art pieces contribute to the understanding of modern art, in that one can see where revolutionaries such as Picasso and Gauguin drew their inspiration.

The museum also shows a variety of art films. During our visit, one film described Australian Aboriginal art, which, like the collection of African art, fascinates by its strangeness and simplicity. Finally, if used within the week, your ticket includes admission to the Seattle Asian Art Museum.

To go down to the Waterfront, take the **Harbour Steps** *(corner of University St. and First Avenue on the western side) down to the Waterfront. To continue Head east on University Street to 4th Avenue.*

As you will learn in the chapter on Shopping (see p 223), Seattle is replete with shopping centres, especially on the outskirts of downtown. One of them, **Rainier Square** *(1301 5th Ave., between University and Union Streets, ☎ 628-5050)*, covers an entire block, from 4th to 5th Avenues from west to east, and

Exploring

between University and Union Streets from south to north. In it you will find men's and women's clothing stores, bookstores, restaurants, even a museum of Native American art. As you head north on 5th Avenue, you will cross another shopping centre, the **City Center** *(1420 5th Ave., between Union and Pike Streets)*. It also includes a range of boutiques, a Planet Hollywood, a movie theatre as well as the Foster/White Art Gallery on the ground floor. Art works exhibited in the shopping centre itself, especially on the first floor, are mostly by artists who belong to the Pilchuck Glass School.

Not all of Seattle's urban design's please everyone in the city. This is notably the case of **Freeway Park ★** *(between Seneca and University Streets, near Highway 5)*. For some, this park was made to bandage part of the ugly urban landscape created by Highway 5, which separates the first posh neighbourhood in Seattle, First Hill, from the downtown area. For others, this park is nothing but a clumsy attempt at reconciling two neighbourhoods

which could no longer peacefully "live together" because of the presence of Highway 5, which, in spite of its breadth, has not solved traffic problems in the Emerald City. Whatever the case, Freeway Park is enjoyed by children who, despite the omnipresent noise of the highway, enjoy playing next to the waterfalls designed by Lawrence Halprin and Angela Danadjiva.

A single lane, the **Pigott Memorial Corridor**, leads from the south to the north of the park, all the way to the **Washington State Trade and Convention Center ★** *(Pike St., corner of 7th Ave.)*. Other than a few fast-food eateries, there is not much to see in this mastodon structure that is mostly used for business purposes. However, this center does showcase **Seattle George**, south of the main lobby, a striking sculpture, created by Lewis Buster Simpson that represents two of the founding fathers of the United States, George Washington and Chief Sealth. The 24 metallic profiles depict-

Seattle George

ing this political Jeckyll & Hyde duo are supported by an inverted conical structure which, in turn, rests on a tripod.

Paths lead around this structure, and the artist also incorporated historical texts on informative plaques.

Belltown (Denny Regrade) and Seattle Center

Just north of downtown, the Belltown district and Seattle Center are markedly different from one another and, to a certain extent, complement each other wonderfully. The first, which begins just north of Pike Place Market and stretches west to east from 1st Avenue to 5th Avenue, was, scarcely 20 years ago, a seedy area to be avoided. But a number of upscale restaurants and hip nightclubs, not to mention pool halls, have since flourished within this four-block radius, bounded by Denny Way to the north.

The district draws a different crowd than downtown, consisting largely of artists, designers and lovers of refined cuisine who gather here to sip beer while taking in a live jazz show. Most establishments cater to the bold and the beautiful without, nevertheless, being too uptight.

Be that as it may, Belltown (also known as Denny Regrade) is where you'll encounter the artsiest crowd in Seattle – with the exception of the "Republic of Fremont", of course. This district is sometimes referred to as Denny Regrade as, at the turn of the century, the mountain-ringed city of Seattle suffered repeated onslaughts of drizzling rain that amounted to veritable downpours. This is why Denny Regrade's forerunner, Denny Hill, was razed and nothing now remains of this bygone hill.

Between 1902 and 1910, the city tore away at Denny Hill with jets of water pumped in from Union Bay, generating a sea of mud as far as the eye could see. This created a highly surrealistic scene as a few residents refused to abandon their homes, which then rested atop a quasi-apocalyptic environment. Today, the Belltown district is often criticized by the poorer segments of the population and blasé artists for its pointless modernity.

You'll see a lot of graffiti denouncing, for instance, the destruction of old buildings sacrificed for high-priced condos offering breathtaking views of the cityscape. Neighbourhood watering holes have also fallen victim to this gentrification, having been replaced by more upscale restaurants. Nevertheless, the bourgeois persona of this area only appears at

Exploring

night as, during the day, it is common to encounter homeless people bumming a little change. Steer clear of 1st Avenue between Wall Street and Blanchard Street, as this stretch of road beneath Highway 99 (or the Alaskan Way Viaduct) is "home" (such as it is) to several vagrants who sleep, drink and ask for change here, which can make it a rather unpleasant spot come nightfall.

North of Denny Way is the heart of Seattle's tourist activity, namely Seattle Center, the site of the 1962 World's Fair. Among the sights to be seen here are the Space Needle, which, much like Toronto's CN Tower, offers a stunning view of the greater Seattle area and its surroundings. Other attractions, such as the Children's Museum are, needless to say, sure to please children. Also on site is the Pacific Science Center, KeyArena and the Opera House.

On warm summer days, musicians and fans of tribal rhythms gather at the **International Fountain** as dogs run around and kites soar under the looming sun above.

● ATTRACTIONS

1. Center on Contemporary Art	7. Children's Museum
2. Tillicum Place Park	8. Flag Plaza
3. Space Needle	9. International Fountain
4. Olympic Illiad	10. Key Arena
5. Pacific Science Center	11. Opera House
6. Center House	

○ ACCOMMODATIONS

1. Commodore Motel Hotel	9. Sixth Avenue Inn
2. Vagabond Inn	10. Ramada Inn Downtown Seattle
3. Kings Inn	11. Holiday Inn Express
4. Seattle Inn	12. Travelodge
5. Best Western Loyal Inn	13. The Warwick
6. Quality Inn & Suites City Center	14. Wall Street Inn
7. Days Inn	15. Vermont Inn
8. Best Western Executive Inn	

● RESTAURANTS

1. Caffe Minnie's	6. Queen City Grill
2. Palmer's Cocktail	7. Avenue One
3. 2218	8. Space Needle
4. Axis	9. El Gaucho
5. Flying Fish	

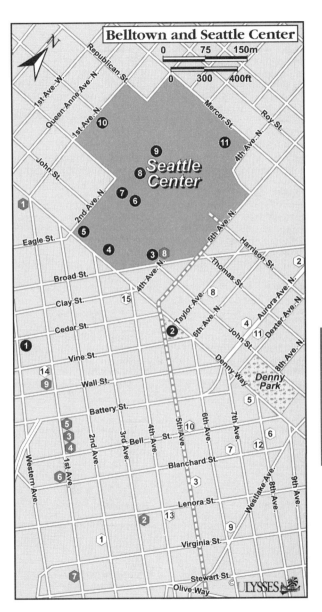

Belltown and Seattle Center

Northwest of the Belltown district stands the **Center on Contemporary Art** ★★ *($2; Tue to Sat 11am to 6pm, Sun noon to 4pm; Cedar St., at Western Ave., ☎/⇒ 728-1980)*, otherwise known as **CoCA**. Adjacent to the Seattle Art Museum since its opening in 1981, the museum moved to its current location in 1995, to the great pleasure of Belltown residents. The **CoCA** prides itself on showcasing the region's newest and most experimental art work, not all of which have pleased the general public.

Indeed, over the years, this museum has boldly allied itself with everything on the so-called fringes of society, featuring tattooed, pierced and chocolate-covered human bodies as well as highlighting all fluids known to humankind, including blood. Some art events have taken on rather unusual forms, such as the one in which body bags were used. Needless to say that conformity is not part of the centre's mandate.

This non-profit arts organization has put on several exhibitions that are now famous in the contemporary art world, such as *Counterfeit Masterpieces of 20th Century Art* in 1989 and, more recently, *Gender Fucked* in 1996. Multimedia installations are an integral part of

the **CoCA**, which would hardly live up to its name without them. At the heart of this contemporary art centre's activities is the art of the Pacific Northwest, though a number of artists from across North America are also invited to exhibit their works. Slovak painters as well as other European artists have also had exhibitions devoted to their work, which only goes to show that the **CoCA**'s focus is indeed international. The centre presents five exhibitions a year.

Head east along Clay Street to the corner of Denny Way.

The triangular-shaped **Tillicum Place Park** ★ *(500 Denny Way, ☎ 684-4075)* honours the memory of the Native American chief after whom Seattle is named, Chief Noah Sealth. At first sight, there is nothing very impressive about this square, save for the copper statue of Chief Sealth sadly sitting enthroned across from Zeek's Pizza. It was probably more impressive when it was unveiled in 1912; the ceremony attended by his great-great grandaughter must have been quite a tearjerker. Unfortunately, history has made an ordinary Native American of the chief, and this sobre park shows it. Today, it merely consists of a few benches where folks can sit to meditate before this wise man's face; the statue is set in a "reflecting pool", with trash littering the surface of the water. Despite this ignominious tribute, we recommend you visit the park nonetheless as, had it not been for Chief Sealth, relations between whites and natives in Seattle would likely have ended in bloodshed.

Once on Denny Way, you'll be just a stone's throw from Seattle Center and its family-oriented tourist attractions. You can also get here by taking the **Monorail** ★ *($1; $25 for a monthly pass; Mon to Fri 7:30am to 11pm, Sat and Sun 9am to 11pm;* ☎ *441-6038, seattlemonorail.com)* from the Westlake Center (see p 224), an "indulgence" that costs nothing more than a dollar. The $3.5 million project was designed by an Italian firm, financed by a Swedish firm, and the cars were built in West Germany, so it could be said that these trains have an international

pedigree ... Built for the 1962 World's Fair, the Monorail runs every 15min, except between 11:30am and 1:30pm, when it comes by every 7min. The enjoyable ride offers a stunning view of the downtown area and Belltown, as supermarkets give way to deserted public gardens, abandoned buildings and construction sites, and this, all the way to your final destination, Seattle Center. The trip only lasts 90 seconds, so make the most of it.

Upon getting off the Monorail, you can't miss the **Space Needle** ★★★ *($9; at 5th Ave. and Broad St.,* ☎ *443-2111,* ⌨ *443-2100, www.spaceneedle.com),* which seems to stand alone in the Seattle sky. It was in 1959 that Edward Carlsson put pencil to scrap of paper to sketch his vision of a tower that would rise high above anything on the horizon. And in 1962, his dream became reality as the tow-

Exploring

Statue of Chief Sealth

ering landmark attracted the gaze of millions from around the world.

Given its spindly silhouette, the Space Needle, though designed to withstand everything Mother Nature could throw its way, has had to close on a few occasions, as it did in December of 1996, when fierce snow storms hit the city. Nevertheless, such occurrences are rare, so you should have no problem getting whisked up to its 200m-high summit, a mere 43-second elevator ride up. A staff member will give you a brief overview of the Space Needle's tumultuous history.

Space Needle

The view from the Space Needle's newly remodeled Observation Deck is absolutely stunning, offering a clear panorama of Puget Sound, Lake Washington, Mount Rainier on cloudless days, Mount St. Helens. Informative signs describe the sights in the distance.

It is, naturally, best to go up on sunny days, when the view is better. However, rainy days should not discourage you from doing so: $9 is a little steep, but if you were in New York, wouldn't you visit the Statue of Liberty? The choice is yours, of course. Also on site are souvenir shops, where Space Needle T-shirts and caps are sold at outrageous prices, and two restaurants.

After having soared into the Seattle sky, head back down to earth and make your way to the western part of Seattle Center, where you can admire the **Olympic Iliad** ★, a public art work created in 1984 by artist Alexander Liberman. Easily spotted given its red colour, which stands in stark contrast to its surroundings, the piece consists of 41 cylindrical iron tubes of various sizes.

Continue your tour of Seattle Center, proceeding west.

Just southwest of the Space Needle is the **Pacific Science Center** ★★★ *($7.50; every day 10am to 6pm; 200 2nd Ave. N,* ☎ *443-2880,* ✉ *443-3631),* a fun-filled "museum" of technology where several hands-on exhibits help visitors understand everyday natural phenomena. Architect

Minoru Yamasaki, who designed Rainier Square (see p 119, 223), saw to the construction of the five buildings that house permanent exhibits like Body Works, which allows you to do such things as test how fast you can pedal a bicycle. Other notable exhibits explain the phenomenon of gravity without being too complex for children (in fact, this centre caters mainly to families, and children in particular, though adults are sure to enjoy it as well).

The Pacific Science Center features a perfect mix of entertainment and education, all parts of the interactive exhibits being simple to operate, without being too simplistic.

The Tech Zone, a room equipped with computers and on-site educators, is designed to empower children with the knowledge of how computers work. Another exhibit, Sound Sensations, allows its visitors to compose their own songs.

The second building features dinosaurs, while the **Smith Planetarium** offers spectacular, starry views of the Northwest sky. Those nostalgic for the 1960s will no doubt make a beeline for the **Laser Fantasy Theater**, the science complex's

fourth building, to enjoy laser light shows sometimes set to the music of The Doors and Jimi Hendrix.

The centre also boasts an **IMAX** theatre (*$2 extra*). Playing here during our visit was, *Everest*, an impressive movie about the famous Himalayan-mountain-expedition..

Head north and enter Center House.

Seattle Center has provided a large space known as **Center House** (*305 Harrison St.*, ☎ *684-8582*) for those looking to have something to eat or drink, though the sustenance offered mostly consists of fast food. It is, however, no ordinary fast-food court, as customers can kick up their heels along with a number of skilled dancers letting loose to the strains of a polka band. Most of the dancers are over 60, which should by not deter you from asking a lady or gentleman to dance!

Also offered on the top floor of Center House are Javanese-music lessons, mostly using percussion instruments which are at the forefront of this Indonesian music? Some stand-up comics also perform here, but, once again, the Center House is primarily geared toward children.

Exploring

Indeed, its main attraction is unquestionably the **Children's Museum ★★** *($5.50, children $4; every day 10am to 5pm; lower level of the Center House,* ☎ *441-1768,* ≈ *448-0910*). The word "museum" is a bit of a misnomer because the place rather consists of a huge playground where kids can play hide-and-seek behind wooden balls or explore a forest whose summit peaks at the restaurant level. Also among the fun hands-on activities are virtual-reality games, including one where kids can enjoy virtual skateboarding, as well as other exhibits, such as *Time Trek,* which allows them to travel back in time, for example to the ancient Mayan civilization. Yet another exhibit spotlights nature, introducing children to our planet's various ecosystems.

Head north to the International Fountain.

After bolting down a few burgers or something of the kind at the Center House, head outside and you'll see **Flag Plaza ★**, where 50 flags flutter freely in the breeze. You may also recall childhood memories upon seeing the **International Fountain ★**, located in the heart of Seattle Center, which shoots jets of water more than 50m up in the air. If you feel the need to cool off, feel free to throw yourself, body and soul, into this cleansing water, and equally reckless souls are sure to follow suit. On warm summer days, musicians fill the air with elusive rhythms, so why not throw your inhibitions to the winds and dance up a storm! During the summer, the Northwest Folk Festival and Bumbershoot bring concerts here, making music lovers jump for joy.

Sports and rock-music fans gather at the **KeyArena ★** *(near N. Harrison St. and 1st Ave. N.,* ☎ *684-7200,* ≈ *684-7342*), the home turf of the Western Hockey League's Seattle Thunderbirds. The KeyArena owes its name to the Key Bank, which bought the building. In addition to presenting exciting ice-hockey games, the stadium welcomes basketball fans who, far outnumbering hockey buffs, flock here to cheer on the Supersonics. Music lovers also come here in droves to see big-ticket concerts by famous acts like Alanis Morissette, Depeche Mode, Andrea Bocelli and Elton John. Keep in mind, however, that like in most American stadiums, food prices are exorbitant; we therefore recommend you have something to eat before taking your seat in the grandstands of KeyArena.

The last, but by no means least, stop in Seattle Center

Lining Occidental Park in Pioneer Square, Duane Pasco's totem poles stand opposite some of Seattle's oldest buildings.
- *Nick Gunderson SKCCVB*

The Waterfront is the perfect contrast to this very modern city, with boats docked next to seafood restaurants.
- *Sean O'Neill*

One of the many ferries crossing Puget Sound, with a superb view of Mount Rainier in the distance. - *Nick Gunderson/SKCCVB*

is the **Opera House** ★ *(at Mercer St. and 3rd Ave. N., ☎ 684-7200, ⇆ 684-7342)*, located in the northeasternmost part of this entertainment centre known as Seattle Center. Speight Jenkins, the opera's general director since 1983, has made full use of his talents, and concerts are often sold out. The opera house's sobre moniker testifies to the austerity of this 3,000-seat amphitheatre. Ballet has been sharing the stage here with opera since 1962, four to five operas being featured annually. Among them is the famous *The Ring of the Nibelung* opera tetralogy by German composer Richard Wagner, whose work has been gaining the public's favour for some time now.

From First Hill to Capitol Hill

First Hill district, the poor cousin of Capitol Hill, which will be explored further on in this section, seems to harbour nothing but hospitals and buildings devoid of any aura or character. This district nevertheless features some of the oldest and loveliest Victorian houses in the Seattle area. But the real high point of First Hill (so named – somewhat pompously –

because the city's first wealthy citizens took up residence here) is its museum, the most conservative of its kind in a city always on the lookout for novelty.

"Conservatism" is not strong enough a word to describe the **Frye Art Museum** ★ ★ *(704 Terry Ave., ☎ 622-9250, www.fryeart.org)*, which for all that is hardly devoid of interest. Outside the museum is a "reflecting pool", a waterfall and a small garden. Once inside, you must cross a rotunda illuminated by a skylight, then an elegant entrance hall, before laying eyes on the Fryes' private collection. The museum's aubergine-and taupe-coloured walls fittingly complement the dark palette of the permanent collections.

Charles and Emma Frye, extremely wealthy late-19th-century Seattle art collectors, purchased a number of paintings by 19th- and 20th-century American artists. Most notable among them were Winslow Homer, Thomas Hart Benton and Edward Hopper. Charles Frye acquired his first European painting at the 1893 Chicago World's Fair, the first of more than 200 paintings that would grace his First Hill home.

This purchase engendered the Fryes' passion for European art, as evidenced by

Exploring

First Hill or Nob Hill

A twist of fate altered the fortune of one of Seattle's many hills, First Hill. On the heels of the gold rush, the well-to-do built homes on this hillock, thereby enjoying the luxury of being close to downtown while basking in the tranquillity of the "suburbs." Before long, this part of town was compared to Nob Hill, a mountainous neighbourhood in San Francisco famous for its wealthy residents. But in 1908, both the Cabrini and Swedish Hospitals acquired land on First Hill. Soon after, sizeable low-rent apartment buildings were built at the foot of the hill, which became known as "Profanity Hill" because of the mud and the steep ascent its residents had to hike up every day. Today, medical clinics abound on the northwest part of the hill and the Wesler Terrace houses the less affluent on the southern side. In short, First Hill lost its former social status despite the addition of Freeway Park, which links it to the rougher Central Area neighbourhood.

the collections of German paintings dating from 1870 to 1900, a period that would serve as a spring-board for the tormented artists of the Expressionist movement (circa 1900-1919). Following in the footsteps of French Impres-sionists, these pre-Expres-sionist German painters depicted the vagaries of nature in all its luminous glory, and panoramas as well as portraits make up the bulk of the collection.

Your artistic neurons may even be roused as you gaze upon *Sin* by Franz Von Struck, an artist well known for his obsessive fear of women and predilection for the morbid. This work de-picts a woman and a snake entwined in such a way as to make it difficult to distin-guish between the two. Troubling, indeed. The mu-seum also houses a 142-seat auditorium.

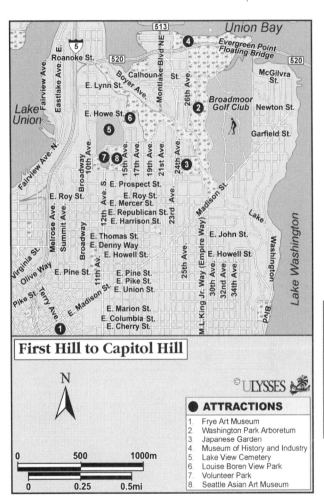

First Hill to Capitol Hill

N

© ULYSSES

● **ATTRACTIONS**

1. Frye Art Museum
2. Washington Park Arboretum
3. Japanese Garden
4. Museum of History and Industry
5. Lake View Cemetery
6. Louise Boren View Park
7. Volunteer Park
8. Seattle Asian Art Museum

0   500   1000m

0   0.25   0.5mi

Exploring

In the easternmost part of the city, the **Capitol Hill** district lies on a hill sloping westward all the way to the downtown area. Separated from downtown by Interstate 5, which bisects the city, this district has been one of Seattle's most pleasant residential districts for some time now, thanks to its laid-back atmosphere and proximity to the business district. However, visi tors will soon realize that there is really very little sightseeing to be done here; but you can stroll around leisurely and, if you're so inclined, mingle with the friendly residents known for striking up lively, pleasant conversations at the drop of a hat. Also worth noting is that this district is the city's unofficial gay village, swarming with shops, bookshops and bars catering to the gay and lesbian community.

In fact, according to certain pundits, Seattle has become the American "pink city" par excellence, even supplanting its neighbour to the south, San Francisco. One of the many gay/lesbian resource guides available in Seattle is *The Pink Pages.*

The high point of Capitol Hill, however, is unquestionably its incredible plethora of shops where you can "shop till you drop". Music stores, bookshops, secondhand and other trendy clothing stores are strategically located here, and the district's distinctly laid-back vibe may even unexpectedly prompt you to head to the nearest tattoo parlor...

Despite its geographically specific name, the **Washington Park Arboretum** ★ ★ ★ *(free admission; every day 7am until dusk, 2300 Arboretum Drive E.,* ☎ *543-8800)* not only features the flora of the Pacific Northwest, but also plant from some 70 countries. This green expanse, which is reached by taking eastbound Madison Street from downtown to Lake Washington Boulevard East, extends from 40th Avenue East and Madison Street to the south, to Highway SR-520 and Lake Washington Boulevard East to the north. With more than 4,800 species on display over 80ha of fittingly landscaped grounds, the arboretum is sure to please nature lovers.

The collections of this living museum, which focuses on trees from the Pacific Northwest, are arranged to highlight their beauty and function within the urban landscape. Educating the public about ecology as well as the diversity of plant species is also among the staff's uppermost concerns. You can even join the non-profit Arboretum Foundation, which relies on a $700,000 annual budget and has over 3,000 members.

You couldn't pick a better season than spring to visit

Birth of a Verdant Eden

Designed in the 1930s by James Dawson a landscape architect with the Olmsted Brothers firm, the arboretum harbours 40,000 trees and vines as well as 139 endangered species - is it any wonder it's called the "tree zoo"? The arboretum was established in 1934, thanks to an agreement between the University of Washington and the City of Seattle, which owned the plot of land, then known as Washington Park. Dawson and Frederick Law Olmsted

Jr. subsequently designed the arboretum as we now know it, though modifications were later made by then director Brian O. Mulligan, who changed the plants' "primitive-to-advanced" plant classification order, which was the norm in the 1930s. He did this by replanting certain species to promote their development, thereby creating the Winter Garden and Woodland Garden, just after World War II.

this huge arboricultural exhibit, when flowers bloom and birds fill the air with song. And there is much more to see here than just magnolias or other common plants, for exotic flora shares the spotlight with the more humble lot of indigenous plants. In deed, you will have the chance to admire Japanese maples, azaleas and rhododendrons. Sharing your passion for flora, Seattleites come here, rain or shine, to stroll along Azalea Way, a sometimes scarcely passable trail that will awaken the "adventurer" in you, or the

more manageable Arboretum Drive East, lined with flowering cherry trees. Maps of the arboretum's various trails are available at the **Donald G. Graham Visitors Center** *(every day 10am to 4pm; 2300 Arboretum Dr. E.)* for those who wish to get a better appreciation for its natural gems. This map also provides information about free guided tours, including those organized Saturday and Sunday afternoons at 1pm.

The crown jewel of this open-air museum is indis-

Exploring

putably the **Japanese Garden** ★ ★ *($2.50; Mar to Nov every day 10am to 4pm, closing time varies according to the season; 1502 Lake Washington Blvd. E.,* ☎ **684-4725**), which is home to turtles, carp and exotic goldfish flitting about in the crystalline waters of a small pond. It was landscape architect Juki Iida who conceived the layout of this 1.4ha formal garden, whose simple, narrow lines make it so very charming. It should be noted that Iida was hardly a newcomer to the art of garden design, having already created more than 1,000 such Japanese gardens! For this particular one, over 500 blocks of granite were extracted from Cascade Range; Iida then decided on the location of each of these blocks and supervised the planting of various trees such as pines, maples, rhododendrons and different plants like moss and ferns. Like at the Seattle Asian Art Museum, visitors can attend a tea ceremony here, held at 1:30pm on the third Saturday of every month from March to November.

From Highway SR-520, you may spot a narrow trail known as the **Arboretum Waterfront Trail**. As insignificant as it may look, it is rife with unexpected treasures, sure to be appreciated by young and old alike. The spectacle graciously offered by Mother Nature also provides a romantic setting, encouraging lovers to whisper sweet nothings to each other. This trail can be taken from the Waterfront Arboretum or the Museum of History and Industry, namely the two places where you can pick up an explanatory brochure on the various species found in this little corner of paradise. Moreover, this exploratory walk will take you no more than an hour, unless, stricken by the beauty of this trail, you linger to enjoy some spectacular view and go so far as to walk all the way back.

The trail runs through **Foster Island** ★, which is home to flora and fauna such as birches, oaks and pines as well as moths, great blue herons, marsh wrens and American blackbirds. More attentive visitors may even spot a foolhardy beaver fleeing a canoeist's oars. You can even explore Montlake Cut by canoe, as these crafts are available for rent at the University of Washington Waterfront Activities Center. What's more, it's not unusual to see clusters of tuberous white water lilies floating in Union Bay, which you can see from the trail or an observation deck built for that purpose. With a little patience, you may also encounter plants, ducks and other birds.

Unfortunately, as is the case for most of the city's parks, traffic, in this case along Highway SR-520 (though it only covers the northern-most part of the trail), spoils the magic of this peaceful haven. At the northernmost tip of the island is a narrow promenade skirting Montlake Cut, where a parade of boats and a few regattas take place every year. You will then cross the largest of Seattle's remaining marshlands, before reaching the parking lot of the Museum of History and Industry (see below).

Just outside the University of Washington campus is another of Seattle's many museums, namely the **Museum of History and Industry** ★★ *($5.50; Mon to Fri 11am to 5pm, Sat and Sun 10am to 5pm; 2700 24th Ave. E.)* And like history itself, this museum is in a constant state of flux, presenting rotating exhibits featuring everything from regional baseball archives to a retrospective of the Pilchuck Glass School. History buffs, particularly those with a penchant for the Pacific Northwest, will be delighted with the museum's vast collection of period photographs *(by reservation only, ☎ 324-1126)*. In the basement is the not-to-be-missed multimedia centre, which reproduces the Great Seattle Fire

of 1889, giving you the impression of actually being in it.

Founded in 1914, the Museum of History and Industry prides itself on being the largest private heritage organization in Washington State. The museum has it all, from nautical equipment to old evening gowns, which admirably characterize the elegant evenings of yesteryear, and relics dating from the late 18th century. However, this museum is also very contemporary, as evidenced by its exhibit on glass blowing, the latest distinctly Seattle trend. The museum provides demonstrations of this craft rooted in ancestral techniques. Also to be seen here is the reconstruction of a street pre-dating the Great Seattle Fire of 1889, as well as some period objects.

As previously mentioned, this museum mainly caters to die-hard history buffs, though everyone should appreciate the artifacts on display here. The museum also features not-to-be-missed curiosities, including *Empathy Belly*, a work produced by a local female artist to give men an inkling of what it's like to be pregnant. And for the price of admission, it's a steal! What's more, you'll have access to 800,000 books, maps, manuscripts and pho

Exploring

tographs inside the museum or on its Web site: ***www.seattlehistory.org***

We know that myths sometimes take on staggering proportions in the United States. The case of Bruce and Brandon Lee is no exception to this golden rule. In fact, you can pay your respects to both the martial-arts master (see p 137) and the cult movie star (see p 137) at the historic **Lake View Cemetery** ★ *(every day 9am until dusk, offices open every day 9am to 4:30pm; at 15th Ave. E. and Garfield St.)*. While it may fail to dazzle or exhilarate visitors, it serves as the final resting place of some of Seattle's celebrities. Besides the two aforementioned megastars of the silver screen, both of whom died under mysterious, not to say bizarre, and tragic circumstances, you can visit the graves of Princess Angeline, daughter of Chief Sealth, Doc Maynard, one of the city's founders, not to mention Asa Mercer, to whom Seattle owes its first generation of true-blue Seattleites. The Denny family, Hiram M. Chittenden, designer of the Ballard Locks, as well as Henry Yesler, the city's first real businessman, to whom Seattle should be grateful, are also laid to rest here.

If visiting the cemetery has dampened your spirits and you feel the need for breathtaking panoramas, head straight to the **Louisa Boren View Park** *(at 15th Ave. E. and E. Olin St.)*, located just across from the entrance to the cemetery. This park has a few notable perks: it is seldom swamped by tourists, and its peaceful environment offers the most sensitive of souls the opportunity to contemplate the beauty of Lake Washington and Lake Union.

Located right in the heart of Capitol Hill, the 16ha green expanse known as **Volunteer Park** ★★ *(winter every day 10am to 4pm, summer every day 10am to 7pm; 1247 15th Ave. E.,* ☎ *322-4112)* was named in honour of those who enlisted to fight in the Spanish-American War of 1898, in the Philippines. The name was thought up by J. Willis Sayers upon his return from the front.

The history of the park is rife with anecdotes – not to mention reorganizations. Indeed, the city acquired the land for the modest sum of $2,000 in 1876. In 1885, the Washelli Cemetery (now known as Lake View Park) and its dearly departed took up residence here for two years. But Leigh Hunt, owner of the *Post-Intelligencer*, one of Seattle's daily newspapers, then had a mystical experience: he heard voices that instructed him to move the bodies of

The Lee Family

Kung-fu superstar Bruce Lee (1940-1973) was born in San Francisco in 1940, the Year of the Dragon. His father, Lee Hoi Chuen, and mother, Grace Lee, named him Lee Jun Fan. Later known as Bruce Lee, he was also nicknamed "Little Dragon" and "Never Sits Still". In 1941, he and his family moved to Kowloon, a district of Hong Kong. At the age of 6, he made his screen debut in *The Beginning of a Boy*, then went on to play various roles in about 20 more Asian films.

At the age of 14, Lee began studying a form of kung-fu known as Wing Chun. Later that year, he had a few run-ins with the Triads, the Chinese mafia. After being involved in numerous street fights, Lee was arrested and his parents decided to send him back to the United States to study. He earned his high-school diploma in Seattle, then enrolled at the University of Washington, where he studied philosophy. He then met the woman he would marry, Linda Emery, dropped out of school, and published his first book, *Chinese Gung Fu, The Philosophical Art of Self Defense.* In 1966, Lee and his new family moved to Los Angeles, where he opened the third branch of his kung-fu school, in Chinatown.

In 1971, Lee was surprised to discover that *Green Hornet,* a TV series in which he had starred, was a big hit in Hong Kong, and that he himself had become an overnight success! Lee then starred in his first "real" films, including *Fists of Fury*, released as *Chinese Connection* in the United States, and the famous *Return of the Dragon*, in which he triumphs over Chuck Norris in the last scene. Bad Feng Shui plagued Lee during the shooting of *Game of Death*, which he never completed. He died July 20, 1973, apparently of cerebral edema; 25,000 people attended his funeral in Hong Kong. He was buried at Lakeview Cemetery in Seattle.

The fate of Bruce Lee's son, Brandon Lee (1965-1993), was just as tragic as his father's. Born in Oakland in 1965, he played his first role in *Kung Fu: The Movie* in 1986 at the age of 21, and made his feature-film debut in *Legacy of Rage*. He also starred in Rapid Fire, but what elevated him to cult status was *The Crow*, a movie during the shooting of which he was fatally wounded. In one scene, a co-star was to fire a gun at Brandon; but a dummy bullet was accidently discharged, hitting and killing him on March 31, 1993. He was buried next to his father at Lakeview Cemetery in Seattle.

the dead as this space was meant for the living.

In 1893, 2.4ha of trees were cut down to make room for the park's first greenhouse. After climbing the 100-odd steps as you enter the park from 15th Avenue, you'll see the water tower, which dates from 1906, though its reservoir was built in 1901.

Once in the park, you can't miss Isamu Noguchi's work, *Black Sun*, which draws globetrotters from far and wide. An irresistible Kodak moment for shutterbugs from the world over, as in the background stands the Space Needle: your photographs are sure to impress your friends! At the top of the steps (106 to be precise), you can enjoy a panoramic view of the city from the water tower's observation deck, and this, at no charge. While this view doesn't compare to the one from atop the Space Needle, you get what you pay for – or just about!

You can also learn about the Olmsted brothers, who created modern-day Seattle's park system, at the park's permanent exhibit, which chronicles the legacy of the famous landscape architects who transformed the face of the city forevermore.

The park also harbours the Victorian-style **Volunteer Park Conservatory** *(winter: every day 10am to 4pm, summer: every day 10am to 7pm)*, reminiscent of London's Crystal Palace. Each of its five houses features a different theme: the Palm House, Bromeliad House, Fern House and Cactus House, as well as the Seasonal Display House. The Olmsted brothers had the conservatory prefabricated, then assembled by the park's employees. The pride and joy of the glass conservatory, however, is its collection of orchids. Because they are very delicate, they are protected by a fence, but can still be seen. The greenhouse was built in 1912 by the Olmsted brothers, who mapped out the entire park. The spring and fall sales, which draw local "greenthumbs", are two of the park's most popular events.

In the 1950s, J. Willis Sayers and some fellow war veterans set up a commemorative plaque to remind everyone why Volunteer Park was so named. The plaque informs visitors that the park is dedicated to the memory of soldiers who died in combat while "liberating the oppressed peoples of Cuba, Puerto Rico and the Philippine Islands".

Volunteer Park is mainly visited on weekends, when people lounge about or run around chasing frisbees; others prefer playing catch, while the more indolent sunbathe to the sounds of tribal rhythms played by local musicians.

The park was home to the Seattle Art Museum from 1933 to 1991. But all is not lost, for the **Seattle Asian Art Museum** ★★ *($3; Tue, Wed and Fri to Sun 10am to 5pm, Thu 10am to 9pm; 1400 E. Prospect St., ☎ 643-3100)* took its place in 1994. Indeed, the museum, housed in an Art-Deco building in the northernmost part of the park, is the centerpiece of Volunteer Park. Lovers of

Exploring

Black Sun

Asian-art will be delighted to know that it contains one of the 10 largest collections of Asian art outside the Far East.

If you plan on visiting the museum at the turn of the millennium, note that a temporary exhibition entitled *Modern Masters of Kyoto: Transformation of Japanese Painting Tradition, Nihonga from the Griffith and Patricia Way Collection* is being held from August 19, 1999 to February 13, 2000. This exhibition spotlights 80 examples of *Kyoto Nihonga* by 40 artists. These paintings span a period of 80 years, from 1860 to 1940. The museum also presents short films, performances and *Free First Saturdays*, when a multitude of activities are offered for the whole family, notably films for children *(11am to 2pm)*.

Also on display here is the art of centuries of dynasties: art works from Southeast Asia, China, Japan, Korea, Vietnam and others, which will delight neophytes and connoisseurs alike. One room is devoted to Chinese funerary art, another to old Japanese kimonos, while yet another stunning one houses the religious stone sculptures of southern Asia. The sculptures dating from the Yuan dynasty (13th century) are each as impressive as the last, be they grave keepers, simple re-

productions of peasants, or warriors. Another room showcases Buddhist art, which can lead to a spiritual experience, as it did for us. The precision and attention to detail that went into the hand-crafted figurines are fascinating. In short, this museum is definitely worth the trip. If you reserve in advance, you can take part in a traditional tea ceremony at the **Tea Garden ★** *(Thu 11am to 5:30pm, Fri to Sun 11am to 4:30pm)*.

University District

Better known as the "U District", the University District offers a superlative studies-oriented environment. Because it is located away from downtown and all the distractions created by the urban life, a distinctly laid-back atmosphere prevails here. The district teems with cafés and restaurants (frequented almost exclusively by a student crowd), avant-garde and trendy shops, to say nothing of scores of bookshops and alternative-newspaper stands.

In fact, so different is the University District from the "real" city that you may well feel as if you've been parachuted into a completely

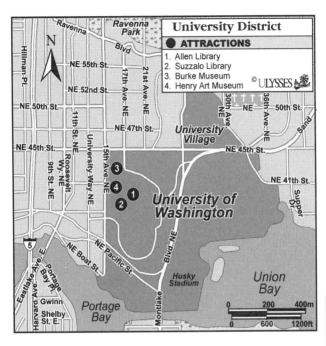

different city, if not another state. Much like Capitol Hill, this district offers little in the way of tourist attractions. Instead, you'll find another, certainly younger face here, far from all those skyscrapers and Starbucks that seem to occupy every downtown street corner.

Though Seattle is not the kind of city where people look down on others, the University District is even more open to the different lifestyles adopted by those who have taken up residence here, whether during their studies or simply to

get away from the urban jungle.

To reach the University District, take Interstate 5, an easy trip that should take you less than 20min, provided you don't get stuck in one of the traffic jams that continue to plague the Interstate. University Way, a.k.a. "The Ave", is mainly where the action is. Indeed, this is where you'll find everything from the latest Korn recording to second-hand clothing stores. In short, this must-visit district of the Emerald City is worth an exhaustive tour, if only

Exploring

for a sunny (if you're lucky) afternoon.

Let us begin the tour with its main attraction: the **University of Washington** ★ *(at NE 45th St. and 17th Ave. NE, ☎ 543-2100)*, where your first stop should be to gather information at the aptly named **Visitor Information Center** *(Mon to Fri 8am to 5pm; 4014 University Way NE)*. Founded in 1861, the university first occupied a single building on what is now known as University Street, located in the heart of modern-day downtown Seattle, an area then known as "Denny Knoll". But the development of the surrounding area forced the powers that be to conclude that the original site was no longer suitable, so they selected an undeveloped piece of land north of Portage and Union Bays. Construction began in 1891, but the project was axed due to lack of funds. However, Regent David Kellogg had Denny Hall, the first building of the new site, built in 1895 and it welcomed the first university students that same year. Designed by George W. Lawton and Charles Saunders, this building houses the

university's original bell, cast in 1861.

The Olmsted brothers were again hired, this time to design the campus: they developed the "Liberal Arts Quadrangle" plan in 1904, but had to postpone its implementation for the 1909 Alaska-Yukon-Pacific Exposition, which was to be held on the site. A few other buildings have been since been added, including the **Allen Library** ★, named after wealthy donor Paul Allen of Microsoft and built by Edward Barnes, stands in sharp contrast to the more Gothic-looking **Suzzallo Library** ★. Today, the campus sprawls over 315ha and welcomes over 30,000 students a year.

The main entrance to the campus is on 17th Avenue NE, and just to the right of one of the university's greatest treasures, the **Burke Museum of Natural History and Culture** ★ *($5.50; Fri to Wed 10am to 5pm, Thu 10am to 8pm; guided tours available by appointment, ☎ 543-5591, 543-5590 or 543-7907, ≠ 685-3039, www.washington.edu/ burkemuseum.)*. At the entrance to the museum stands a native totem pole similar to those in Vancouver, Canada. After crossing the museum's light-filled entrance hall, you will see a life-size replica of one of our long-lost predecessors, a dinosaur. A dozen metres farther are some 40 artifacts, each as fascinating as the last, which offer a fine overview of the captivating quantity of relics the museum contains (it is said to house more than 4 million artifacts, and we'll just have to take their word for it!). One of the museum's highlights is definitely its impressive collection of Native American art from some 30 aboriginal communities, which recounts the history of Washington State from the dinosaur age to the earliest human presence in the region.

There is also a permanent exhibit entitled *Pacific Voices*, which explores the culture and language of West Coast nomadic communities. Another permanent exhibit, the *Life and Times of Washington State* chronicles the natural history of Washington State over a period of 500 million years. After your enlightening tour of the museum's treasures, you can refuel on a good caffe latte at the in-house café, **The Boiserie** (☎ 543-9854).

Take Memorial Way (the continuation of 17th Avenue NE) to Denny Hall, on your left. Continue eastward to Red Square.

Designed in the 1960s, Central Plaza, or **Red Square**, was the site of a number of civil demonstrations during the era of "peace and love". Offering quite a contrast from Red Square, the **Suzzallo Library** has been dubbed the "cathedral of books" because of its size and the amazing amount of books it contains. Those who visit it will soon understand why it is so named, its ceilings reaching staggering heights. East of the Suzzallo stands the Allen Library, while at the southernmost end of the campus is the gushing Drumheller Fountain, also known as "Frosh Pond", surrounded by the university's famous rose gardens.

Farther west is **Meany Hall**, which was rebuilt after being heavily damaged by an earthquake in 1965. Recitals and chamber-music concerts are presented here. The stairs next to the building lead to the Henry Art Gallery.

Located on campus since 1927, the **Henry Art Gallery ★** *($5; Fri to Sun, Tue and Wed 11am to 5pm, Thu 11am to 8pm; at 15th Ave. NE and NE 41st St.,* ☎ *543-2280,* ≈ *685-3123, www.henryart.org)* was renovated and greatly expanded in 1997, more than quadrupling its size. Its most significant collections of 19th- and 20th-century art include everything from photography and painting to textiles.

The museum's permanent collections are upstairs in the small North Gallery. Unlike the Burke Museum, whose focus is more historical (see above), the North Gallery spotlights contemporary art. The alterations made in 1997 included a 100-seat auditorium as well as a large space named the S. Gallery, where various contemporary art works are exhibited along with multimedia installations. The temporary exhibits change at warp speed, so you'll be hard-pressed to see the same piece more than once unless you return within the same week. Noteworthy among the temporary exhibitions we enjoyed was *Coming to Life: The Figure in American Art 1955-1965*, which explored the evolution of the body in art from Abstract Expressionism to Pop Art.

Bald-Headed Eagle

The Outskirts of Seattle

North of Seattle

North of Seattle Center are two bodies of water named **Lake Union** and **Green Lake**, which are surrounded by quiet residential neighbourhoods perfect for outdoor activities. Many area residents make no secret of their athletic side, taking advantage of their surroundings by running, in-line skating and even sailing.

Those travelling with children are sure to venture into this part of the city, as it is home to the **Woodland Park Zoo** ★★ (*$8; every day 9:30am to 4pm; 5500 Phinney Ave. N., ☎ 684-4800, ≈ 233-7278*). The zoo shelters an impressive number of endangered species, such as the bald-headed eagle, Asian and African elephants, grey wolves, jaguars, ocelots, orang-outangs, snow leopards and a Sumatran tiger. Also among the zoo's residents is a young lion whose roar makes all the other animals quiver. Habitats include the African Savannah, which features such animals as giraffes and zebras.

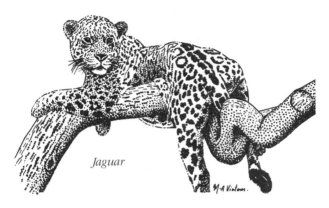

Jaguar

The zoo also sees to the conservation of certain plants, including 13 varieties of orchids.

While at the zoo, visitors can have something to eat at the charming little Rain Forest Cafe. The **Woodland Park Rose Garden** ★ (☎ **684-4040)**, which harbours more than 5,000 carefully tended roses over a little less than 1ha, can also be visited here.

Northwest of Seattle

The remote districts of Fremont and Ballard are not exactly your run-of-the-mill neighbourhoods. In fact, some zealots have designated the former the "Artists' Republic of Fremont", or the "Center of the Uni-verse", which says it all: Fremont is the artsiest of districts. Despite its pretensions, at least we can say that here, as is rarely the case, public art reflects the community's originality.

Located west of Fremont, Ballard has had a strong Scandinavian flavour for a little over a century, being heavily populated by people from Denmark, Sweden, Finland, Iceland and Norway. The district even puts on an annual Norwegian Constitution Day Parade on May 17 to remind the 19th-century immigrants' great-grandchildren of their Scandinavian heritage.

The district's premier tourist attraction is the **Ballard Locks** *(free admission; every day 7am to 9pm; 3015 NW 54th St.,* ☎ *783-7059)*. In 1917, the **Hiram M. Chittenden Locks**, as they are officially named, were finally completed after

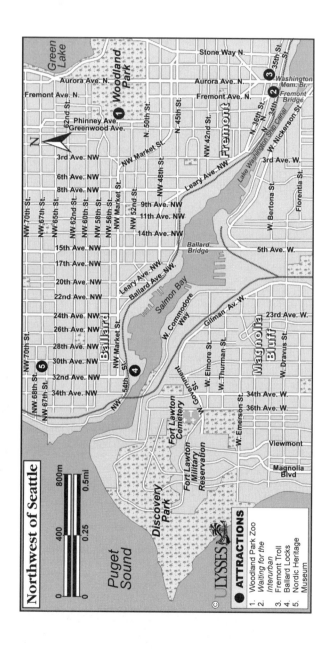

Northwest of Seattle

Green Lake

Woodland Park

Stone Way N.

35th St.

Aurora Ave. N.

Aurora Ave. N.

Washington Mem. Br.

Fremont Ave. N.

Fremont Ave. N.

Fremont Bridge

32nd St.

Phinney Ave.

Greenwood Ave.

N. 50th St.

N. 45th St.

NW 42nd St.

N

Fremont

N. 36th St.

N. 34th St.

N. Nickerson St.

Lake Washington Ship Canal

W. Nickerson St.

3rd Ave. NW

NW Market St.

NW 48th St.

Leary Ave. NW

3rd Ave. W.

6th Ave. NW

W. Bertona St.

8th Ave. NW

9th Ave. NW

Florentia St.

NW-70th St.

NW-67th St.

NW-65th St.

NW-62nd St.

NW-60th St.

NW-58th St.

NW-56th St.

NW 52nd St.

NW Market St.

11th Ave. NW

14th Ave. NW

15th Ave. NW

Ballard Bridge

5th Ave. W.

17th Ave. NW

20th Ave. NW

Leary Ave. NW.

22nd Ave. NW

Ballard Ave. NW.

Salmon Bay

Ballard

24th Ave. NW

W. Commodore Way

Gilman Av. W.

23rd Ave. W.

26th Ave. NW

28th Ave. NW

NW Market St.

W. Elmore St.

W. Thurman St.

Magnolia Bluff

30th Ave. NW

NW 54th St.

W. Gov't St.

32nd Ave. NW

W. Dravus St.

34th Ave. NW

NW-70th St.

NW 68th St.

NW 67th St.

Fort Lawton Cemetery

34th Ave. W.

36th Ave. W.

Fort Lawton Military Reservation

W. Emerson St.

Viewmont

Magnolia Blvd

Discovery Park

Puget Sound

400   800m

0   0.25   0.5mi

© ULYSSES

ATTRACTIONS

1. Woodland Park Zoo
2. Waiting for the Interurban
3. Fremont Troll
4. Ballard Locks
5. Nordic Heritage Museum

Statues and Monsters...

A work entitled *Waiting for the Interurban* ★★, completed in 1979, represents five people patiently waiting for the bus. These aluminium individuals sit at the corner of Fremont Avenue N. and N. 34th Street, just north of the *Fremont Bridge* ★, the most-travelled drawbridge in the world according to the Guinness Book of World Records. Area residents enjoy (literally) dressing the figures of the *Waiting for the Interurban* statue, especially during Christmas time and the winter season. A little farther east is the Aurora Bridge, under which stands the *Fremont Troll* ★★★, a strangely featured character who, with his inordinately large face, flaring nostrils and monstrous fingers, seems straight out of a B movie. Despite its hideous appearance, the character is actually quite pleasing. Perhaps, like us, you will find him vulnerable and innocuous, clutching an old VW Bug in his left fist.

years of labour, and it is here that the salt water of Puget Sound and the fresh water of Lake Washington commingle – a phenomenon rarely seen in the world. If you visit the locks between June and August, you'll have a good chance of seeing salmon migrating upstream to their freshwater spawning grounds. You will also get to watch dozens upon dozens of boats go by, pleasure crafts and commercial vessels alike, navigating from one body of water to the other.

If you venture farther north, you can visit one of Seattle's distinctive museums, the **Nordic Heritage Museum** ★ *($4; Tue to Sat 10am to 4pm, Sun noon to 4pm; 3014 NW 67th St., ☎ 789-5707).* Located at the corner of 30th Avenue NW and NW 67th Street, it recounts the early days of the Scandinavian immigrants who settled in Seattle as of the mid-19th century. On display are the costumes, tools and textiles

Exploring

of various northern European countries, as well as an exhibit on the third floor highlighting Danish, Finnish, Swedish, Norwegian and Icelandic culture.

The northwesternmost tip of Seattle includes the Magnolia district and is primarily visited for its marvellous verdant expanse, **Discovery Park** ★★ (see p 79).

South of Seattle

The districts south of Pioneer Square have little of vital interest, consisting primarily of an industrial area stretching over several kilometres along the Waterfront. It is nonetheless worth visiting, if only to check out the **Museum of Flight** ★★ *($8; Fri to Wed 10am to 5pm, Thu 10am to 9pm; 9404 E Marginal Way S., ☎ 764-5720, www.museumofflight.org*), one of Seattle's most celebrated museums.

Located on a former Boeing base, this air and space museum showcases awe-inspiring aircraft, with several authentic vintage models on display in the **Great Gallery**. Eighty years ago, this museum-to-be was known as the "Red Barn", Boeing's original airplane factory. Children are sure to enjoy the hands-on exhibits; in fact, the sometimes bizarre, downright wacky and/or concertingly original planes can be appreciated by one and all. As such, the museum is worth a visit, even for those with only a fleeting interest in aviation...no pun intended.

Accommodations

Seattle is hardly in short supply of hotels, making it easy for visitors to find somewhere to stay among the city's plethora of establishments.

However, because the city is experiencing major economic growth, finding a room that is both decent and inexpensive can be something of a challenge. Nevertheless, a number of establishments offer magnificent views of Elliot Bay, Puget Sound or the downtown area, and sometimes even Lake Washington.

Most hotels are located downtown, whereas other districts have virtually none. Those scattered throughout Seattle Center offer standard comfort and a close-up view of the Space Needle. Pike Place Market harbours one of the city's youth hostels as well as a marvellous "boutique hotel", a charming little hotel reminiscent of those found in Europe. (See p 161) You may sometimes have to get off the beaten path to find the establishment that best meets your needs. We therefore invite you to peruse this chapter carefully, and recommend that you consider districts with a smaller selection of hotels.

Ulysses' Favourite Accommodations

All prices mentioned in this chapter apply to double-occupancy rooms before taxes during peak tourist season, namely from April to October. In fact, the hotel occupancy rate is exceptionally high during this period. Those who anticipate visiting Seattle in season are thus strongly advised to reserve their room a few months in advance. Most hotels require a credit-card number to guarantee reservations. During the low season, from November to March, many hotels rent out rooms at lower prices, but the harsher climate may well make your stay less pleasant.

Pioneer Square

Pioneer Square Hotel
$99 to $159
77 Yesler Way, WA 98104
☎ *340-1234*
☎ *800-800-5514*
⇄ *467-0707*
The only hotel in this district is the aptly named Pioneer Square Hotel, taken over and restored by the Best Western chain in 1995-96. Built in 1914, the establishment sports a turn-of-the-century look that is sure to please fans of the Roaring Twenties, as will both the furnishings and the lobby. Located in the western part of the historic district, the hotel is within easy reach of the Waterfront, which lies farther west along Yesler Way.

Waterfront

The Edgewater
$130 to $250
2411 Alaskan Way, Pier 67 at Wall St., WA 98121
☎ *728-7000*
☎ *800-624-0670*
⇄ *441-4119*
Built in the 1960s, The Edgewater is Seattle's only waterfront hotel. Renovated in 1997, the hotel has 236 rooms, whose décors recall Western Canadian lodges. Depending on the room you choose, you will have a striking view of Elliot Bay, the islands of Puget Sound or the Olympic Mountains; the rooms facing east provide an unparalleled view of the city's skyscrapers and the Space Needle. You may hesitate at first to venture into The Edgewater as it seems very secluded from the city itself; but think again, as all the tourist attractions – particularly Pike Place Market – are just a stone's throw from this one-of-a-kind hotel.

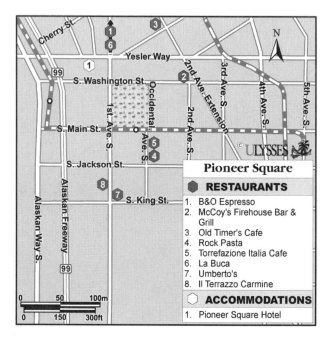

Pioneer Square

RESTAURANTS

1. B&O Espresso
2. McCoy's Firehouse Bar & Grill
3. Old Timer's Cafe
4. Rock Pasta
5. Torrefazione Italia Cafe
6. La Buca
7. Umberto's
8. Il Terrazzo Carmine

ACCOMMODATIONS

1. Pioneer Square Hotel

Pike Place Market

Green Tortoise Hostel
$15 to $40
1525 2nd Avenue, WA 98101
☎ *340-1222*
☎ *888-4AHOSTEL*
⇄ *623-3207*
The Green Tortoise Hostel, which primarily draws young travellers, is only steps away from Pike Place Market. Internet access as well as laundry facilities are just two of the services provided here.

Inn at the Market
$155 to $345
≡, ℝ
86 Pine St., WA 98101
☎ *443-3600*
☎ *800-446-4484*
www.inatthemarket.com
Located in the heart of Pike Place Market, the Inn at the Market is a fine choice for those who prefer charming little hotels to their big-chain counterparts. The spacious, well-lit rooms afford an excellent view of Puget Sound: those who get the chance to see the sunrise will have this glorious image etched on their cere-

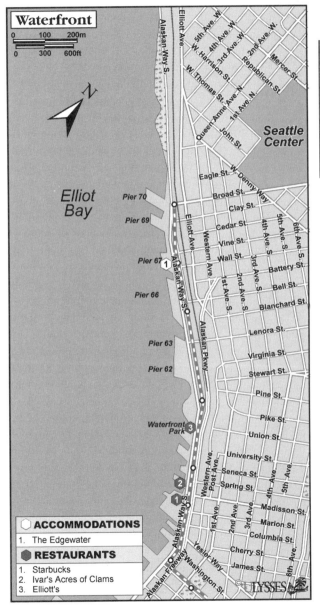

Waterfront

| 0 | 100 | 200m |
| 0 | 300 | 600ft |

Elliot Bay

Seattle Center

Pier 70
Pier 69
Pier 67 **1**
Pier 66
Pier 63
Pier 62

Waterfront Park **3**

2
1

Elliott Ave.
Alaskan Way S.
Elliott Ave.
Western Ave.
Alaskan Way S.
Alaskan Pkwy.
Western Ave.
Post Ave.
Alaskan Way S.
Alaskan Freeway

5th Ave. W.
4th Ave. W.
3rd Ave. W.
2nd Ave. W.
Mercer St.
Republican St.
W. Harrison St.
W. Thomas St.
1st Ave. N.
Queen Anne Ave. N.
John St.
Eagle St.
W. Denny Way
Broad St.
Clay St.
Cedar St.
Vine St.
Wall St.
4th Ave. S.
3rd Ave. S.
Battery St.
2nd Ave. S.
1st Ave. S.
6th Ave. S.
Bell St.
Blanchard St.
Lenora St.
Virginia St.
Stewart St.
Pine St.
Pike St.
Union St.
University St.
Seneca St.
Spring St.
4th Ave.
5th Ave.
Madisson St.
Marion St.
1st Ave.
2nd Ave.
3rd Ave.
Columbia St.
Cherry St.
6th Ave.
James St.
Yesler Way
Washington St.

⬡ **ACCOMMODATIONS**
1. The Edgewater

⬢ **RESTAURANTS**
1. Starbucks
2. Ivar's Acres of Clams
3. Elliott's

©ULYSSES

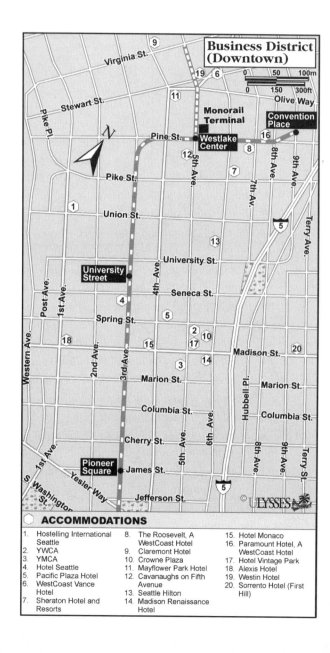

Business District (Downtown)

ACCOMMODATIONS

1. Hostelling International Seattle
2. YWCA
3. YMCA
4. Hotel Seattle
5. Pacific Plaza Hotel
6. WestCoast Vance Hotel
7. Sheraton Hotel and Resorts
8. The Roosevelt, A WestCoast Hotel
9. Claremont Hotel
10. Crowne Plaza
11. Mayflower Park Hotel
12. Cavanaughs on Fifth Avenue
13. Seattle Hilton
14. Madison Renaissance Hotel
15. Hotel Monaco
16. Paramount Hotel, A WestCoast Hotel
17. Hotel Vintage Park
18. Alexis Hotel
19. Westin Hotel
20. Sorrento Hotel (First Hill)

bral cortex for a long time to come – our word of honour!

The establishment favours sombre blue and taupe hues as well as silky sheets to slip into for a good night's sleep. Guests can also warm up by the fireplace or sip coffee while reading a daily paper or a novel in the cozy lobby. For a great dinner, head to the Campagne Restaurant (see p 185), adjoining the hotel, where the seafood is out of this world. A staff member will be delighted to reserve a table for you.

Downtown

Hostelling International – Seattle
$15 to $17 for members
$18 to $20 for non-members
84 Union St., at 1st Ave., WA 98101
☎ *622-5443*
⇄ *682-2179*
www.hihotels.com
Young travellers may well want to spend a night at the Hostelling International – Seattle, the city's youth hostel. The 199-bed establishment has private rooms available; groups are also welcome, but should reserve in advance. Making reservations is also a good idea for those visiting between June and September, when the demand is so high that only members are accepted.

YWCA
$33 to $50
≈, ☺
1118 5th Ave., WA 98101
☎ *461-4860*
One of the least expensive places to stay is, of course, the YWCA, though only women are welcome. While the rooms are rather tiny and unimaginatively decorated, this is unlikely to deter women travellers in search of peace and quiet from appreciating the establishment. Besides, they can take a dip in the indoor swimming pool or let off steam in the fitness centre. Weekly rates are also available.

YMCA
$60
≈
909 4th Ave., WA 98104
☎ *382-5000*
For simple accommodations and a friendly welcome, head to the YMCA, whose slogan says it all: "The nicest people stay with us!" Located right in the heart of downtown Seattle, the "Y" offers well-lit, medium-sized rooms to its guests, who can rest easy as they won't be bothered by impudent night owls. Boarders can relax in the TV room, play a game of racquetball or squash, or swim a few laps in the indoor swimming pool. All this and a truly gracious staff, too!

Hotel Seattle

$90 to $120

315 Seneca St., at 3rd Ave., WA 98101

☎ *623-5110*

☎ *800-426-2439*

⇌ *623-5110*

The 11-storey Hotel Seattle offers basic comfort. Every room has nice furnishings, a television and a VCR. And for more comfort, a few small chairs and a lovely bedside table adorned with a standard lamp, enhance a décor that could, nevertheless, use a make over. Indeed, the grey wallpaper's "cross-fading" leaf pattern and the dark ceiling, which makes the room impossibly dim, are hardly the highlights of the hotel. On the other hand, the bathrooms have been completely redone and each is fitted with a standard bath/shower; a large closet, at the entrance of the room, also proves very useful. Guests can have breakfast at Bernard's on Seneca (see p 185), located in the hotel's basement.

Pacific Plaza Hotel

$90 to $125, bkfst

400 Spring St., at 4th Ave., WA 98104

☎ *623-3900*

☎ *800-426-1165*

⇌ *623-2059*

Renovated in 1980, the Pacific Plaza Hotel was originally built in 1929 by architect A. O. Baumgartner. The historic, if old-fashioned, little guestrooms were being renovated (again!) during our visit. A few of the rooms offer a view of bustling 4th Avenue, and all have a 60cm television set, modem hookup and voice mail. The tiny bathroom is fitted with a rudimentary shower. The hotel is connected to the Red Robbin Pub (see p 185) as well as a Starbucks outlet.

WestCoast Vance Hotel

$135

620 Stewart St., WA 98101

☎ *441-4200*

☎ *800-426-0670*

⇌ *441-8612*

www.westcoasthotels.com/vance

Take Stewart Street from Pike Place Market and you can't miss the WestCoast Vance Hotel, which occupies the southern stretch of Stewart Street and a considerable chunk of 7th Avenue. This is yet another hotel that was designed in the 1920s, and restored in 1990. A very turn-of-the-century cachet still pervades the establishment, as evidenced by its lobby and frosted windows. The carefully conceived décor and warm-coloured rooms make this a very tasteful, highly recommended hotel. If Italian food makes your mouth water, head to the hotel restaurant, Città Ristorante. All of this makes the WestCoast Vance an affordably priced luxury hotel – what more could you ask for?

Accommodations

Sheraton Hotel & Resorts
$135 to $650
≈, ⊛
1400 6th Ave., at Pike St., WA 98101
☎ *621-9000*
⇄ *621-8441*
www.sheraton.com
To say that the Sheraton Hotel & Towers is a luxury hotel is to put it mildly. Money is clearly no object for the owners of this establishment, which has recently undergone $11 million worth of renovations. The 840 rooms provide everything you could possibly wish for in terms of splendour, from voice mail to a magnificent desk, as well as in-house facilities such as the indoor swimming pool and whirlpool. What's more, the hotel also offers 108 suites that are sure to be appreciated by business travellers. One of the hotel's high points (literally!) is unquestionably its observation deck on the 35th floor, which affords a breathtaking view of the cityscape and the surrounding area.

WestCoast Roosevelt Hotel
$135 to $180
≡, ⊘
1531 7th Ave., WA 98101
☎ *621-1200*
☎ *800-426-0670*
⇄ *233-0335*
westcoasthotels.com/roosevelt
Located on the same block as Niketown, The Roosevelt, a WestCoast Hotel, harks back to the bygone

days of the 20th century with its sombre-coloured lobby, and the furnishings of its rooms recall the 1920s – an era that seems very much in fashion in Seattle. The 151 rooms will satisfy the needs of solo travellers such as businesspeople, who can hold meetings in one of four conference rooms set aside for that purpose. In the lobby stands a piano whose ivory keys have been dallied by a few celebrated musicians. Guests can also enjoy a martini, the house specialty, in the social atmosphere of Von's Grand City Cafe.

Claremont Hotel
$139 to $199
⊘
2000 4th Ave., at Virginia St., WA 98121
☎ *448-8600*
☎ *800-448-8601*
⇄ *441-7140*
www.claremonthotel.com
The very classy Claremont Hotel has a classic look, modelled after turn-of-the-century European hotels. The lobby is graced with high ceilings as well as a classical decor of marble and bronze. Most rooms afford a view of the cityscape or Puget Sound. And, aah, the bathrooms! You could easily spend half a day in there, reading USA Today as you luxuriate in everything from the plush bathrobe to the complimentary toiletries. Guests also have access to state-of-the-

art fitness equipment. Also at the Claremont is Very Italian Assaggio, a three-star Italian restaurant that has garnered a multitude of gastronomic awards (see p 186).

Crowne Plaza
$140 to $240, bkfst
☉
1113 6th Ave., WA 98101
☎ *464-1980*
☎ *800-2CROWNE*
⇄ *340-1617*
www.crowneplaza.com

The Crowne Plaza occupies the northeast corner of the block between 5th and 6th Avenues, at Seneca Street. Business travellers are sure to appreciate the exquisite hotel's nine conference rooms, just as leisure travellers will cherish the in-house health club and the impressive view provided by the panoramic windows of the 415 rooms. Guests will find these rooms equipped with several modern conveniences, such as an iron and ironing board, and those feeling peckish can enjoy skilfully prepared dishes at the City Views restaurant or a latte at the Espresso Cart. Music lovers in the mood for syrupy jazz can have an early-evening drink at the Sax on Seneca Lounge.

Homewood Suites Hotel
$149 to $209, bkfst
K, ℝ
206 Western Ave., between John St. and Thomas St., WA 98119
☎ *281-9393*
☎ *800-225-5466*
⇄ *283-5022*
www.homewood-suites.com

Visitors seeking out-and-out luxury need look no further than the Homewood Suites Hotel, which looks right onto Elliot Bay and the Olympic Peninsula. The comfort of guests is the staff's number-one priority and they certainly don't skimp on it: each of the suites is comprised of two rooms with a king-size bed, a kitchenette, a microwave oven, a refrigerator, a dishwasher (!), a coffee maker as well as place settings and cutlery. These large suites do lack imagination, however, the walls needing to be livened up somewhat. Then again, who could complain when the only flaw is the décor?

Mayflower Park Hotel
$150 to $365
≡, ☉
405 Olive Way, WA 98101
☎ *623-8700*
⇄ *382-6997*
www.mayflowerpark.com

The Mayflower Park Hotel, which adjoins the Westlake Center shopping mall (see p 224), is a real bargain, considering the service and the quality of its rooms.

In fact, the spacious guest quarters, which have a separate living room and bedroom, provide a homey feeling that is seldom found in other Seattle hotels. Most of the establishment's twenty suites come with a minibar, but what makes this hotel one of our favourites is the attentive service of the staff, who will be happy to recommend a nightclub where you can dance until the break of dawn. The hotel's magnificent lobby makes it a choice place in which to daydream until hunger gets the better of you, or simply chat with your fellow travellers who, like you, will have only positive things to say about this exquisite establishment. You can also relax over one of the best martinis in town at Oliver's (see p 188) and, when dinner time rolls around, satisfy your palate – and then some – at the Andaluca Restaurant (see p 188).

Cavanaughs on Fifth Avenue
$155 to $225
1415 5th Ave., between Pike St. and Pine St.,
WA 98101
☎ *971-8000*
⇄ *971-8100*
www.cavanaughs.com
Strategically located between the Westlake Center and Rainier Square shopping centres, Cavanaughs offers opulent accommodations with a view of Puget Sound to the west and the Space Needle to the north. In business since 1996, the hotel has 297 rooms with refined décors, a lovely desk on which to plan out your day, as well as all the necessary toiletries. Each of the oversized rooms has a very comfortable bed and a large living room with cable TV, VCR and CD player. A coffee maker as well as an iron and ironing board are also at guests' disposal. The in-house restaurant, the Terrace Garden, provides a lovely view of Elliot Bay and serves typical Northwest cuisine, while the soft melodies of live jazz can be heard in the lounge.

Seattle Hilton
$155 to $500
ℝ, ☺
1301 6th Ave., between University St. and Union St.,
WA 98101-2304
☎ *624-0500*
☎ *426-0535*
⇄ *682-9029*
www.seattlehilton.com
Business travellers opt for the Seattle Hilton because of its close proximity to the Washington State Convention and Trade Center (see p 117). The breathtaking view from the top of the 237-room luxury hotel will leave you awestruck as you gaze upon the Olympic Peninsula and Puget Sound. The in-room amenities are the norm in Seattle for this category of hotel, consisting

of a hair dryer as well as an iron and ironing board, not to mention a refrigerator. The exercise room, on the 29th floor, will allow you to keep your muscles in peak condition and work off those extra pounds gained from eating the delicious fare at the in-house Asgard Restaurant.

Renaissance Madison Hotel
$160 to $220, bkfst
☺
515 Madison St., at 6th Ave.,
WA 98104
☎ *583-0300*
☎ *800-HOTELS-1*
⇰ *624-8125*
www.renaissancehotels.com
Located just west of Inter-state 5, the Renaissance Madison Hotel offers rooms with spectacular views of the Olympic Mountains, the downtown area or Elliot Bay. Decorated with pastel-coloured paintings, they are fitted with a few couches, eggshell-white walls and a king-size bed with silky inviting sheets. Guests also receive complimentary coffee or tea along with a daily newspaper. Those who enjoy video games can order one (at their expense) and play to their hearts' content on the in-room cable TV. All rooms are also graced with a large closet, a hair dryer, an iron and iron-ing board, as well as a minibar. The hotel also boasts health-club facilities, an indoor swimming pool and whirlpool on the 20th floor, and a restaurant on the 28th floor.

Hotel Monaco
$195 to $775
⌂, ☺
1101 4th Ave., at Spring St
WA 98101
☎ *621-1770*
☎ *800-945-2240*
⇰ *624-0060*
www.monaco-seattle.com
Part of the Kimpton Group hotel chain, Hotel Monaco is a gem with all modern conveniences. What's more, you will have the chance to enjoy some of the best wines produced by the state of Washington. In fact, guests are invited to a wine tasting every day from 5pm to 7pm. This takes place in the magnificent lobby, finely decorated by Los Angeles designer Cheryl Rowley, who combines the Ancient-Greek style classic lines with the typical mo-dernity of the "City of An-gels". The chandelier sus-pended from the high ceil-ing confers a sophisticated atmosphere upon the lobby, where the wine se-lection is remarkably di-verse. As for the rooms, the hotel shows originality and has wisely painted the walls in warm colours, unlike many of its counterparts in Seattle. Moreover, you can help yourselves to the minibar as you listen to your favourite tunes on the in-room CD stereo. Having provided sustenance for

your soul, you can then do the same for your body at Sazerac (see p 188), which serves fine Northwest cuisine.

The Paramount Hotel
$200 to $225

⊛

724 Pine St., at 7th Ave., WA 98101
☎ 426-9500
☎ 800-426-0670
⇄ 292-8610
westcoasthotels.com/paramount
Situated in the northeastern limit of the downtown area, the Paramount, despite its original style, is probably the easiest hotel to overlook in Seattle. However, its location takes nothing away from its definite charm. Indeed, a magnificent view of the Space Needle and Lake Washington awaits, as do charming rooms well decorated in a sobre style. Each of the 146 rooms offers the standard Seattle conveniences (iron and ironing board, hair dryer and coffee maker), while the suites are enhanced with whirlpool baths for the weary traveller.

Hotel Vintage Park
$200 to $435

⊘

1100 5th Ave., at Spring St., WA 98101
☎ 624-8000
☎ 800-624-4433
⇄ 623-0568
hotelvintagepark.com
Located on busy 5th Avenue, Hotel Vintage Park is another "boutique hotel" where European charm and American modernity come together in perfect harmony. Much like its sister establishments belonging to the Kimpton Group chain (Hotel Monaco and Alexis Hotel), Hotel Vintage Park offers wine tastings featuring vintages from Washington State in its intimate lobby, where you can chitchat by the fireplace with fellow travellers from around the world. The genial staff members will do their utmost to make your stay a memorable one. The hotel's 126 rooms are decorated in rich, dark hues, with a television set ensconced in a lovely piece of cherrywood furniture. Guests can also treat their palates to fine Italian cuisine at Tulio Ristorante (see p 188).

Alexis Hotel

$210 to $625

♨, ®,

1007 1st Ave., at Madison St.,
WA 98104

☎ **624-4844**

☎ **800-264-8482**

⇌ **621-9009**

www.alexishotel.com

The 100-odd rooms of the Alexis Hotel, the third link in the Kimpton Group chain, offer a romantic decor where you can lounge blissfully under the covers while sipping the drink of your choice. You can then enjoy a relaxing bubble bath in the spacious bathroom, before hitting the streets of Seattle. Some suites have a fireplace, while others have a two-person whirlpool bath; in short, the comfort and luxury of this hotel make it a regular favourite with those seeking high-quality accommodations. Guests can relax their tense muscles in the whirlpool on the 6th floor, then dine on so-called "New American Cuisine" at The Painted Table, adjoining the hotel.

Westin Hotel

$240 to $350

P, ≈, ⌂, ☉, ®, 🐾, ❧

1900 5th Ave., at Stewart St.,
WA 98101

☎ **728-1000**

☎ **800-228-3000**

⇌ **728-2007**

Architect John Graham has made the Westin Seattle, which takes up the entire block between Stewart and Virginia Street, and 5th and 6th Avenue, one of the most impressive hotels in town. Parking your car will be no problem as the hotel, is comprised of two huge towers (the first of which was built in 1969 and stands 40 storeys high on the corner of Stewart Street, while the second, to the north, is 47 storeys tall and was built in 1981) linked by a walkway to the Westin Building, which has a multi-level parking lot. The word "luxury" describes this establishment in a nutshell. Its 800 rooms, overlooking either Puget Sound, the Space Needle or Safeco Field, lack nothing at all: a private bar, a coffee maker, an iron and ironing board, cable TV and voice mail, not to mention the beautiful desk on which you can plan your day's itinerary. The hotel is home to three restaurants, namely Roy's Seattle, Nikko and the Golden Bagel Cafe, as well as the largest ballroom (the Grand Ballroom) north of San Francisco and west of

Mississippi, with 20m-high ceilings and room for up to 2,000 guests. As luxury dictates, you can relax in the indoor swimming pool, the sauna, the whirlpool, or build up your muscles at the health club.

Belltown (Denny Regrade) and Seattle Center

Commodore Motel Hotel
$39 to $65
2013 2nd Ave., between Virginia St. and Lenora St.,
WA 98121-2215
☎ *448-8868*
⇄ *269-0519*
www.commodorehotel.com
Well situated in the centre of town, the Commodore is one of the least expensive hotels in Seattle. Despite their rather unimaginative décor, the rooms are decent and a sound choice for budget travellers.

Vagabond Inn
$55 to $100
🐾, ≈, ⊛, ℝ, △
325 Aurora Ave. N., WA 98109
☎ *441-0400*
The opening of the Vagabond Inn coincided with the 1962 World Fair, though it was renovated in 1998. Its best-equipped rooms come with a refrigerator and microwave oven. A worthwhile option for those who wish to stay a little outside the downtown area while

remaining less than 5min from all the city's major tourist attractions.

Kings Inn
$60 to $100
ℝ
2106 5th Ave., WA 98121
☎ *441-8833*
☎ *800-546-4760*
⇄ *441-0730*
www.travelbase.com/destinations /seattle/kings-inn
Guest at the Kings Inn are guaranteed gracious service as well as clean and comfortable rooms but the décor could use a little freshening up. The staff will provide you with a microwave oven or a refrigerator upon request, conveniences that come in rather handy if you wish to have something to eat without having to leave your room.

Seattle Inn
$70 to $100
≈
225 Aurora Ave. N., WA 98109
☎ *728-7666*
⇄ *567-5265*
Located opposite the Holiday Inn Express, the Seattle Inn stands out because of its huge indoor swimming pool, though guests will be disappointed with the tasteless rooms. The establishment mainly relies on its location, which provides an okay view of the Space Needle.

Accommodations

Best Western Loyal Inn
$75 to $105, bkfst
⌂, ⊛, ≈
2301 8th Ave., WA 98121
☎ *682-0200*
⇄ *467-8984*
The service and hospitality of the staff at Best Western Loyal Inn are the highlights of this well-known hotel chain. Noteworthy among the conveniences offered are voice mail, a sauna and a whirlpool, (accessible around the clock), as well as the complimentary copy of *USA Today* guests receive every morning.

Quality Inn & Suites City Center
$79 to $159, bkfst
⌂, ⊛, 🐕, 🖊
2224 8th Ave., WA 98121
☎ *624-6820*
☎ *800-228-5151*
Another practical, if austere, hotel, the Quality Inn & Suites City Center caters to those who wish to explore the streets of Seattle by bike as it rents them out. Comfort and basic amenities are provided for guests, who can relax those sore muscles in the hotel's sauna or whirlpool at any time of the day or night.

Days Inn
$89 to $139
P
2205 7th Ave., WA 98121
☎ *448-3434*
⇄ *441-6976*
Staying at the Days Inn has just one real advantage: you will be but a stone's throw from the Space Needle and Seattle Center. The minimal comfort and the nondescript decor of the rooms are not particularly inspiring. Truth be told, their only distinguishing feature is a large mirror and certainly not the view, which ranges from 7th Avenue ("lively" but hardly very romantic) to - worse yet - the parking lot!

Best Western Executive Inn
$99 to $149
200 Taylor Ave. N., WA 98109
☎ *448-9444*
☎ *800-351-9444*
⇄ *441-7929*
www.exec-inn.com
As its name suggests, the Best Western Executive Inn caters to business travellers, providing a large conference room for conventions. However, tourists will enjoy the view of the Space Needle from the rooms facing north. The hotel also supplies guests with an iron and ironing board, a coffee maker and, above all, two queen-size beds in many of its rooms.

Sixth Avenue Inn
$100 to $120, bkfst
P
2000 6th Ave., between Virginia St. and Lenora St.
WA 98121
☎ *441-8300*
☎ *800-648-6440*
⇄ *441-9903*
The 160-odd well-lit rooms of the Sixth Avenue Inn,

Accommodations

located just south of the Space Needle, make it a choice hotel. Provided for your leisure are cable TV, a VCR and myriad copies of Reader's Digest, not to mention the ubiquitous Bible. The somewhat dull, very beige decor of the rooms is fortunately enhanced with period photographs, wicker chairs and a table. A practical closet in which to store your luggage as well as a standard, but rather small, bathroom with a bath/shower and a little shelf (of sorts) for your toiletries round out the room's amenities. Guests with east-facing rooms can enjoy a view of Queen Anne Hill from the comfort of their cozy beds. The flawless, courteous service, as well as access to the restaurant of the same name are sure to make your stay here a memorable one. Breakfast is served from 7am to 11am.

Ramada Inn Downtown Seattle
$100 to $165
2200 5th Ave., WA 98121
☎ *441-9785*
⇄ *448-0924*
www.ramada.com
Occupying the entire block between 5th and 6th Avenues all the way up to Blanchard and Bell Streets, the Ramada Inn Downtown Seattle offers 120 somewhat tacky-looking rooms that could use a makeover. Be that as it may, non-smokers will definitely appreciate

the fact that 75 per cent of the rooms are smoke-free. Moreover, the cleanliness of the rooms as well as the outstanding service certainly compensate for the glaring lack of taste that prevails in the guestrooms and the in-house restaurant, Big Cliff's.

Holiday Inn Express
$119 to $159, bkfst
≈, ☉, ®, ዼ
226 Aurora Ave. N., WA 98109
☎ *441-7222*
☎ *800-HOLIDAY*
⇄ *441-0786*
Open since early 1998 and offering a low-angle view of the Space Needle, the Holiday Inn Express is a sound choice for travellers with rather limited budgets who wish to stay in a respectable hotel. The establishment has 195 rooms, 45 of which are suites, including 10 with a whirlpool bath. Each room has a coffee maker as well as an iron and ironing board and guests can choose to sit down to a complimentary continental breakfast which is graciously offered in the hotel's lobby. A small indoor pool and fitness centre are also available. The hotel mainly welcomes families, but it also suits business people as it houses two conference rooms, namely the Pike Place Room and the Pioneer Square Room. What's more, the impeccable service is sure to make

your stay here a very pleasant one.

Travelodge
$119 to $159, bkfst
®, ≈
200 6th Ave., WA 98121
☎ *441-7878*
☎ *800-578-7878*
⇄ *448-4825*
Travelodge
$60 to $90
2213 8th Ave.
☎ *624-6300*
☎ *800-578-7878*
⇄ *233-0185*
www.travelodge.com
The Travelodge is another one of those big-chain hotels that offer decent but rather bland accommodations. The Travelodge has two locations in Seattle. Coffee (or tea) and a continental-style breakfast are offered on the house. An indoor swimming pool and a whirlpool round out the hotel's facilities.

The Warwick
$140 to $380
☺, ≈, △
401 Lenora St., at 4th Ave.
WA 98121
☎ *443-4300*
☎ *800-426-9280*
⇄ *441-9488*
www.warwickhotel.com
The Warwick Hotel houses some 220 rooms, finely decorated with Italian marble and carefully chosen fabrics. Athletic types can stretch their legs at the fitness centre or in the swimming pool, followed by a

steam bath in the sauna. The hotel staff is particularly obliging, so don't hesitate to ask questions. What's more, those itching for a taste of luxury can opt for one of the suites, which could satisfy even the most demanding of aristocrats. The hotel's restaurant, Liaison, combines the subtle flavours of Northwestern cuisine with a quintessentially European-bistro ambiance.

Wall Street Inn
$150 to $209, bkfst
K
2507 1st Ave., WA 98121
☎ *448-0125*
☎ *800-624-1117*
⇄ *448-2406*
There are few hotels along 1st Avenue in the Belltown District, so the Wall Street Inn has no competition to speak of in the area. All of the B&B's rooms are flooded with natural light, and the view of Puget Sound and the waterfront alone makes this hotel a good option. Guests here can also enjoy a continental breakfast along with a good cup of coffee as they read the daily paper in a family-like ambiance. The inn has wisely set up a fireplace in its lobby, which is much appreciated by guests on rainy days. Note that five of the 20 rooms are set aside for guests who wish to stay on for an extended period of time.

Accommodations

Vermont Inn
$299 to $425
☺, *K*
2721 4th Ave., at Clay St.,
WA 98121
☎ *441-010*1
Set back from the traffic of
Denny Way, the Vermont
Inn has been offering apartments or studios that can
only be rented by the week
(*$299 to $425*) or the month
(*$795 to $1195*) for the past
five years. Its standard
apartments with common-
place décor are fitted with
comfortable sofa beds, an
iron and ironing board, a
refrigerator, a microwave
oven and everything else
you may require to cook for
yourselves. There is a laundry room in the basement
and a terrace on the roof
that affords a lovely view of
Elliot Bay on sunny days. In
short, this is just the place
for those for who don't
need luxury. Exercise
equipment is also available
to visitors and "residents" of
the hotel.

Queen Anne

Inn at Queen Anne
$110 to $160
K
505 1st Ave. N., WA 98109
☎ *282-7357*
☎ *800-952-5043*
⇌ *217-9719*
www.pacificws.com/iqa
Conveniently located near
Seattle Center, the Inn at
Queen Anne stands at the
end of Queen Anne Ave-
nue. The establishment
prides itself on the cleanliness of its rooms, well laid
out for your comfort. All
offer voice-mail service as
well as a kitchenette with a
microwave oven. Weekly
and monthly rates available.

MarQueen Hotel
$159 to $219
K, ℝ, ℜ
600 Queen Anne Ave. N.,
WA 98109
☎ *282-7407*
☎ *888-445-3076*
⇌ *283-1499*
If you have the opportunity
to stay in a charming little
"boutique hotel", make it
the MarQueen Hotel, which
gets our prize for the warm-
est of its kind. Housed in an
elegant building dating
from 1918, the establish-
ment was renovated in
1998, thereby enhancing its
European character. When
you enter the sumptuous
lobby, you will see a large
staircase that leads to the
two floors above, where
spacious, well-lit rooms
looking out on the magnifi-
cence of Puget Sound await
you. Guests may well have
trouble leaving their rooms,
with their oh-so-charming
furnishings and captivating,
refined canopy beds. Then
again, there may be no
need to, as you can prepare
your own culinary delights
in the kitchenette, complete
with refrigerator, while lis

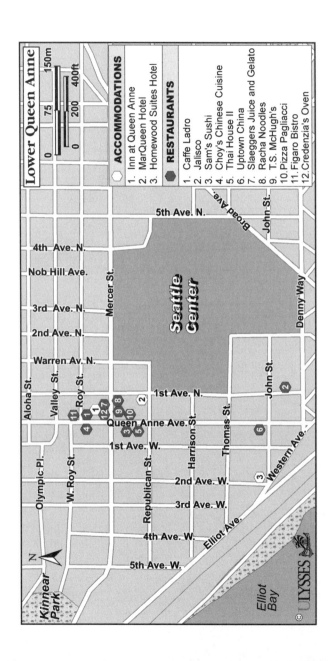

Lower Queen Anne

tening to your favourite tracks on the CD stereo.

First Hill

 **Sorrento Hotel**
$225 to $1,200

®

900 Madison St., WA 98104-1297

☎ *622-6400*

☎ *800-426-1265*

≈ *343-6155*

www.hotelsorrento.com

Perched on First Hill, the Sorrento Hotel is the oldest luxury hotel in Seattle, having opened its doors in 1909. It was restored to its original Italian Renaissance glory in 1981. The result? Guests will be charmed by the elegance of the hotel, whose lobby combines Honduran mahogany with antiques and other luxurious touches. The rooms themselves have it all, including a fax machine, two-line phones with voice mail as well as a modem connection. Those with the means and opportunity to stay in the penthouse suite will also be treated to the regenerative properties of its whirlpool bath, not to mention the incredible view of Puget Sound. The rooms are more like small apartments, with doors between the master bedroom and living room providing privacy. The hotel also attends to the culinary needs of their guests' palates with the Hunt Club (see p 194),

a highly acclaimed Seattle restaurant. What's more, those who wish to enjoy an aperitif can retire to the Fireside Room, where a fireplace creates a very warm atmosphere.

University District

University Plaza Hotel
$85 to $150

≈, ⅄

400 NE 45th St., WA 98105

☎ *634-0100*

☎ *800-343-7040*

≈ *633-2743*

www.travelbase.com/destinations /seattle/univ-plaza

The University Plaza Hotel offers some 130 ordinary-looking, though comfortable, rooms. A laundry room is at guests' disposal, as is an outdoor swimming pool so that those who visit Seattle during the summer can enjoy a refreshing dip. The lobby is graced with a Steinway on which pianists demonstrate their savoir-faire. The hotel is also home to the Excalibur restaurant, whose cuisine will satisfy the most discriminating of palates. To reach the hotel, take Interstate 5, then westbound Exit 169.

Accommodations

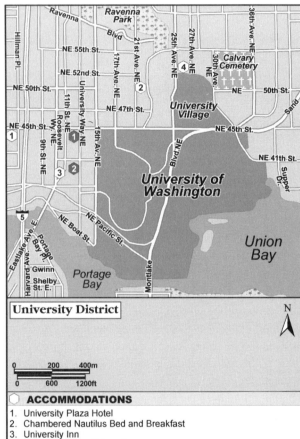

University District

N

| 0 | 200 | 400m |
| 0 | 600 | 1200ft |

ACCOMMODATIONS

1. University Plaza Hotel
2. Chambered Nautilus Bed and Breakfast
3. University Inn
4. Silver Cloud Inn University

RESTAURANTS

1. All American Sports Bar & Grill
2. Big Time Brewery & Ale House

Accommodations

Chambered Nautilus Bed and Breakfast

$99 to $115, bkfst
pb, ℜ
5005 22nd Ave., at NE 50th St.,
WA 98105
☎ 522-2536
☎ 800-545-8459
≠ 528-0898
www.bed-breakfast-seattle.com

If you're looking to stay in homier surroundings, check into the Chambered Nautilus Bed and Breakfast, where your hosts Karen, Steve and Joyce will welcome you into a house of Georgian architecture dating from 1915. Before entering the lobby, which is full of antiques, take the time to admire the well-tended gardens in front of the house. The establishment has six rooms, all of which have a private bathroom, with a charming teddy bear comfortably seated on each of the beds. A tip: those who reserve in advance may even be fortunate enough to snap up the only room with a fireplace!

University Inn

$95 to $145, bkfst
⊛, ≈, ☺
4140 Roosevelt Way NE, WA 98105
☎ 632-5055
☎ 800-733-3855
≠ 547-4937
www.universityinnseattle.com

The 102 rooms of the University Inn are comparable to those at the most notable hotels in the downtown area. Each one is equipped with a data modem port as well as a view of Portage Bay, Lake Union and the posh neighbourhoods in the western part of the city. Guests can also get sustenance at the Portage Bay Cafe while reading the daily paper, graciously provided by the establishment. During the summer, you can relax in the small outdoor swimming pool. To reach the inn, take Interstate 5, get off at westbound Exit 169, then take southbound Roosevelt Way NE to NE 42nd Street.

Silver Cloud Inn - University District

$110 to $150
≡
5036 25th Ave. NE, WA 98105
☎ 800-551-7207
www.scinns.com

Located near the University of Washington and University Village (see p 140, 224), the Silver Cloud is renowned for its hospitable and gracious staff, who will fill you in on the highlights of the University District. The establishment offers about 180 rooms, spread over four floors, all of which come with a coffee maker and a hair dryer. An iron and ironing board as well as a microwave oven and modem hookup are also available on request.

Near the Airport

Georgetown Inn
$55 to $155, bkfst
⊛, ⊘, △, K
6100 Corson Ave. S, Interstate 5
Exit 162
WA 98108
☎ 762-2233
⇄ 763-6708

South of town, near Boeing Field, stands the Georgetown Inn. Built in 1993, it is a worthwhile choice for those with no intention of heading all the way downtown after a long flight. The hotel offers standard rooms with nondescript decor, but suites and luxury rooms are also available, some even come with a kitchenette. What's more, you can wish to unwind can use the whirlpool (in the fitness centre) or the sauna. An added bonus: guests can wash their clothes in the laundry room at no extra cost.

Comfort Inn & Suites
$70 to $170, bkfst
≈, ⊘, ⅊
19333 Pacific Highway S, south of
188th St.,
WA 98188
☎ 878-1100
☎ 800-228-5150

The Comfort Inn & Suites offers standard rooms providing the customary comfort of this hotel chain, but has also recently been fitted out with comfortable, fairly luxurious suites that will satisfy travellers after their journey through the skies. A range of amenities is also at hand, including an indoor swimming pool and an exercise room, and those under 18 stay for free.

Days Inn
$75 to $135, bkfst
⊛, ℝ, ⊘
19015 International Blvd. S,
WA 98188
☎ 244-3600
☎ 800-DAYS-INN
⇄ 241-4556

After an arduous flight, out-of-towners can head to the Days Inn, which offers shuttle service from the airport 24 hours a day. A decent hotel, most of its rooms come with a microwave oven and a refrigerator. Noteworthy among the many services to which guests have access are a fitness centre and laundry facilities, as well as relaxing in-room whirlpool baths. The knowledgeable staff will be glad to help you plan out your itinerary or steer you toward the best restaurants in town.

Clarion Hotel
$110
⊛
3000 S. 176th St., Interstate 5,
Exit 152,
WA 98188
☎ 242-0200
⇄ 242-1998
www.hotelchoice.com

Visitors who want to stay near the airport can do so

at the Clarion Hotel, which offers 210 soberly decorated rooms. The hotel also provides a few services and amenities such as an indoor swimming pool, a whirlpool bath and even a beauty salon. Shuttle service from the Sea-Tac International Airport is available 24 hours a day.

Holiday Inn – Sea-Tac
$100 to $130
☺, ⊛, ≈
17338 International Blvd.,
WA 98188
☎ *242-1000*
⇄ *242-7089*

Right across from the airport, the Holiday Inn – Sea-Tac happily welcomes visitors - who won't find better for the price in the airport area - to one of its 260 rooms. The hotel also offers exercise facilities, a whirlpool and an indoor swimming pool, to say nothing of the courteous service, all of which makes this hotel a good choice.

Radisson Hotel Seattle Airport
$130 to $300
≈
17001 Pacific Highway S.
WA 98188
☎ *244-6000*
☎ *800-333-3333*

The advantage offered by the Radisson Hotel Seattle Airport is its very large outdoor swimming pool, surrounded by a terrace surrounded by greenery where guests can enjoy basking in the sun. The hotel has some 160 rooms, including a few luxury suites with modern conveniences. However, the rooms, though standard and comfortable, sport a dull décor.

Doubletree Hotel
$135 to $500
☺, △
18740 Pacific Highway,
WA 98188
☎ *246-8600*
☎ *800-222-TREE*
⇄ *431-8687*
www.doubletreehotels.com

The Doubletree Hotel offers everything expected from a high-class hotel. Indeed, the establishment boasts 838 rooms, 12 suites, a swimming pool, a fitness centre and a sauna. Airport shuttle service is also provided round the clock.

Some of Ulysses' Favourite Restaurants

Restaurants

Whether you're looking for a seafood restaurant or excellent French cuisine, you will have a hard time deciding where to eat, as the city abounds in all manner of original restaurants with enticing menus and charming ambiances.

This chapter offers a sampling of the city's restaurants, listed in alphabetical order by district and by price. Note that it is difficult to have a full meal for less than $10; the tradeoff, however, is that you are almost sure to be satisfied with your meal and the service (the city's rather laid-back attitude generally ensures that those who wait on you will do so politely and, above all, with a smile!). The least expensive restaurants (**$**) offer meals for under $10 for one person before drinks, tax and tip, but the food served in such places sometimes (though by no means always) leaves something to be desired.

Prices at mid-range eateries (**$$**) vary from $11 to $20, with very cordial service. Establishments with menus in the $21-to-$30 range (**$$$**) should, in theory, please one and all. Last but not least (especially where money is concerned), Seattle's finest dining establishments (*$$$$*) offer refined cuisine and impeccable service, but will set you back at least $31.

Restaurant Prices

$	$10 and less
$$	$11 to $20
$$$	$21 to $30
$$$$	$31 and up

Bon appétit!

Pioneer Square

B&O Espresso
$
103 Cherry St.
☎ *621-9372*
For a quick coffee to be enjoyed by a cozy fire in the hearth, B&O Espresso is a lovely opportunity to savour something other than Starbucks...

McCoy's Firehouse Bar & Grill
$
173 S. Washington St.
☎ *652-5797*
⇆ *652-5798*
On the corner of South Washington Street and 2nd Avenue stands McCoy's Firehouse Bar & Grill, where, the tantalizing

aroma of the colossal T-bone and Peppercorn New York steaks compete with those of simple burgers and salads. Late risers can also have breakfast here until 3pm.

Old Timer's Cafe
$
620 1st Ave.
☎ *623-9800*
The Old Timer's Cafe primarily draws sports fans who come in to have a beer and watch a game. But you can also fill up on American southern-style cooking, Louisiana cuisine inspiring the chef here.

Four Seas Restaurant
$-$$
Sun to Thu 10:30am to midnight
Fri and Sat 10:30am to 2am
Sun 10:30am to 3pm
714 S. King St.
☎ *682-4900*
The Four Seas Restaurant offers diners a great dim-sum experience, though unfortunately not much else is very enticing, except good ribs. In fact, this large, easy-going restaurant would do well to refine the taste and presentation of its dishes.

Rock Pasta
$-$$
322 Occidental Ave. S.
☎ *682-ROCK*
www.wsim.com
Sports fans often gather at Rock Pasta during Mariners, Sonics or Seahawks games.

This large restaurant has a small mezzanine set aside exclusively for non-smokers, and serves dishes cooked in a wood-fired brick oven which serves as a centrepiece to a rather uninspired décor. The pizzas, however, will make you forget this detail, particularly The Blues, a pizza that combines Italian sausage, hot peppers and tomato sauce.

Torrefazione Italia Cafe
$-$$
320 Occidental Ave. S.
☎ **624-5847**
⇄ **625-0287**
Located in the heart of Pioneer Square, Torrefazione Italia Cafe welcomes those seeking a quiet place to enjoy a good coffee with Viennese bread and buns, in a simple yet warm setting graced with high ceilings.

 La Buca
$$
102 Cherry St.
☎ **343-9517**
A rather eclectic ambiance awaits diners at La Buca, located just below Cherry Street level. The trattoria's ebullient owner, Luigi, never tires of regaling patrons with stories and jokes, so don't be surprised if he comes by your table to shoot the breeze while you enjoy a selection of authentic Italian pasta. Indeed, the generous penne, fettucine

and rigatoni dishes are sure to satisfy those who don't worry about their cholesterol level! La Buca often welcomes groups celebrating a birthday or nuptials. Moreover, the restaurant's cosmopolitan staff will be happy to steer you toward the city's not-to-be-missed nooks and crannies.

Umberto's
$$
100 S. King St.
☎ **621-0575**
⇄ **621-8554**
Those in search of a family restaurant with a grade-A decor and menu need look no further than Umberto's, where a fine meal awaits. Try the simple yet satisfying and delicious pomodoro pizza or the *farfalle tutta di mare*, composed of crab, shrimp and shellfish bathed in a sherry sauce – a real treat!

Il Terrazzo Carmine
$$-$$$
411 1st Ave. S., at King St.
☎ **467-7797**
Open since 1984, this trattoria is appreciated by Seattle residents who never tire of its classic Italian cuisine. The ambiance that prevails here may remind you of some Godfather scenes – without the requisite murders, of course! Noteworthy among the dishes recommended by the chef is the sauté of veal with capers.

Restaurants

Waterfront

Starbucks
$

every day 7am to 7pm
Pier 52

Starbucks cafés are all over Seattle, for it was here that the chain originated. Indeed, at first sight, one wonders if these establishments might not have a total monopoly on the coffee industry. If you're in the Waterfront area, more specifically at Pier 52, you can warm up with a good latte while waiting to take the ferry to the island of your choice.

Ivar's Acres of Clams
$$-$$$
Pier 54
☎ 624-6852

The best-known restaurant on the Waterfront, Ivar's Acres of Clams will please families and all those who wish to gaze upon Puget Sound. Gracing the entrance is a huge painting depicting Ivar Haglund, the now-deceased founder of the establishment. As might be expected, the fishhouse offers good portions of fish and seafood, namely a medley of crab, shrimp, halibut and salmon. The smiling and hospitable service pleasantly complements the meal and the view offered by the eatery, which is much appreciated by many visitors. The place

also features a good wine list ranging in price from $15 to $55. Sporting events are sometimes broadcast at the small in-house bar.

Elliott's
$$-$$$$
Pier 56
☎ 623-4340

Another favourite with out-of-towners, Elliott's offers a lively atmosphere and good-quality seafood that is truly worth the trip. The restaurant's magnificent view of Puget Sound leads many to partake of salmon or excellent oysters. The crab is also a good choice, while those who prefer chicken or beef can sample the filet mignon with mushrooms and blue cheese. All this, combined with the exemplary service, makes this restaurant a sound choice.

Pike Place Market

Bacco Juice Bar
$
86 Pine St.
☎ 443-5443

Next to the Inn at the Market (see p 152), the Bacco Juice Bar is just the place to start off your day on the right foot as it serves up the ultimate in health food. Featured on the menu are 11 kinds of fruit juices named after Greek gods such as Zeus, Pluto, Pan and Cupid. These various

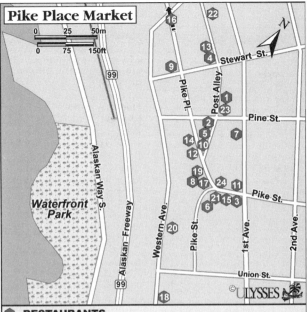

Pike Place Market

0 25 50m
0 75 150ft

©ULYSSES

Restaurants

RESTAURANTS

1. Bacco Juice Bar
2. Cinnamon Works
3. Les Crêpes de France
4. Le Panier Very French Bakery
5. Mr. D's Greek Deli
6. No Boundaries Cafe
7. Pike Place Bagels
8. Pike Place Bakery
9. Starbucks Cafe
10. Three Girls Bakery
11. Pike Pub and Brewery
12. Athenian Lunch Seafood
13. Japanese Gourmet Restaurant
14. Lowell's
15. Alibi Room
16. Etta's Seafood
17. Maximillien French Market Cafe
18. Emerson's on Western
19. Place Pigalle Restaurant and Bar
20. Wild Ginger
21. Il Bistro
22. The Pink Door
23. Campagne and Cafe Campagne
24. Chez Shea and Shea's Lounge

elixirs, composed of oranges, papayas and pineapples, and other ingredients, are divine palate rousers. For breakfast, the eggs Benedict is tops. And, at lunch, you can choose from a range of panini or sandwiches made from the freshest of ingredients.

Cinnamon Works
$
1530 Pike Place
☎ **583-0085**
As its name suggests, Cinnamon Works offers cinnamon-and-raisin rolls to feast on. The very good blueberry-oatmeal pie is also worth a few greenbacks. Takeout orders only.

Les Crêpes de France
$
95 Pike St.
☎ **624-2195**
Just west of the newsstand is Les Crêpes de France, where you can tuck into scrumptious crepes stuffed with everything from mozzarella or ricotta and fresh tomatoes to cinnamon or strawberries and a multitude of other delectable ingredients that literally melt in your mouth. Vanilla, cream, sugar...

Le Panier Very French Bakery
$
1902 Pike Place, at Pine St.
☎ **441-3669**
At the Le Panier Very French Bakery, in the Triangle Market, you can buy delicious croissants or, if

you really want to splurge, an Opera cake, a Charlotte, French baguette, a round loaf, a ring-shaped loaf, etc.

Mr. D's Greek Deli
$
1518 Pike Place
☎ **622-4881**
Mr. D's Greek Deli sells all kinds of pastries, cinnamon bread, croissants and Bavarian sausages. Also up for grabs are ham-and-cheese sandwiches with spinach as well as quiches.

No Boundaries Cafe
$
Economy Market Atrium
Solo diners can treat themselves to a soup or a sandwich at the No Boundaries Cafe without worrying about being pestered by any tiresome characters.

Pike Place Bagels
$
1st Ave., at Pine St.
Pike Place Bagels makes good bagels, and the ones with smoked turkey are particularly delicious. Also offered here is a variety of meats such as roast beef, ham and other cold cuts. Several kinds of bread are also available: garlic, low-fat, plain, mixed-herb, etc. The young and friendly employees – who seem to be genuinely glad to serve you with a smile – as well as the view of 1st Avenue make this place a wise and inexpensive choice.

Pike Place Bakery
$
Main Arcade
The Pike Place Bakery also offers cinnamon treats; its yummy apple pretzels go like hot cakes, as do its scrumptious little cherry croissants.

Starbucks Cafe
$
1912 Pike Place
☎ 448-8762
The market boasts the first Starbucks ever to have seen the light of day. Takeout orders only.

Three Girls Bakery
$
1514 Pike Place, stand no. 1
☎ 622-1045
The oldest business in the market, the Three Girls Bakery serves soup and cold-cut sandwiches for a pittance. Several kinds of bread are available, and there's no shortage of condiments. Whether you're in the mood for salami or bacon, there's something for you here. The staff is fairly young and friendly and a bottomless cup of coffee will cost you a mere $.085.

Pike Pub & Brewery
$-$$
1415 1st Ave.
☎ 622-6044
⇌ 622-8730
www.pikebrewing.com
Spread over two floors, the Pike Pub & Brewery serves local suds as well as five

home-brewed beers known as Pike Ales. This large bar-restaurant with a black-and-white checkerboard floor welcomes people of all descriptions, who come here to puff on stogies in the cigar lounge, shoot pool on one of four tables or simply have a bite to eat washed down with a few beers.

The restaurant's pub-style decor suits it to a tee – to say the least. Featured on the menu are selections such as Capitol Hill Crab Chowder, Caesar salad and artichokes with beer (weiss Bier!), to say nothing of the very good crab terrine and the pizzas. Scotch and other hard liquors also have pride of place in the downstairs room, where you can read a daily paper, a novel, or chat with other patrons while seated in a comfortable armchair. What's more, the establishment also hosts Organic Farmers Days in the Pike Place Market, from mid-June to late October (see p 37, 106).

Athenian Inn
$-$$
1517 Pike Place
☎ 624-7166
Many visitors come to enjoy a meal at the Athenian Inn, their curiosity roused by the view of Puget Sound and the funky mess that adorns the establishment – including tanks in which lobsters waddle, oblivious to what

Restaurants

fate has in store for them. People also come here to have a cocktail and watch the ferries go by or to have breakfast, the Golden Rhodes Eggs stealing the show.

Japanese Gourmet Restaurant
$-$$
82 Stewart St.
☎ *728-6204*
⇄ *728-8805*
Well situated in the Pike Place Market, the Japanese Gourmet Restaurant whips up little Japanese-inspired dishes enhanced according to the whims of the chef. A wonderful opportunity to sample sashimi, sushi or dumburi. Sayonara!

Lowell's
$-$$
1519 Pike Place
☎ *622-2036*
Located in the Campus Market, this three-floor restaurant offers seafood but the quality of the food is no match for the view of Puget Sound. Crowded with tourists, the establishment relies on a young, enthusiastic staff to serve patrons halibut burgers, salads or crab sandwiches at the speed of light. Also to be sampled here are a few microbrews from the region and beyond, including Anchor Stream, Red Hot E.S.B., Sierra Nevada Stout (New Mexico) and Shutz Mirror Pond Pale Ale.

Alibi Room
$$
85 Pike St.
☎ *623-3180*
Located below the market between the Economy Atrium and the Main Arcade, the Alibi Room offers an unparalleled romantic and relaxing experience. The bread is freshly baked every day, and the wide array of red and white wines will further enhance the quality of your meal: bottles cost from $20 to $40. You can enjoy a glass of muscatel, sherry, port, sangria, Pinot Noir, etc. The menu features simple yet delicious and reasonably priced starters such as salads and soups, "crostinis", baked brie, mousses and roasted vegetables. The main dishes are also simple, with vegetarian selections and a Mexican offering, the chicken burrito; the spinach pie, pirogies and vegetarian lasagna also come highly recommended. Creative minds gather here to have a drink and discuss theatre and cinema in a sometimes jazzy, sometimes disco ambiance. The slender, wooden beams propping up the ceiling give the place a warm appearance, though the large windows unfortunately look out onto the imposing modern building that houses the Hill Climb Chiropractic Clinic, blocking the view of Elliot

Bay in the process. Courteous and hospitable service.

Etta's Seafood
$$
2020 Western Ave.
☎ *443-6000*
≈ *443-0648*
For a splendid view of Puget Sound and Victor Steinbrueck Park (see p 109), not to mention a good meal, head to Etta's Seafood, a favourite with Seattleites. The clam chowder is unrivalled, while the Alaskan halibut is one of the menu's highlights. You can sample a few local or imported beers before your meal, notably the delicious Ayinger Jarhundert, a one-litre titan.

Maximillien French Market Cafe
$$
closed Mon
81A Pike St.
☎ *682-7270*
Located between the Economy Market and the Main Arcade (right near the Bronze Pig), this eatery offers starters such as Coquille St-Jacques and Rockefeller oysters for somewhat unpalatable prices. Renovated in 1997, the restaurant welcomes a business clientele at lunch, tourists mingling with regulars to admire Puget Sound from its large windows. Try the market bouillabaisse or the sea perch with rum; the lobster dishes are also recommended. Maximillien

also serves breakfast every day and brunch on Sundays from 9:30am to 3:30pm, when patrons can enjoy good fresh-fruit dishes, brioches, ham and cheese, as well as breakfast specialties such as smoked salmon, eggs Benedict and Rothschild.

Emerson's on Western
$$-$$$
1010 Western Ave.
☎ *682-1918*
Housed in an official historic building, Emerson's is suitable for either a classy dinner or a casual meal with friends. The chef prepares Italian- and American western-style dishes. Because of the rather carefree atmosphere, if the menu fails to rouse your interest, you can make a special request to your server who will indulge your little culinary whim if at all possible! In the lounge and bar area, live jazz can be heard pounding from the piano's black and white keys.

Place Pigalle Restaurant & Bar
$$-$$$
81 Pike St.
☎ *624-1756*
The ambiance at Place Pigalle, reminiscent of Parisian bistros, is sure to charm anyone who dines here. The restaurant affords a picture-postcard view of Elliot Bay and prides itself on offering excellent steamed mussels, calamari bathed in mustard cream

Restaurants

sauce and good crab dishes, which both residents and visitors eat their fill. Patrons here can also enjoy good, affordably-priced soups and salads. Depending on the season, you can also feast on boyourdone-style pork chops or braised halibut served on a bed of udon noodles paired with shitake mushrooms. Another highly recommended dish is the scallops with red peppers.

Wild Ginger
$$-$$$
1400 Western Ave.
☎ *623-4450*
⇋ *623-8265*

One of the hottest places in town, Wild Ginger specializes in the American and Asian fusion cuisine. The place also offers another special culinary treat known as satay, an Indonesian word meaning grilled and skewered. This spacious but lovingly decorated and downright bewitching establishment offers diners an outstanding culinary experience. The noodle dishes, like those served with duck, are highly recommended and, if no tables are immediately available, you can have a drink at the bar frequented by thirty-somethings and Asians in their twenties.

Il Bistro
$$$
93A Pike St.
☎ *682-3049*

Located below Pike Place Market, this cozy little Italian restaurant will please the tender-hearted and lovesick couples. The subdued lighting and low ceilings confer a unique, suitably romantic ambiance upon the place, which has been in business for more than 30 years. You can sit at the bar and sip the drink of your choice, the cellar boasting an impressive stock of the best regional wines. You will have a hard decision to make when it comes to your palate, however, as the veal, the ribs and the finely prepared pastas all literally melt in your mouth.

The Pink Door
$$$
1919 Post Alley
☎ *443-3241*

Not all Pike Place Market restaurants are tourist traps. One good example is the Pink Door which is illusively located in the alley east of the market and offers quality cuisine. The primarily Italian menu offers affordably priced soups, antipasti and risotti. In addition to such delicious starters are the main-course paninis, the house specialty. The cheerful decor, despite the beat-up (if rustic) ceiling, bestows undeniable charm upon the place. In summer, patrons dine on its outdoor terrace, which affords a breathtaking view of Puget Sound and its islands.

Campagne
$$$$
86 Pine St.
☎ 728-2800
Cafe Campagne
$$-$$$
In the Pike Place Market area, you won't find better than the Campagne restaurant and its more affordable and casual counterpart Cafe Campagne, both of which offer the finest in French country cuisine. Out-of-towners and local gourmets alike gather here to feast on dishes inspired by French traditions and enhanced with typical Nortwestern American touches in the hushed atmosphere of the dining room or bar. Chef James Drohman offers a tasty menu that consists of country-style beef, eggplant and veal-liver pâté followed by delicious smoked-trout raviolis, not to mention the perfectly creamy cheeses.

Chez Shea
$$$$
94 Pike St., Suite 34
☎ 467-9990
One of the best restaurants in Seattle is also one of the hardest to find. Tucked away on the third floor of the Corner Market building, this hidden gem specializes in fine French cuisine, where every ingredient is market-fresh. Owner Sandy Shea has made this romantic hideaway an absolute must, by creating just the right ambiance and decor, complete with candlelight and a breathtaking view of Elliot Bay.

Shea's Lounge
$$$
Just below Chez Shea is Shea's Lounge, a very charming little bistro that serves Spanish and Mediterranean fare. Prices here, however, are more palatable than those of its more upscale sister establishment.

Downtown

Bernard's on Seneca
$
317 Seneca St.
Located in the basement of the Hotel Seattle (see p 156), Bernard's on Seneca is a typical American diner offering omelets, spinach salads, burgers and fish & chips.

Red Robbin Pub
$
At Spring St. and 4th Ave.
☎ 474-1909
A statue of Chief Sealth occupies a place of honour at the entrance to the Red Robbin Pub, a deli with a lively atmosphere where seemingly well-acquainted patrons mainly come to

Restaurants

have a drink at the bar and watch televised sports matches. But good sandwiches, salads and burgers can also be enjoyed in the dining room, where the pennants of local sports teams adorn the back of the establishment. The draught beer and happy hours (every day 3:30pm to 6:30pm and 9:30pm until closing) are a big draw.

Elephant & Castle Pub & Restaurant
$-$$
1417 5th Ave.
☎ *624-9977*
⇄ *624-9944*

Situated between Pine and Pike Streets, the Elephant & Castle is a typical pub where shepherd's pie, burgers and salads make up most of the menu. Also offered are a good Caesar salad and lavish pasta dishes. Pacific Northwestern cooking is also spotlighted, the halibut and fish & chips proving very popular. This is just the place to enjoy a Guinness (or several different brands of imported beer) in a vivid setting where the brick walls and lovely woodwork make it an inviting place to drink and chat.

Rock Bottom Brewery
$$
1333 5th Ave.
☎ **623-3070**
www.rockbottom.com

A twenty-something crowd flocks to the Rock Bottom Brewery to enjoy the festive, typical brasserie atmosphere or simply to watch a televised sports match while playing a game of pool. Come sink your teeth into the house specialties, the pizzas and ribs, and find out why this restaurant chain has such a large following. In fact, about fifteen Rock Bottom establishments dot the American landscape from Chicago to the west coast.

Very Italian Assaggio
$$
2010 4th Ave.
☎ *441-1399*

The Assaggio is a very charming haunt with rococo-style decor that is unequalled in Seattle. The close-set tables and noisy atmosphere foster sharing and encounters with your fellow patrons at the surrounding tables who, like you, will feast on dishes prepared with finesse. Statues of angels and madonnas give the space an almost-ethereal look and the reproduction of a Michelangelo painting gives the decor a crowning touch.

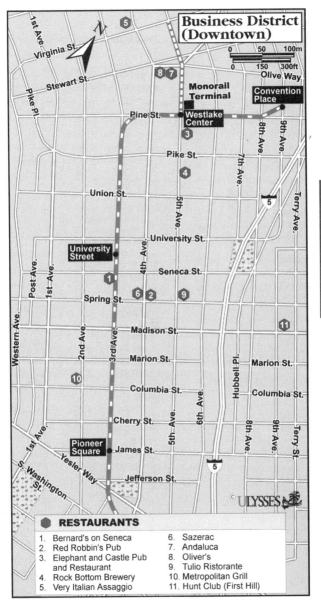

Business District (Downtown)

RESTAURANTS

1. Bernard's on Seneca
2. Red Robbin's Pub
3. Elephant and Castle Pub and Restaurant
4. Rock Bottom Brewery
5. Very Italian Assaggio
6. Sazerac
7. Andaluca
8. Oliver's
9. Tulio Ristorante
10. Metropolitan Grill
11. Hunt Club (First Hill)

It is best to reserve in advance, given the trattoria's growing popularity. The restaurant offers an affordable, fixed-price menu (*$12*), including linguini with home-made pesto that is slowly but surely savoured.

🌴 Sazerac
$$-$$$
1101 4th Ave.
☎ 624-7755
⇄ 624-0050

Pleasantly situated in the Hotel Monaco (see p 160), the Sazerac restaurant a Californian décor, designed by Cheryl Rowley. The high ceilings give you the impression of being in the open air while you sample the dishes of Jan "Big Dawg" Birnbaum, who has an affinity for cuisine from the Deep South, particularly Louisiana. If you only get the chance to eat here once, be sure to order the New York Strip Steak with buttermilk onion rings, sazy sauce and cheese. The place also serves breakfast until 10am.

🌴 Andaluca
$$$
407 Olive Way
☎ 382-6999

Set up in the west wing of the Mayflower Park Hotel, Andaluca is another one of those romantic dining establishments where subdued lighting reflecting on the rosewood walls creates a very warm, stylish atmosphere. The restaurant's European look heralds Old World dishes, but it is rather the proximity of the sea that inspires the chef to concoct mainly seafood dishes. Sweethearts can share mushroom tartlets or crisp duck cakes or selections from the main-course menu including chicken in spicy Moroccan sauce as well as Zarzuela Shellfish Stew, composed of shrimps, scallops, mussels and octopus. The impeccable service of this smoke-free establishment gives it a unique cachet.

Oliver's
$$

Also located in the Mayflower Park Hotel, Oliver's serves good halibut sandwiches and crab cakes, though people come here to enjoy one of the best – if not the very best – martinis in town.

🌴 Tulio Ristorante
$$$
1100 5th Ave.
☎ 624-5500

One of the best reasons to stay at the Vintage Park Hotel (see p 161) is unquestionably its Italian restaurant Tulio Ristorante, which draws both residents and visitors seeking outstanding Italian food. Seated at one of the tables looking out on 5th Avenue, you will have a fine view of the bustling thoroughfare. Those who prefer "tête-à-tête" dining, however, can request a more private table at the back of the establishment, finely decorated with sombre-coloured woodwork. The menu is distinctly Italian, as expected, and the hospitality and service are flawless. Patrons can enjoy a few antipasti like the roasted asparagus with prosciutto or the sweet-potato gnocchi. And, as a main course, there's the Zafferano risotto with shellfish, basil and orange zest. The chef also turns out excellent steaks, such as the Grilled Marinated Ribeye, and grilled veal chops with prosciutto and mozzarella.

Metropolitan Grill
$$$-$$$$
820 2nd Ave.
☎ *624-3287*
If there's a restaurant renowned for its steaks, it's the Metropolitan Grill, which has garnered countless "best steak in town" awards from the local dailies. This colossal steakhouse is tasteful and classy through and through. The chef personally attends to procuring the best steaks in town and prepares meats that are sublime in all respects. You can give in to such culinary delights as the meal for two, consisting of a porterhouse steak or the Double Top Sirloin. Excess being the maxim in such places, liquor flows like

water at the bar, particularly the bourbon, scotch and whiskey.

Belltown and Seattle Center

Caffe Minnie's
$-$$
at 1st Ave. and Denny Way
☎ *448-6263*
Perfectly situated where Belltown, the Seattle Center, the Waterfront and Lower Queen Anne converge, Caffe Minnie's is a worthy representative of American diners and is open round the clock. This is the place to meet after attending a concert at the KeyArena (see p 128) or to gaze up at the Seattle sky from the top of the Space Needle. Neighbourhood regulars also gather here to feast on burgers, salads and seafood.

Palmer's Cocktail, A Gathering Place
$-$$
2034 3rd Ave., at Lenora St.
☎ *728-2337*
The food offered at this Irish pub can hardly be described as the epitome of imaginative cooking, as it consists of burgers, sandwiches and salads. University students and people of all ages and descriptions nonetheless flock here to spend a pleasant evening at the welcoming bar, where waitresses and patrons alike hobnob as they watch a

Restaurants

televised game or listen to rock music. Several Irish whiskeys are available.

2218
$$
2218 1st Ave.
☎ 441-2218
www.2218.com

The 2218 restaurant, which turns into a trendy bar after 10pm, sports a minimalist décor recalling Andy Warhol's Factory, but on a much smaller scale. The grilled salmon and the penne rigate are enlightened choices, while the dessert table, which includes New York Cheesecake, is positively mouthwatering.

Axis
$$-$$$
Sun to Thu 5pm to midnight
Fri and Sat 5pm to 3am
2214 1st Ave.
☎ 441-7924

At Axis, where Asian and American traditions intermingle, you will feel right at home. The unpretentious restaurant features one of the most acclaimed wine lists in town, to say nothing of its feverishly imaginative "post-fusion" cuisine. The grilled octopus, much like the ahi draped in guava sauce, is worth getting over the initial feeling you may get of being an outsider, as this place is mostly frequented by regulars. But once you strike up a conversation with the single

person of your choice and realize that the place welcomes as many uptight artist types as it does blue-collar workers hunger for cleverly prepared dishes, you should find yourself very much at ease.

Flying Fish
$$-$$$
2234 1st Ave.
☎ 728-8595

Open since 1995, the Flying Fish is saturated with a subdued ambiance seemingly suspended in time. You can watch the chef prepare your meal behind the huge wood-burning oven, and whether you opt for the Red King salmon, the grilled escolar or the dishes of appetizers to be shared, you will not be disappointed. Should you fail to meet someone with whom to strike up a conversation, you can look around the place and admire its warm, orange-hued decor while drinking one of the 200 wines offered.

Queen City Grill
$$-$$$
2201 1st Ave.
☎ 443-0975

The Belltown district is spoiled when it comes to restaurants, and the Queen City Grill is no exception to the rule. A casual thirtysomething crowd gathers here to enjoy an aperitif at the bar followed by delicious crab cakes, a good New York Steak or a plate of grilled vegetables. Also a joy to dig into is the lemon meringue pie and, to top off the night, what could be better than one of the ten varieties of port available?

Avenue One
$$$
1921 1st Ave.
Open for almost two years now, the excessively lit Avenue One restaurant has a very light-hearted atmosphere and welcomes people in their 30s who come here to have a bite to eat and listen to good, live jazz. You can enjoy a cocktail ($7) at the bar or at your table in this very romantic (and smoke-free, except the bar) restaurant with warm, orange-hued colours. There are six booths, separated by handsome beams, but try to reserve a table by the magnificent brick wall at the south end of the eatery. A huge painting of the restaurant, which you can't miss, heralds the class and tastefulness that pervades this fine establishment. Romantics can opt for the very intimate blue room at the back, which provides a lovely view of Elliot Bay. Praised to the skies by a multitude of food magazines, notably the November 1998 issue of Bon Appétit, Avenue One offers first-rate Northwest- and Italian-inspired dishes and a wine list to match: Chardonnay, Pinot Gris, Riesling, Sauvignon Blanc, Cabernet Sauvignon, Merlot and Pinot, as well as about ten kinds of champagne ($50 to $320 a bottle). The kitchen closes at 11pm, when patrons head to the bar for a drink and a chat with the owner. The place also hosts jazz shows every Tuesday night at 9pm, and local singer Kelly Johnson sometimes performs here.

Space Needle Restaurant
$$$-$$$$
Seattle Center
☎ 443-2100
The Space Needle Restaurant's recipe for success? Location, location, location. Indeed, the revolving restaurant's panoramic view is the only justification for the exorbitantly priced, altogether disappointing dishes. The decor, however, fares a little better in a style somewhat reminiscent of classy Asian restaurants, where the rooms are separated by elegant screens. An aquarium, at the elevator exit, will fascinate the younger set as they gaze in awe at the fish of all colours. But in the end, this restaurant offers very little value for the money.

El Gaucho
$$$$
2505 1st Ave.
☎ 728-1337
≈ 728-4477
"Conviviality" and "swanky" are terms that simply do not

do justice to the atmosphere that prevails at El Gaucho. In fact, you will come across just about every type of person at this welcoming restaurant, from tattooed bikers to opera divas and business magnates to writers in search of inspiration. The pianist mercifully eschews "muzak", taming the room with his dexterous fingers when asked for his rendition of a Duke Ellington or Bill Evans piece. Your server will ensure that everything is to your satisfaction (do not hesitate to order a mimosa, for instance; you are the boss here!), after which you can satisfy your taste buds. As a starter, you can choose between a cocktail or a crab cake, clam chowder or the Gaucho salad with shrimp. Next comes the main course, consisting of juicy steaks, lobster or pasta, which you can wash down with the drink of your choice. The selection is positively dizzying... To end the night with a flourish, head to the main floor, where the Pampas Room (see p 215) sometimes presents cabaret-like shows.

Lower Queen Anne

Caffe Ladro
$
600 Queen Anne Ave. N.
☎ 282-1549
Think orange. Visiting Caffe Ladro, where the atmosphere is a cross between *Trainspotting* and *The Cook, the Thief, His Wife and Her Lover*, is akin to eating an art exhibit. What's more, the dazzling array of pastries, improvised salads and excellent coffee here will tempt gourmands and gourmets alike. A feast for the senses!

Jalisco
$
122 1st Ave. N.
☎ 283-4242
Mexican fare holds sway at the Jalisco *taquería*, where tostadas, burritos and enchiladas make up the greater part of the menu. The eatery's contrasting colour scheme evokes Méjico even more vividly.

Sam's Sushi
$
521 Queen Anne Ave.
☎ 282-4612
Between 2nd Avenue North and Queen Anne Avenue North are a multitude of Asian restaurants with decors recalling China and Thailand. Noteworthy among these is Sam's Sushi, which offers good *yakisoba*.

Choy's Chinese Cuisine
$
601 Queen Anne Ave. N.
☎ 283-1598
Choy's Chinese Cuisine is well known for its mu-shu chicken served with crepes!

Thai House II
$
517 Queen Anne Ave. N.
☎ 284-3700
The Thai House II's ginger pork is an enlightened gastronomic choice.

Uptown China
$
200 Queen Anne Ave. N.
☎ 285-7710
Uptown China is the place to go for vegetarian dishes, our favourite being the Buddha's Delight.

Slaeggers Juice and Gelato
$
12 Mercer St.
☎ 285-7557
⇔ 285-7597
For a refreshing fruit juice or sorbet, slip into Slaeggers Juice and Gelato, which has a very welcoming, high-ceilinged space a most original décor.

Racha Noodles
$-$$
537 1st Ave. N.
☎ 281-8833
The Lower Queen Anne district is chock-full of Asian restaurants. Our favourite is Racha Noodles, which offers a wide variety of Thai dishes served by polite, efficient servers who weave their way through the tables at lightning speed. Try the *tom ka* soup, made of coconut milk, oyster mushrooms and kafir leaves. As a main course, the curry dishes are a good alternative to the noodle selections.

T.S. McHugh's
$-$$
21 Mercer St.
☎ 282-1910
T.S. McHugh's, whose Gaelic motto is Céad Mile Fàilte!, is named after Thomas Shannon McHugh, an Irishman from Galway who settled in Seattle sometime in the 20th century. The institution is famous for its clam chowder as well as its T-bone steak, which is made even tastier by a heavenly mustard sauce. The establishment also prides itself on offering an impressive array of beers from the Emerald Isle (not to be confused with Seattle's namesake, the Emerald City), which you can enjoy while chatting with a regular or a fellow globetrotter. The place also welcomes a few avid sports fans with eyes glued to the television screens as college or university games are broadcast live.

Restaurants

Pizza Pagliacci
$$
550 Queen Anne Ave. N.
4529 University Way
426 Broadway E.
☎ *285-1232*

Craving a pizza? Then head to Pizza Pagliacci, which has not only earned a multitude of awards, but also been mentioned in the renowned food magazine Bon Appétit. The tasty thin-crust pizzas dripping with cheese are famous for nothing; just thinking of the one with goat cheese still makes our mouths water!

 Figaro Bistro
$$
11 Roy St.
☎ *284-6465*

Owners Philippe Bollache and Laurent Gabrel, two Frenchmen who have adopted the Emerald City, are the masterminds behind this gem of a restaurant. It should then come as no surprise that the Figaro Bistro, located next to the MarQueen Hotel (see p 167), has all the hallmarks of an absolutely charming Parisian bistro, with its high ceilings, carefully conceived decor and French-style service. Patrons can feast on classic French bistro fare such as Breton clams, Provençal shrimps or vegetable pâté as starters. Highly recommended as a follow-up is the Norman-style veal laced with a creamy apple and Calvados sauce. A culinary delight fit for the gods and goddesses!

Credenzia's Oven
$$-$$$
10 Mercer St.
☎ *284-4664*
↝ *284-4854*

Chef-owner Laura Dewell has recently turned the former Credenzia Village Bakery into a full-fledged restaurant, now known as Credenzia's Oven. Despite a somewhat mismatched decor, the brand-new eatery offers refreshingly different food you won't find anywhere else in Seattle. In fact, Laura has a particular affinity for food from the Mediterranean and the Caucuses, particularly that from Georgia.

First Hill

Hunt Club
$$$$
900 Madison St.
☎ *343-6156*

Housed in the Sorrento Hotel (see p 169), one of the most prestigious hotels in Seattle, the Hunt Club is largely frequented by businesspeople but will also please couples in search of a romantic setting. In fact, this dining establishment, with its Italian Renaissance decor will help transport you to Italy and has something on the menu for everyone: the meats are succulent, the seafood artfully prepared and the service among the most gracious in town. The freshest of ingredients goes into the palaterousing Pacific Northwestern dishes, with a menu that changes on a weekly, sometimes daily, basis. And to top off your meal, what could be better than a glass of cognac – the crowning touch to a great evening.

University District

All American Sports Bar & Grill
$
4333 University Way NE
☎ *545-7771*
Located in the very heart of the University District, the All American Sports Bar & Grill offers an appetizing, if thoroughly conventional, menu where steak and burgers steal the show.

This is a predictably popular spot with university students, who come here to drink a draught beer (or two, or three, or...).

Big Time Brewery & Ale House
$
4133 University Way NE
☎ *545-4509*
The pub-like atmosphere of the Big Time Brewery & Ale House encourages patrons to sample one of the many beers brewed right on the premises. The place also serves typical pub grub such as shepherd's pie, steaks and burgers, and fills up by 9pm.

Entertainment

This chapter offers myriad ways to enjoy yourself in Seattle, be it at the movies, the theatre or the opera.

Also included are the various bars and clubs we have visited, listed by district and in alphabetical order for your convenience.

Sports fans need not fret, however, for we have also covered the various venues in which the Mariners, Seahawks and Super-Sonics play against their rivals.

Seattle offers visitors and residents alike countless entertainment possibilities. Classical-music lovers can take in first-rate concerts at the **Seattle Center's Opera House**, which boasts amazing acoustics. Those who prefer the theatre will also be spoiled for choice as the Belltown and Capitol Hill districts have plenty of theatres where classic and fringe plays are put on alternately. As far as bars are concerned, Seattle positively bursts at the seams with unpretentious establishments where conversation is the focus of nighttime gatherings. Moreover, those looking to "trip the light fantastic" will have no problem finding a dance club, most of which cater to the gay community. Though "straights" are tolerated in these clubs, they will be hard-pressed to find worthwhile places that solely cater to them.

B ecause of the 2am closing time dictated by Washington State laws, people go out rather early in Seattle, unlike other major American cities. Indeed, for many, the evening often starts off with happy hour, between 5pm and 7pm. Party hounds will nevertheless find a few establishments that close later, though these after hours clubs do not serve alcohol after 2am.

To keep abreast of what's going on in and around the city, consult the local *Seattle Times* (*www.seattletimes.com*) and *Seattle Post-Intelligencer* (*www.seattle-pi.com*) dailies, both of which have a first-rate "Arts & Entertainment" section in their weekend editions. If you happen to venture into the **Pike Place Market**, be sure to pick up a copy of the *Pike Place Market News*, available throughout the famous market. To find your way around the historic quarter, pick up the *Discovering Pioneer Square Map & Guide*, available in various places, including the **Elliot Bay Book Co.** (see p 18, 231)

For more alternative yet equally valid sources, grab a copy of the *Seattle Weekly* (*www.seattleweekly.com*) or *The Stranger* (*www.thestranger.com*), both top-notch cultural weeklies. They come out every Thursday and offer a slew of information on restaurants worth checking out, the hottest bars, upcoming concerts, etc. These free publications are available at newsstands, in shopping centres and select shops throughout the city.

Gay and lesbian visitors may also want to pick up *The Lesbian & Gay Pink Pages*, published in the spring and fall, or check out the *Seattle Gay News Online* (*www.sgn.org*) web site, another great source of information.

For precise maps or any other kind of tourist information, contact the *Seattle-King County News Bureau*, located at the **Washington State Convention Center**. Tickets can also be purchased through the bureau.

Seattle-King County News Bureau
520 Pike St., Suite 1325, Seattle, WA 98101
☎ *461-5840*
www.seeseattle.org

27: The Number of the Beast...

No one who lived through the 1960s revolution can deny having hummed, at least once, the opening lines of Purple Haze, the signature song of guitar-legend Jimi Hendrix, who died September 18, 1970. Born in Seattle on November 27, 1942, this proud Pacific Northwest Native American (his father was African American and his mother Cherokee) first took the music world by storm in 1966 with his debut album, *Are You Experienced?*. Discovered in a seedy little New York bar by British producer Chas Chandler, Hendrix, before creating revolutionary music, played back-up guitar for flamboyant soul piano-player Little Richard, singer of *Good Golly Miss Molly*, until Richard kicked him out of his band for upstaging him!

Hendrix reached the height of his popularity in 1969 during the now-famous Woodstock concert, where he played his subversive, scathing rendition of *The Star Spangled Banner*, the American national anthem, and *Voodoo Child*, leaving his fans stunned by his dexterity, awesome prowess and blues-inspired passion.

Jimi Hendrix died in London, choking on his own vomit after ingesting a heavy dose of sleeping pills. He was only 27 years old. Like many of his contemporaries, he died before the age of 30, well before his time.

27: The Number of the Beast, Part 2

Kurt Cobain grew up in a dysfunctional family in a poor suburb of Seattle, and cut his teeth on punk bands like the Sex Pistols and Richard Hell & the Voidoids. Like Hendrix, he dropped out of school in his early teens, in no small part due to his parents' divorce. He slowly developed a passion for music and began writing his own anguish-fueled songs, which he wailed in various Seattle bars. Meanwhile, several bands burst onto the Seattle scene, including Pearl Jam and Soundgarden, the latter being pioneers of the "grunge" sound. It was through the small Sub Pop Records indie label that Cobain led Nirvana, very much in spite of himself, to the top of the U.S. music charts with the hit-single "Smells Like Teen Spirit", named after an actual brand of deodorant worn by teens at the time! This unwelcome fame engendered a sometimes stormy relationship between Cobain and the media, which blithely focused on and attacked Cobain's private life: heroin, that evil mistress, would lead him into a deep depression.

Nirvana recorded several unrecognized albums before *Nevermind,* which propelled the band to the forefront of contemporary rock. The band's official sophomore album, *In Utero,* pushed bitter sarcasm even further, to the point of cynicism. Two songs from the album, namely "Rape Me" and "Heart-Shaped Box", became big hits, before Cobain took his own life (though some claim otherwise) in April 1994.

Somewhat ironically, Kurt Cobain achieved even greater fame by dying, like Jimi Hendrix, at the tender age of 27, thereby attaining legendary status without ever having wanted to...

TicketMaster Counters

There are TicketMaster counters (known as Ticket Centers) throughout the city.

TicketMaster
☎ *628-0888*

Downtown

RITE AID
319 Pike St.
☎ *223-1128*
☎ *223-0512*

Seattle Center and Surrounding Area

KeyArena
305 Harrison St.

Tower Records
500 Mercer St.
☎ *283-4456*

Pioneer Square

Seahawks EndZone Store
88 S. King St.
☎ *682-2900*
⇄ *808-8314*

University of Washington District

Tower Records
4321 University Way

Capitol Hill

Wherehouse
206 Broadway E.
☎ *628-0888*

Classical Music, Theatre and Cinema

Classical Music

Opera House
at 3rd Ave. and Mercer St.
☎ *684-7200*
⇄ *684-7342*
The Opera House, where the Wagnerian classics performed by the Seattle Opera Company are often sold out, is located in Seattle Center.

Pacific Northwest Ballet
301 Mercer St.
☎ *441-9411*
Classical ballet lovers can take in a performance of the Pacific Northwest Ballet Company, one of the best dance troupes in America, at the **Opera House**.

Benaroya Hall
200 University St.
☎ *215-4700*
☎ *215-4747*
⇄ *215-4748*
No longer travelling around from one place to another to satisfy classical-music aficionados, the Seattle Symphony has just recently found a home at Benaroya Hall, a concert hall that can accommodate up to 2,500 music lovers.

Entertainment

Theatre

5th Avenue Theatre
1308 5th Ave.
☎ *625-1417*
Seattle boasts a thriving and diversified theatre scene: some playhouses focus on contemporary plays while others concentrate on big Broadway hits. The 5th Avenue Theatre, which has a superbly decorated hall belongs to the latter genre.

Cabaret de Paris at Crepe de Paris
1333 5th Ave.
☎ *623-4111*
Fans of cabaret-style theatre are sure to appreciate the shows presented by the Cabaret de Paris at Crepe de Paris, located downtown in the **Rainier Square Shopping Centre** (see p 119, 223).

A Contemporary Theatre
700 Union St.
☎ *292-7676*
www.acttheatre.org
A Contemporary Theatre (ACT) favours socially relevant, always-contemporary productions.

Belltown Theatre Center
115 Blanchard St.
☎ *728-7609*

Annex Theatre
1916 4th Ave.
☎ *728-0933*
The Belltown District is chock-full of alternative theatres and boasts a few halls, including the **Belltown Theatre Center** and the Annex Theatre which was looking to relocate at press time. Both showcase fringe theatre.

Children's Museum Theater
Seattle Center House
Not to be outdone, the lower Queen Anne District harbours an original theatre located on the grounds of The Seattle Center: the Children's Museum Theater (see "**Children's Museum**", p 128), which, of course, caters to children.

Intiman Theatre
north of the Seattle Center, on Mercer Street
☎ *269-1901*
www.seattlesquare.com/intiman
Of Swedish origin, the Intiman Theatre Company presents the classics of Scandinavian and Eastern-European countries, such as plays by Henrik Ibsen and Gogol.

Market Theater
1426 Post Alley
☎ *587-2414*
In the Pike Place Market District, you can check out the tiny Market Theater, whose specialty is improv as well as multimedia and art films.

Broadway Performance Hall
1625 Broadway E.
☎ *325-3113*
Capitol Hill, where art is a
way of life, also has its fair
share of theatres, including
the Broadway Performance
Hall, which welcomes local
up-and-coming amateurs
and more venerable theatre
troupes alike.

Cornish College of the Arts
710 E. Roy St.
☎ *323-1400*
The plays staged by the
Cornish College of the Arts
are highly original. In fact,
students work on plays that
they then produce. Subject
matter primarily highlights
the political and social
problems of our times.

Cinema

Nicknamed "Hollywood
North", Seattle harbours a
great many cinemas, with
more than 70 theatres scattered throughout the greater
metropolitan area.

Seattle has also enjoyed a
certain amount of success
through Hollywood produc-
tions that have featured the
city, such as *Sleepless in
Seattle*, starring Tom Hanks
and Meg Ryan. In *It Hap-
pened at the World Fair*, in
which "the King", Elvis
Presley, a talented singer
with limited acting abilities,
shared top billing with the
Space Needle. Because of

the many hills that surround
the Emerald City, several
Hollywood movies that
ostensibly take place in San
Francisco are actually shot
here. Unfortunately, inde-
pendent films or *films
d'auteur* have some difficulty penetrating the Seattle
market, a few cinemas having even closed their doors
for lack of profit. Such was
the case with the Casbah
Cinema, among others.

911 Media Arts Center
117 Yale Ave. N.
☎ *682-6552*
Though primarily renowned
for its trendy nightclubs and
restaurants, the Belltown
District is also home to a
few cinemas. Notable
among these is the 911 Media Arts Center, whose 50-
odd-seat amphitheatre hosts
multimedia events and art
films.

Cinerama Theatre
2100 4th Ave.
☎ *441-3653*
The Cinerama has been
showing repertory films
since late April 1999,
screening such gems as the
science-fiction classic *Star
Wars*.

Boeing IMAX Theater
200 2nd Ave. N.
☎ *443-4629*

Laser Fantasy Theater
200 2nd Ave. N.
☎ *443-2850*

Entertainment

The lower Queen Anne District, which harbours part of the Seattle Center, boasts one IMAX-style cinema, namely the **Boeing IMAX Theater**. The Laser Fantasy Theater features multi-coloured laser light shows set to the music of bands such as Pink Floyd, the Jimi Hendrix Experience and the Beastie Boys. Both cinemas are located in the **Pacific Science Center** (see p 126).

Uptown Cinemas
511 Queen Anne Ave. N.
☎ *283-1960*
The latest Hollywood blockbusters are featured at the Uptown Cinemas.

City Center Cinemas
1420 5th Ave.
☎ *622-6465*

Meridian 16 Cinemas
1501 7th Ave.
☎ *622-2434*

Pacific Plaza 11
600 Pine St.
☎ *652-2404*
The downtown area abounds in shopping centres, and several cinemas have been built within these very dens of consumption. Among these are the **City Center Cinema**, the **Meridian 16 Cinemas**, one of the newest and most high-tech, and Pacific Plaza 11. All three screen the usual big box-office hits.

Omnidome
Pier 59
☎ *622-1869*
In the Waterfront District, cinephiles can enjoy high-brow film fare at the Omnidome (IMAX theatre). Shorts and feature-length films centered around the themes of nature and the environment make up the greater part of the programming here, with such films as *Alaska: Spirit of the Wild* and *Eruption of Mount St. Helens* being featured.

Broadway Market Cinemas
Broadway Market
401 Broadway E.
☎ *323-0231*
Capitol Hill, a veritable temple of nonconformism, has the greatest concentration of cinemas. Therefore most most repertory houses are located here, as well as a few cinemas featuring foreign films. The largest of them, The Broadway Market Cinemas, offers both indie and foreign films.

Egyptian Theater
801 E. Pine St.
☎ *323-4978*
The Egyptian, which owes its name to its decor reminiscent of the land of the Pharaohs, showcases repertory films such as Ridley Scott's *Blade Runner*, a tried-and-true cult classic.

Little Theater
608 19th Ave. E., at E. Mercer St.
☎ *675-2055*

Harvard Exit Theater
807 E. Roy St., at Broadway
☎ *323-8986*
The Little Theater features
foreign films, while the
Harvard Exit Theater
favours repertory films.

Bars and Pubs

Finding a good place to
spend the evening in Seattle
is hardly a challenge. Indeed, the city harbours
great Irish, Scottish and
Welsh-style pubs. Moreover,
because of the always-re-
laxed and rarely stuffy ambiance, visitors will feel at
ease in most establishments
listed here, with a few ex-
ceptions. In fact, it's not
unusual for someone sitting
alone to be asked to play a
game of pool or simply
share a pitcher of beer.
Such encounters are com-
mon in Seattle, and the
city's friendly nature is sure
to charm a fair share of
visitors. The Belltown district, which now boasts the
majority of trendy bars,
was, not so very long ago,
so seedy even the locals
shunned it. But all that
changed about 10 years
ago, to the great delight of
all. The university crowd as
well as twenty-something
travellers, hang out more in
the Pioneer Square district,

where an $8.95 cover
charge provides access to
10 neighbourhood bars.
Most of these places offer
live music on weekends
and sometimes during the
week, featuring everything
from blues and reggae to
rhythm & blues and jazz.

Seattle having a rather sizeable gay population, it was
only natural that one of the
city's districts welcome this
very social crowd. The
Capitol Hill district has the
majority of gay clubs,
though "straights" are welcome, too. One could say
the two camps are as thick
as thieves, though that may
be stretching it a little... This
district also has the best
dance clubs in town,
though we're talking quality
vs. quantity here. As such,
hetero dance-floor divas
wishing to "shake their
groove thang" to disco or
techno will have to rely on
the hospitality of the gay
clubbing community.

Pioneer Square

Rock Pasta
322 Occidental Ave. S.
☎ *682-ROCK*
www.wsim.com
A festive ambiance prevails
at Rock Pasta, which fills up
with a feverish crowd root-
ing for their local team
during televised sports
matches.

Entertainment

Courtney Love

Courtney Love (1964-), the widow of legendary rock-star Kurt Cobain, rose to fame thanks to her punk-rock/grunge band Hole, made up almost exclusively of women. A former stripper now known for her on-stage antics, including stage-diving into the mosh pit (a space on the dance floor where frenzied fans slam dance during concerts), Love went to Los Angeles to become a rock star. She also spent time in Liverpool, England, where she hung out with the legendary Julian Cope, and even had a brief stint as the lead singer of the band that would become Faith No More and achieve a certain degree of success in the 1990s. Love also pursued an acting career, giving a memorable performance in *Sid and Nancy* (1986), a movie about the sadistic relationship between Sex Pistols bassist Sid Vicious and his girlfriend Nancy Spungen. Love formed Hole in Los Angeles in 1989 and, despite rave

reviews, the band's first album, *Pretty on the Inside*, was only a modest commercial success. The historic turning point of her career occurred in 1991, when she befriended Cobain, who had a huge hit with Nirvana's first "official" album, the seminal *Nevermind*. In 1992, the two lovers married, and the pregnant Love was accused (rightly or wrongly?) of having taken heroin during her pregnancy. Love reached the pinnacle of her notoriety when Cobain committed suicide in April 1994: there were rumours that Love had hired a hitman to kill the tortured singer, but this has never been proven. A few arrests (overdoses...) later, Love returned to the silver screen in *Feeling Minnesota*, starring alongside Keanu Reeves, and was a big hit with the critics in Milos Forman's highly controversial *The People* vs. *Larry Flint*, about the rise and fall of the founder of the porn magazine *Hustler*.

Torrefazione Italia Cafe
320 Occidental Ave. S.
☎ **624-5847**
A reasonable alternative for those who prefer to have a good coffee in an informal ambiance or to drink beer while listening to blaring music.

Bohemian Cafe
111 Yesler Way
☎ **447-1514**
Those who want to dance to reggae, ska, disco or hip hop need look no further than the Bohemian Cafe, where university students cut loose to the latest radio hits on the small dance floor. The place is divided into two rooms, the second playing host to bands. You can also sample delicious Jamaican cuisine at the back of this highly regarded café.

Pioneer Square Saloon
73 Yesler Way
☎ **628-6444**
One of the oldest watering holes in Seattle, the Pioneer Square Saloon sports a bygone look reminiscent of John Ford westerns. Patrons can sit at the bar and knock back one of the many local brews, such as Pyramid or Full Sail, while a few pool sharks show off their skills at the back of the establishment. Happy hour is especially popular here.

New Orleans Restaurant
114 1st Ave. S.
☎ **622-2563**
Both the spirit and cuisine of Louisiana hold sway at the New Orleans Restaurant, as does jazz of course. This bar-restaurant, which has walls strewn with photographs of true jazz luminaries like Louis Armstrong — who has pride of place at the entrance — presents very colourful shows that draw an ecstatic crowd of connoisseurs along with neophytes studiously joining in the fun.

Larry's Greenfront Cafe
209 1st Ave. S.
☎ **624-7665**
At Larry's Greenfront Cafe, expect an ambiance of radiating melancholic blues. People primarily come here to listen to live blues, have a quick burger and a few beers, which disappear at the speed of light given their very affordable prices.

Old Timer's Cafe
620 1st Ave.
☎ **623-9800**
The Old Timer's Cafe is just the place to enjoy a beer or coffee on the terrace looking out on Pioneer Square Park (see p 91). Featured here are blues and occasional reggae shows appreciated by a clientele in their 20s and 30s.

Entertainment

Zasu
608 1st Ave.
☎ *682-1200*
Zasu resonates with jazz. The two-storey establishment, adjacent to Doc Maynard's (see below), has a sombre but charming décor enhanced by brick walls. On weekends, DJs spin dance music as well as current rock hits.

Central Saloon
207 1st Ave. S.
☎ *625-1265*
The Central Saloon is a choice place to catch local jazz or rock and blues bands. Cigar afficionados also gather here to puff Fidel's delicacies.

Colourbox
113 1st Ave. S.
☎ *340-4101*
The locus of alternative music, Colourbox fills up with a young crowd seven nights a week. This is your chance to listen to the best (and not-so-best) indie rock has to offer, as punk-rock and alternative bands perform here every night. The high ceilings and brick walls counterbalance the riotously powerful sounds shaking the bar's foundations, and the cheap beer and animated chatter give the place an eclectic and vibrant ambiance.

Doc Maynard's Pub
610 1st Ave.
☎ *682-4646*
Named after one of the city's founders, Doc Maynard's attracts a lively and very diverse crowd of devoted rock 'n' roll and heavy Mississippi blues fans. The two-storey bar is adjacent to Zasu (see p 208).

The Fenix & Fenix Underground
315 2nd Ave. S.
☎ *467-1111*
Along with the Colourbox, the Fenix and Fenix Underground bars are good choices for fans of punk, goth music and all manner of other musical genres. A largely leather-clad, nonconformist crowd congregates here to listen to local Jimi Hendrix and Marilyn Manson cover bands. The downstairs dance floor of this huge, two-storey institution, swarms with a high-energy breathless crowd slamming for all it's worth.

Comedy Underground
222 S. Main St.
☎ *628-0303*
Pioneer Square is home to all kinds of nightclubs, including one where comedy reigns supreme. Indeed, the Comedy Underground presents some of the nation's best stand-up comics every night of the week. A boisterous crowd attends these shows, demonstrating its displeasure remorselessly

by heckling those who fail to tickle its funny bone.

Ned's
206 1st Ave. S.
☎ 340-8859
Tina Beacher is the proud and very colourful owner of Ned's, a bar that draws a 20-something clientele here to play pool, darts, or simply listen to 90s music. Happy hour attracts scores of revellers who chug down a few beers before heading out to bar hop in Pioneer Square.

Waterfront

Elliott's
Pier 56
☎ 523-4340
Though the waterfront doesn't have many notable establishments, the bar at Elliott's restaurant offers a lively ambiance enjoyed by the neighbourhood working class crowd, who come here to finish off the night with a televised game and a beer.

Pike Place Market

Athenian Inn
1517 Pike Place
☎ 624-7166
Draught-beer lovers will enjoy the selection offered by the Athenian Inn, where the view of Puget Sound is well worth the trip (see p 11).

Place Pigalle Restaurant and Bar
81 Pike St.
☎ 624-1756
Place Pigalle offers a dazzling view of Puget Sound, as well as a warm ambiance in which to drink – a rewarding experience whether alone or with friends (see p 11).

The Owl 'n Thistle
808 Post Ave.
☎ 621-7777
In this cozy, unpretentious, Irish-style pub with a typically American ambiance, the Guinness flows like water. The Owl 'n Thistle will primarily please those with a penchant for cheap beer and baseball or football games.

Il Bistro
93A Pike St.
☎ 682-3049
One of the most romantic spots in Seattle, Il Bistro is a great choice for those who wish to have a few glasses of wine in charming company. Patrons mainly come here to eat in the dining room, but those who settle at the bar cand don't care about the food, can engage in subtle flirting.

The Pink Door
1919 Post Alley
☎ 443-3241
The Pink Door is just the place to sip a martini while admiring the sun setting on Puget Sound from a terrace

Entertainment

overhanging Pike Place Market. The establishment also has a good wine list.

Campagne
86 Pine St.
☎ **728-2800**
The Campagne restaurant is our favourite place to end the night on a high note, with a scotch in one hand and a cigar in the other. The restaurant's large, panoramic windows look out on Elliot Bay and, whether at the bar or comfortably seated at one of the small tables, you will be served like the boss' own son or daughter.

Shea's Lounge
94 Pike St., N⁰ 34
☎ **467-9990**
Located upstairs from Chez Shea (see p 185), Shea's Lounge is another very romantic place with an unforgettable view of the ferries on Elliot Bay. The handful of elegant tables and very subdued lighting give the place a unique ambiance.

Pike Pub and Brewery
1415 1st Ave.
☎ **622-6044**
To enjoy local brews while comfortably seated in large leather couches, there's no beating the Pike Pub and Brewery, which brews five of its own beers known as Pike Ales.

Alibi Room
85 Pike St.
☎ **623-3180**
One of our favourite places, the Alibi Room, which has a laid-back and convivial ambiance going for it, draws artists and university students who come to exchange tips on film shoots, or read from their latest literary or movie scripts.

Downtown

Jersey's Sports Bar & Grill
2004 7th Ave.
☎ **343-9377**
Pool sharks are spoiled for choice in Seattle, and those who hang out at Jersey's Sports Bar & Grill can also enjoy sports in the larger sense, as the place offers televised Sonics games and other local matches. Also available here is a selection of ten beers on tap.

Rock Bottom Brewery & Restaurant
1333 5th Ave.
☎ **623-3070**
The festive ambiance at the **Rock Bottom Brewery & Restaurant** draws a young crowd who knock back local beers and socialize while playing pool or watching televised sporting events.

Red Robbin Pub
at Spring St. and 4th Ave.
☎ **474-1909**
The televised sports matches at the Red Robbin

Pub bring in a range of sports fans who come to drink a few pitchers of beer and cheer on the Mariners or the Seahawks.

Elephant & Castle Pub & Restaurant
1417 5th Ave.
☎ *624-9977*
You can relax and chat with the patrons of the Elephant & Castle, a place made all the more charming by its young and eager staff, amid a décor worthy of the best Irish pubs (see p 214). Indeed, the lovely woodwork and the Guinness and Smithwick's posters give the place a cachet recalling passages of James Joyce's *Ulysses*. The pool tables at the entrance round out the bar-restaurant's amenities.

Oliver's
407 Olive Way
☎ *382-6999*
People primarily come to the bar at Oliver's restaurant to enjoy what the local regulars have declared "the best martini in town". A 30- to 40-something crowd frequents the establishment, which has a little bar is that is the scene of many an animated conversation.

Belltown

Dimitriou's Jazz Alley
2033 6th Ave.
☎ *441-9729*
One of Seattle's best jazz clubs, Dimitriou's is the place to catch the jazz greats in action while enjoying a good meal. During our visit, McCoy Tyner, John Coltrane's former pianist, performed here, to the great delight of the 30 to 40 year-old patrons who appreciate the laid-back and very classy ambiance.

Timberline Tavern
2015 Boren Ave.
☎ *622-8807*
Clad in cowboy hats and boots, gays and lesbians come to dance a few quadrilles at the popular Timberline Tavern, a true-blue country & western watering hole. On Sundays, drinks go for downright ridiculous prices, drawing an avid beer-drinkin' crowd.

Lava Lounge
2226 2nd Ave.
☎ *441-5660*
Another neighbourhood bar, the Lava Lounge positively revels in kitsch, as evidenced by the Chinese lanterns, miniature Tiki gods and Godzilla himself, who occupies a place of honour behind the bar!

Entertainment

The jukeboxes here offer an eclectic medley of songs that provide an alternative to the jazz and blues hits that sound from many of Seattle's other bars.

Sit & Spin
2219 4th Ave.
☎ *441-9484*
The highly original concept behind Sit & Spin allows you to do your laundry while sipping a beer or a coffee. This delightfully off-beat high-ceilinged and subtly lit establishment is mainly frequented by young hipsters, though it's not uncommon to meet families and seniors humming a bygone tune here.

Speakeasy Cafe
2304 2nd Ave.
☎ *728-9770*
Whether you're pining for your friends and family and wish to get in touch by e-mail or simply want to surf the Net, the Speakeasy Cafe is the place to go. The walls adorned with local art and the somewhat beat-up furniture give the place undeniable charm, and the drinks are cheap to boot.

2218
2218 1st Ave.
☎ *441-2218*
Those not averse to a lack of decor will feel right at home at 2218, where the memory of great jazz luminaries is honoured. Lively patrons come here on the weekends, when DJs play dance music that positively roars from the loud-speakers.

Two Bells Tavern
2313 4th Ave.
☎ *441-3050*
Artists in search of inspiration and other artistically inclined folk gather at the Two Bells Tavern, a quirky local hangout known for its great burgers. The large windows look out on 4th Avenue, allowing patrons to take in the night-time crowd parading by while nursing a glass of home-brewed beer.

Virginia Inn
1937 1st Ave.
☎ *728-1937*
Though a neighbourhood bar, the Virginia Inn comes off as somewhat hoity-toity when the time comes to order a drink. The service is not always obliging and smokers may well be displeased as smoking is prohibited. However, those who snag a table on the little terrace may get a good view of the Olympic Peninsula – depending on Mother Nature's mood, of course.

The Vogue
2018 1st Ave.
☎ *443-0673*
A hip young crowd gathers at The Vogue with the hope of seeing the next Nirvana play here, for this is the place where the cult-status band once dazzled its legions of loyal fans. The

trend has since changed somewhat though, dance music having usurped indie rock's throne, to the great displeasure of local punk rockers. Courtesy is hardly the trademark.The place also hosts reggae nights.

Pampas Room
90 Wall St.
☎ 284-5003
For those with well-stuffed wallets, Pampas Room offers 15-odd draught beers several of which are brewed in Washington State. Located in El Gaucho (see p 191),, the club occasionally hosts shows, that become something of a cabaret – one that frustrated smokers will no doubt enjoy as the place gets so smoky it's sometimes hard to see your hand in front of your face.

Belltown Billiards
90 Blanchard St.
☎ 448-6779
Without a doubt the best pool room in all Seattle, Belltown Billiards, with its woodwork and 12 pristine pool tables cherished by serious players, is located at the corner of 1st Avenue. The beer is a tad expensive, but the first-rate service will soon banish the cost of that Alaskan Amber from your mind.

Belltown Pub
2322 1st Ave.
☎ 728-4311
The Belltown Pub, where locals gather to treat themselves to a few drinks amidst the warm ambiance, wins our prize for the best neighbourhood watering hole. Indeed, the unparalleled service and, above all, handsome brick walls and high ceilings make the place a most relaxing little haven.

Five Point Cafe
415 Cedar St.
☎ 448-9993
The Five Point Cafe, yet another neighbourhood bar-restaurant, doesn't offer much beyond a view of Chief Sealth's statue. Non-smokers may well want to steer clear of the place, for its slogan says it all: "Smokers Welcome, Non-Smokers Beware". This only goes to show that the city has yet to be wholly afflicted with the scourge of political correctness...

Hurricane Cafe
2230 7th Ave.
☎ 623-5750
Despite its ordinary ambiance, the Hurricane Cafe provides regulars with round-the-clock if slow and surly, service. This, combined with the decor of period photographs, gives the diner an atmospher like the film *Natural Born Killers* and will please the most jaded of customers.

Entertainment

211 Billiard Club

2304 2nd Ave.

☎ *443-1211*

Named for its former location on Union Street, the oldest billiards club in the city is strategically located on 2nd Avenue. The unpretentious establishment welcomes players of all stripes who enjoy shooting a few games of pool or snooker for the lowest prices in town. Hotheads and degenerates are not tolerated, however, as the staff here are known to put players lacking good manners in their place.

Lower Queen Anne

T.S. McHugh's

21 Mercer St.

☎ *282-1910*

A typical Irish-pub ambiance is keenly felt at T.S. McHugh's, which is also a restaurant (see p 193). Here you can sample some 15 beers on tap in a lively atmosphere made up of noisy patrons sipping Guinness as they watch a televised sports match.

Slaeggers Juice and Gelato

1 Mercer St.

☎ *285-7557*

Tee-totalers can enjoy delicious fruit juices at Slaeggers Juice and Gelato, which has a vivid and dazzling décor making it all the more pleasant to visit.

Capitol Hill (Gay Clubs)

Bauhaus Books & Coffee

301 E. Pine St.

☎ *625-1600*

With its board games and good latte, Bauhaus Books & Coffee is a pleasant place in which to leaf through a book, play checkers or take in the occasional show featuring local performers.

Rudy's Barbershop

614 E. Pine St.

☎ *329-3008*

Feeling the urge to get a tattoo? Then head to Rudy's Barbershop, where, in addition to getting the icon of your choice emblazoned on your skin forevermore, you can get a haircut, too! You can also buy tickets for local shows here, as well.

ARO.space

925 E. Pike St.

☎ *320-0424*

The ultimate dance- and techno-music experience until the break of dawn, ARO.space essentially caters to a gay clientele, though "straights" are also welcome. This fabulous night club, where the hippest of dancing queens hang out, also offers electronic- and techno-music concerts, with bands like Daft Punk performing here on a regular basis.

Neighbours
1509 Broadway
☎ *324-5358*
A popular spot with Seattle's gay community, Neighbours features theme nights showcasing techno, disco, drum & bass as well as new wave. Though the place's main asset is its huge dance floor, patrons here can also play pool or pinball.

R Place
619 E. Pine St.
☎ *322-8828*
www.rplaceseattle.com
Spread over three floors, R Place is a friendly and laid-back mostly-male cruising hot spot with a unique atmosphere. Just the place for those wishing to play a few games of pool, watch videos or sing themselves hoarse imitating Madonna or George Michael during karaoke nights organized every Sunday on the top floor.

Beatbox
722 E. Pike St.
☎ *322-4024*
One of the most popular afterhours clubs in Seattle is the Beatbox, which draws a trendy young crowd. The place opens its doors at 10pm and stays open until the wee hours of the morning so that patrons can dance till they drop to old house, funk and all kinds of imaginable beats.

C.C. Attle's
1501 E. Madison St.
☎ *323-4017*
C.C. Attle's is the place for leather-clad men of all ages, who flock here in such numbers that pushing your way through the crowd to cruise and drink cheap beer can be quite a task.

Thumper's
1500 E. Madison St.
☎ *328-3700*
Just opposite (in more ways than one) C.C. Attle's, Thumper's is the complete antithesis of its neighbour, as somewhat older men come here to warm up by the fireplace at the entrance and drink a few beers in a casual, tavern-like ambiance.

Rosebud Restaurant & Bar
719 Pike St.
☎ *323-6636*
www.halcyon.com/sage/
In no way a reference to Orson Welles' famous Citizen Kane, the Rosebud mainly caters to women who come here to enjoy a few fresh dishes and happy hour, a very popular draw as drinks go for a paltry $2.

Four Angels Cafe
1400 14th Ave.
☎ *329-4066*
A gay and lesbian clientele frequents the Four Angels Cafe, where spoken-word performances and concerts are held on weekends. The place also serves a few sal-

Entertainment

ads and sandwiches, but closes at 11pm.

Elysian Brewery
1221 Pike St.
☎ *860-1920*
Come taste the beers brewed by the Elysian Brewery, a pub where the beer flows like water and a mixed crowd sits on chairs (if any are available!) or right on the floor to listen to local bands perform. The high ceilings and large windows give the place an airy atmosphere.

University District

Big Time Brewery & Alehouse
4133 University Way NE
☎ *545-4509*
To sample some home-brewed beers, head to the Big Time Brewery & Alehouse, where a slew of beers such as Atlas Amber, Coal Creek and Bhagwan Bitter disappear at the speed of light. The woodwork and small back room attract a Marlboro-smoking student crowd.

Spectator Sports

KeyArena
At 1st Ave. N. and N. Harrison St.
☎ *684-7200*
⇋ *684-7342*
*www.seattlesquare.com/seattlece
nter/keyarena.htm*
One of the hottest tickets in town is for the SuperSonics,

Seattle's NBA team. Their local games are played at the KeyArena, where concerts are also held by many of today's biggest performers. The amphitheatre is also home to the Thunderbirds, part of the WHL (World Hockey League). Though this team is made up of young players aged 17 to 21, their games are just as exciting (if not more so) as those of their professional NHL counterparts.

Safeco Field
south of the Kingdome
201 S. King St.
☎ *346-4001*
☎ *(206) 682-2800*
Part of the American Baseball League, the Seattle Mariners now face their rivals at the brand-new Safeco Field ballpark, which opened on July 15, 1999. Mariners all-stars like Ken Griffey Jr., Alex Rodriguez and Jay Buhner offer a "grand-slam fest" to those who wish to take in a major-league baseball game under the open sky.

Kingdome
201 S. King St.
☎ *(206) 682-2800*
www.metrokc.gov/stadium
The Seattle Seahawks football team has the home-field advantage at the Kingdome, which opened in 1977 but is slated to close in January 2000. From then on, the Seahawks will play local games at Safeco

Field, located just south of the Kingdome.

Festivals and Annual Events

Revellers have a slew of festivals and events to choose from all year round in Seattle (see the list following listing). It is advisable to contact the various organizations responsible for the exact dates of a particular event as these change every year.

January

2000 Seattle Boat Show
last week of January
$7.50
3-day pass - $9.95
☎ *634-0911*
www.seattle.boatshow.com
This boat show is held in two places simultaneously, namely at the New Exhibition Center (201 S. King St.) and Pier 66 (2205 Alaskan Way).

Chinese New Year's Celebration
mid-January
☎ *382-1197*
A parade featuring traditional Chinese dragons and various activities winds its way through the city, especially in the International District.

Martin Luther King Jr. Day
mid-January
☎ *684-7284*
Festivities at the Seattle Center honour the memory of outspoken civil-rights leader Dr. Martin Luther King Jr.

February

Northwest Flower & Garden Show
first week of February
☎ *789-5333*
☎ *800-229-6311*
www.gardenshow.com/nw/ index.html
Held at the Washington State Convention & Trade Center (*at Pike St. and 9th Ave.*), this annual exhibition is one of the city's most popular, having drawn more than 80,000 people in 1999.

Festival Sundiata
mid-February
free admission
Seattle Center
☎ *684-7200*
The three-day Festival Sundiata (pronounced Soon-jah-tah) celebrates every aspect of African-American culture with exhibitions and live entertainment. Though admission to the festival itself is free, there is an entry charge for some concerts.

Entertainment

Fat Tuesday
mid-February
Pioneer Square
☎ *622-0209*
Seattle has its very own week-long Mardi Gras, during which the historic district feels much like Louisiana.

March

Irish Week
mid-March
☎ *(425) 865-9134*
www.irishclub.org/stpats.htm
About a dozen events, including an Irish film festival and a Celtic-music festival, are organized during the week leading up to St. Patrick's Day.

Annual Oyster Olympics
late March, $65
3:30pm to 9pm
Anthony's HomePort
6135 Seaview Ave NW
☎ *286-1309*
Oyster lovers attend this bivalve blowout to feast on the slithery little molluscs, of course, but also to see the "enchanted-oyster magician" and watch the "oyster fashion show"!

April

Seattle Cherry Blossom
mid-April
Seattle Center
☎ *684-7200*
This festival celebrates Japanese art and traditions, allowing participants to do such things as attend a tea ceremony and admire the works of brilliant calligraphists.

May

Opening Day of Yachting Season
first Saturday in May
Seattle Yacht Club
1807 E. Hamlin St.
☎ *325-1000*
www.seattleyachtclub.org
Some 200,000 people attend the opening day of sailing season, when yachts and kayaks hit the waters of Montlake Cut.

Maritime Week Waterfront
mid-May
from Pier 48 to Pier 70
☎ *443-3830*
Two weeks of festivities are held on the waterfront, including maritime competitions and concerts.

Seattle International Film Festival
mid-May to early June
$7.50
six-film pass $39
one-week pass $125
☎ *324-9996*
≠ *324-9998*
www.seattlefilm.com/siff/default
American and foreign films are screened during this citywide festival (*General Cinema Pacific Place 11 Theater, Cinerama Theater, The Egyptian Theater, Harvard Exit Theater and Broadway Performance Hall*). The

festival celebrated its 25th anniversary in 1999 and since 1995 has held a forum for film-makers to discuss their craft.

University District Street Fair
mid-May
During this great fair, held in the streets of the university district, students and merchants offer goods and refreshments.

Northwest Folklife Festival
May 26 to 29, 2000
May 25 to 28, 2001
free admission
305 Harrison St.
☎ *684-7300*
⇌ *684-7190*
www.nwfolklife.org/folklife
This festival is one of the nation's biggest events celebrating traditional art. More than 6,000 regional and international artists and performers participate, sharing their traditions with some 200,000 visitors through live music, visual art, dance, etc. at the Seattle Center. Workshops are also offered.

Pike Place Market Festival
Memorial Day weekend
Several activities at the centre of this festival remind us that this historic landmark was almost razed to the ground roughly thirty years ago. Adults can check out the blues and jazz shows featured while kids enjoy making puppets, necklaces or kites. Arts, crafts and

cooking are also integral parts of the festival.

Greek Festival
late May to early June
St. Demetrios Greek Orthodox Church
2100 Boyer Ave.
☎ *325-4347*
☎ *706-4144*
greece.org/FDF/sympseat1.html
As you may have guessed, Greek culture is highlighted during this festival with organized symposiums and workshops.

June

Seattle International Music Festival
mid-June to early July
☎ *233-0993*
Chamber music, and classical music in general, resound throughout Seattle during this two-week festival.

Fremont Fair
mid-June
In downtown Fremont, near the Washington State Ship Canal
☎ *633-4409*
www.speakeasy.org/frefair
This annual community fair, which attracts artists and performers of all stripes, is the most eclectic celebration in Seattle. It features the latest musical talents and handicrafts. Several non-profit organizations also participate in the fair, providing information about their social functions. The liveliest of crowds attend

Entertainment

this event, with more than 100,000 people visiting it every year.

Northwest Microbrewery Festival

Father's Day weekend
From Seattle, take Highway 90 East until Exit 22 for Preston/Fall City. Drive through Preston to Fall City. Once you reach a Y-shaped lane, turn left and pass the green bridge. The Herbfarm, which hosts the festival, is located about 1km farther.
☎ *784-2222*
☎ *800-866-4372*
www.nwbrewfest.com
Microbrew aficionados come to celebrate the summer season by chugging down the beers of over 50 wonderful Northwest microbreweries, which have absolutely nothing in common with the likes of Bud.

July

Bite of Seattle

mid-July
free admission
Seattle Center
☎ *684-7200*
More than 400,000 people attend this food festival to sample inexpensive little dishes (*all of which are priced under $5*), provided by 50-odd restaurateurs just waiting to dazzle you with their culinary treats!

August

ArtsBallard

mid-August
☎ *782-4596*
www.inballard.com
This festival, whose theme is Industrializingart, features live music, spoken word, theatre and films projected on a giant screen in the streets of Ballard.

Seattle Boats Afloat Show

last week of August
$6
Wed to Fri noon to 8pm, Sat 10am to 8pm, Sun 10am to 6pm
Shilshole Bay Marina
7000 Seaview Ave. NW
www.seattle-boatshow.com
This boat show features yachts and booths staffed by specialists providing information about boating.

September

Bumbershoot

Labor Day weekend
☎ *281-7788*
www.bumbershoot.com
This arts festival beautifully rounds off the summer season. Indeed, more than 2,000 regional, national and international artists and performers participate, including musicians, artisans and writers, the whole shebang taking place at the Seattle Center over four days. A one-day pass goes

for $14 ($10 in advance), a two-day pass for $18, while a four-day pass will set you back $32.

October

Coffee Fest
late October
Seattle Center Exhibition Hall
☎ *232-2982*
The American coffee capital is clearly required to have a "caffeine festival". The Coffee Fest takes place at the Seattle Center, introducing visitors to the roasting process.

November

Bon Marché Holiday Parade
late November
Westlake Center
☎ *506-7556*
Downtown Seattle celebrates the start of the Christmas season with a huge tree illuminating Westlake Center and a Santa Claus parade winding its way along 5th Avenue to the great delight of children.

December

New Year's Eve
December 31st
Space Needle
☎ *443-2111*
All of Seattle gathers at the Space Needle to ring in the new year.

Shopping

S eattle positively bursts at the seams with lovely shops where buying clothes or shoes is like a dream come true.

I n fact, everywhere you look there are shops, especially in the downtown area. This chapter will help you find your way around this shopping maze, where "shop-till-you-drop" consumers will think that they are in paradise.

Shopping Centres

Broadway Market
Broadway E., between E. Harrison St. and E. Republican St.
In the heart of the gay district is the Broadway Market, a shopping centre with trendy shops, restaurants and a multiplex cinema.

City Center
1420 5th Ave.
☎ 624-8800
While at the City Center, shoppers can admire glassware from the **Pilchuck School**. Located all over the shopping centre, these pieces impart a lofty cachet to this den of consumption. Also here, of course, are lovely shops such as

Benetton (see p 236) and Ann Taylor (see p 235), as well as a multiplex cinema.

Rainier Square
1301 5th Ave.,
Between 4th & 5th Avenues and Union Street and Universtiy Streets
☎ 628-5050
The four-floor Rainier Square shopping centre houses such shops as

Channel 9 Store (see p 228) and Eddie Bauer (see p 236). Also on site are a few good restaurants as well as a museum of Native-American art.

Westlake Center
at 4th Ave. and Pine St.
☎ *467-1600*

The Westlake Center is the place to take the Monorail (see p 125), which goes to Seattle Center. The place also has scores of shops, including the Disney Store (see p 229), Brentano's Bookshop (see p 231) and Jacob Laurent, SM (see p 233), which sells attractive and original watches.

Uwajimaya
519 6th Ave. S.
☎ *624-6248*
☎ *800-889-1928*
⇒ *624-6915*

Located in the International District, the sprawling Uwajimaya market place harbours numerous restaurants and Asian arts-and-crafts shops.

Pacific Place
600 Pine St.
☎ *405-2655*
www.pacificplaceseattle.com

A brand-new addition to the Seattle landscape, Pacific Place, located between Pine Street and Olive Way to the south and north and 6th and 7th Avenue to the west and east, boasts over 50 rather preppy shops. Among these are clothing

stores for children, women and men and a Barnes & Noble bookstore (see p 230), as well as a multiplex cinema.

University Village
2673 NE University Village Mall
☎ *523-0622*

University Village is probably the most appealing shopping centre in the city. Located in the University District, it is more festive looking than its downtown counterparts. Among the shops to be found here are a Gap store, a Barnes & Noble bookshop (see p 230) and an Eddie Bauer outlet (see p 236).

Au Bon Marché
1601 3rd Ave., at Pine St.
☎ *344-2121*

Founded in 1890, the Au Bon Marché shopping centre offers clothing for the whole family, as well as a host of beauty products and children's toys.

Art Galleries

A real art craze hit Seattle a few years ago. This craze combined with the opening of new art galleries and the successful work of the Pilchuck Glass School has carried Seattleites away in a search for the inexpressible. The city even instituted the Gallery Walk, which takes place on the first Thursday of every month, when both

This pagoda, a gift from the city of Taipei to the city of Seattle, is located in Hing Hay Park in the International District.
- *Nick Gunderson SKCCVB*

Seattle's monorail, which starts at the Westlake Center, was built for the 1962 World's Fair.
- *SKCCVB*

The Space Needle towers above everything else
in the "Princess of the Northwestern United States". - *Camirique*

locals and visitors have free access to some 15 art galleries. What's more, alcoholic refreshments (wine and beer) and nibbles (sandwiches and pâté) are sometimes offered as well. An added bonus: the Seattle Art Museum also offers visitors free access during Gallery Walk. Listed below are the Pioneer Square galleries that participate in Gallery Walk:

Azuma Gallery
530 1st Avenue South
Seattle, WA 98104
☎ *622-5599*

Bryan Ohno Gallery
155 South Main Street
Seattle, WA 98104
☎ *667-9572*

Collusion
163 South Jackson Street
Seattle, WA 98104
☎*657-5209*

D'Adamo/Hill Gallery
307 Occidental Avenue South
Seattle, WA 98104
☎ *652-4414*

Emerald City Fine Arts
317 1st Avenue South
Seattle, WA 98104
☎ *623-1550*

Flury & Company
322 1st Avenue South
Seattle , WA 98104
☎ *587-0260*

Foster/Whyte Gallery
123 South Jackson Street,
Seattle, WA 98104
☎ *622-2833*
1420 5th Avenue, Suite 214
Seattle, WA 98101
☎ *340-8025*

G. Gibson Gallery
122 South Jackson Street, Suite 200
Seattle, WA 98104
☎ *587-4033*

Garde Rail Gallery
312 1st Avenue South, #5
Seattle, WA 98104
☎ *623-3004*

Glasshouse Studio Gallery
311 Occidental Avenue South
Seattle, WA 98104
☎ *682-9939*

Greg Kucera Gallery
212 3rd Avenue South
Seattle, WA 98104
☎ *624-0770*

Kurt Lidke Gallery
318 2nd Avenue South,
Seattle, WA 98104
☎ *623-5082*

Lead Gallery
1022 1st Avenue,
Seattle, WA 98104
☎ *623-3034*

Linda Hodges Gallery
410 Occidental Avenue South,
Seattle, WA 98104
☎ *624-3034*

Northwest Fine Woodworking
101 South Jackson Street,
Seattle, WA 98104
☎ *625-0542*

Shopping

Stonington Gallery
119 South Jackson Street,
Seattle, WA 98104
☎ *405-4040*

Tule Gallery
316 1st Avenue South
Seattle, WA 98104
☎ *748-9904*

Lisa Harris Gallery
1922 Pike Place
☎ *443-3315*

This last gallery is one of
our favourites. Located in
Pike Place Market, the **Lisa
Harris Gallery** exhibits paintings by local and international artists. At press time,
a very austere exhibit was
featured, recalling the
works of Ernst Ludwig
Kirchner, one of the founders of the German *Die
Brücke* (The Bridge) expressionist art movement.

Travel Accessories

La Valise Luggage
1902 4th Ave.
☎ *340-0066*
University Village
☎ *525-9055*
Should you be unfortunate
enough to have your lug-
gage stolen, you can always
find some measure of con-
solation at **La Valise Luggage**,
which specializes in good-
quality attaché cases and
leather suitcases.

Antiques and Curios

Antique Importers
closed Sun
640 Alaskan Way
☎ *628-8905*
Located in front of Pier 54,
the hodge-podge of old-
fangled objects that is Antique Importers has no
equal when it comes to
finding bygone articles like
a wardrobe, a wooden ten-
nis racket or a magician's
trunk.

Ye Olde Curiosity Shop
Pier 54, 1001 Alaskan Way
☎ *682-5844*
The best-known curio shop
in Seattle is unquestionably
Ye Olde Curiosity Shop,
where mummies and
shrunken heads upstage
more "current" articles.

Rugs and Arts of Asia
213 1st Ave. S.
☎ *622-0102*
Pioneer Square has several
rug shops such as Rugs and
Arts of Asia, a large, high-
ceilinged store where you
can acquire - what else?
Asian handicrafts and huge
rugs.

Jewellery and Deluxe Accessories

Goldman's Jewelers
1521 1st Ave.
☎ 682-0237
www.goldmansjewelers.com
Goldman's Jewelers' pieces are made with finesse and grace. Consumers seeking simplicity can purchase plain, unadorned items, the jeweler having a penchant for classical and more-minimalist shapes.

Swissa
1518 5th Ave.
☎ 625-9202
⇄ 625-0215
www.swissa.com
In business since 1973, this family firm makes gold and platinum rings, pendants and earrings. Diamonds are also front and centre at this jeweller's shop, renowned for its reasonable prices.

Ben Bridge Jewelers
At 4th Ave. and Pike St.
☎ 628-6800
Another jeweller's where you'll find everything to satisfy your "better half", Ben Bridge Jewelers, founded in 1912, is conveniently located at the corner of two of the busiest streets in town.

Hats

Eclipse Hat Shop
1517 1st Ave.
☎ 623-2926
Sharon Hagerty, owner of the Eclipse Hat Shop, restores and repairs old hats, transforming them into wonderful headgear for both women and men. New hats are also available.

Shoes

Clog Factory
217 1st Ave. S.
☎ 682-CLOG
⇄ 624-1617
If you're looking for reasonably priced, comfortable shoes, head to the Clog Factory, which offers a good selection of **Kickers** and **Doc Martens**. Also up for grabs are clogs, of course, and all manner of hip footwear.

Chocolate Shops

Godiva Chocolatier
400 Pine St., Suite 214
☎ 622-0280
Don't know what to bring back for your sweetheart? Not to worry, Godiva should do the trick. Indeed, this chocolate-maker has long had a rock-solid reputation in North America for its top-of-the-range chocolates.

Shopping

Bernard C. Chocolates
1420 5th Ave.
☎ *340-0396*
Those with a craving for pralines and Belgian chocolate need look no further than Bernard C. Chocolates, which has garnered a multitude of awards for its quality goodies. A chocoholic's dream come true!

Cigars

Cigar Pavilion
1501 Western Ave., Suite 301
☎ *621-1980*
On the way down the stairs leading to the Waterfront from Pike Place Market (see p 37, 106), stands the Cigar Pavilion, a treasure trove of everything to do with cigars. Several brands of cigarettes are also available.

Condoms and Sex Shops

Cigar Pavilion
1501 Western Ave., Suite 301
☎ *621-1980*
The most original condom store in Seattle is the Cigar Pavilion (let's dispense with the obvious jokes, shall we?), whose motto is "Save the Humans". The place stocks condoms of all aphrodisiacal flavours and colours, but also sells run-of-the-mill "rubbers" for more-circumspect stud muffins.

Toys in Babeland
711 E. Pike St.
☎ *328-2914*
Conquer your inhibitions and drop by Toys in Babeland, a decidedly atypical sex shop. Indeed, the glum atmosphere usually found in such establishments is refreshingly absent here, so go ahead and admire or perhaps buy whatever gadget turns you on.

Convenience Stores

Louie's on the Pike
1926 Pike Place Market
☎ *443-1035*
⇌ *443-0389*
At Louie's on the Pike, you'll find everything you need to get by: cheap wine, crackers, chips, and even imported beer! In short, a good, convenient place in the heart of the historic market.

Eclectic

Channel 9 Store
1308 4th Ave., at Union St.
☎ *682-8198*
2560 NE University Village
☎ *526-5074*
Not to be confused with the famous perfume, Channel 9 Store sells travel guides, magnetic poetry and lunar charts! This charming store donates some of its proceeds to KCTS, the local public-television station.

Florist

R.D. Adams Flowers
1001 4th Ave., Suite 525
☎ *623-9649*
☎ *800-753-5695*
⇌ *340-1304*
www.rdavidadams.com
There's nothing better than a bouquet of flowers to brighten up a rainy day. And R.D. Adams Flowers is the best choice when it comes to buying lovely roses, whether for yourself or that special someone...

Toys and Board Games

Westlake Disney Store
400 Pine St., Suite 238
☎ *622-3323*
Those looking to please little tots could do worse than buying a Mickey Mouse or Goofy toy at the Westlake Disney Store, where the brainchildren of Donald Duck's famous creator are sold at reasonable prices.

Turn Off the TV
400 Pine St., Suite 230
☎ *521-0564*
One of the most unique stores in Seattle is without a doubt Turn Off the TV, which, as its name suggests, advocates shunning the "boob tube" in favour of board games. The place offers educational games, puzzles and interactive games.

FAO Schwarz
1420 5th Ave.
☎ *442-9500*
⇌ *343-9040*
www.faoschwarz.com
Remember the toy store Macauley Culkin ventured into during his improbable trip to New York City in *Home Alone 2: Lost in New York?* Though more modest, Seattle's FAO Schwarz, with its huge teddy bear occupying a place of honour outside the store, is sure to tickle children pink. Among the cornucopia of toys here are Star Wars figures, which you can purchase for your kids or simply keep for yourselves!

Warner Bros. Studio Store
1516 5th Ave.
☎ *467-1810*
⇌ *467-9728*
The Disney Store's greatest rival is probably the Warner Bros. Studio Store, a colossal icon of Daffy Duck gracing the entrance to the emporium. Cartoon lovers can stock up on shirts, pajamas and other items emblazoned with the images of Bugs Bunny, Elmer Fudd and the like.

Shopping

Newspapers

Read All About It
At 1st Ave. and Pike St.
☎ *624-0140*
Those looking to read foreign newspapers should
find fulfillment at the Read
All About It newsstand.

Lamps

Antique Lighting Company
1000 Lenora St., Suite 314,
at Boren Ave.
☎ *622-8298*
⇄ *233-0237*
The Antique Lighting Com-
pany stocks an impressive
array of lamps of all kinds,
and its staff is sure to find
you a chandelier or ceiling
light to add that crowning
touch to your living room
or bedroom's décor.

Z Gallerie
1308 4th Ave., at Union St.
☎ *749-9906*
Located in the heart of
Rainier Square (see p 119,
223), Z Gallerie boasts one
of the city's best selections
of furnishings, lamps,
knick-knacks and kitchen-
ware. This large store will
please those who prefer not
to be pestered by overly
attentive service...

Bookshops and Music Stores

Barnes & Noble
600 Pine St., Suite 107
☎ *264-0156*
⇄ *264-0489*
2700 NE University Village
☎ *517-4107*
Located in the brand-new
Pacific Plaza Mall (p 224) ,
Barnes & Noble is probably
the largest bookstore of its
kind in Seattle. Spread over
two huge floors, the sheer
size of the place pretty
much ensures you'll find
any book you're looking
for. If you're in the market
for titles by Seattle authors,
ask a salesclerk to steer you
toward the works of Tess
Gallagher, Tom Robbins,
Ann Rule and Earl Emerson.

Beyond the Closet Bookstore
518 E. Pike St.
☎ *322-4609*
Positively the biggest
gay/lesbian/bisexual/trans-
gender bookshop in Seattle,
Beyond the Closet Book-
store not only stocks books
by "queer" authors, but
biographies and safe-sex
guides, as well.

BLMF
1501 Pike Place, Suite 324
☎ *621-7894*
On the third basement level
of Pike Place Market, the
BLMF bookshop offers a
good range of secondhand
books dealing with every-
thing from contemporary

music and esotericism to cooking and biographies. The bookshop is also used for literary discussion groups and readings.

Borders Books & Music
1501 4th Ave.
☎ 622-4599
☎ 622-6799
⇌ 622-8570
Definitely one of the best bookshops in Seattle, Borders Books & Music follows in the footsteps of Barnes & Noble, offering scores upon scores of books covering every subject under the sun. Also available are the latest CDs from popular artists such as Céline Dion and Cypress Hill.

Brentano's
222 Westlake Center
400 Pine St.
☎ 467-9626
The Mayflower Park Hotel (see p 158) is connected to the Westlake Center, where you can browse through the collection of books at Brentano's. The bookshop carries several travel guides on the region as well as best-sellers, thrillers and horror novels.

Disc Go Round
532 Queen Anne Ave. N.
☎ 285-4605
111 Broadway E.
☎ 323-7374
4527 University Way NE
☎ 632-7713
If you've got a soft spot for the 1980s and are really into the glum-cum-neon music for which the decade is famous, head straight to Disc Go Round. For half the going rate, this alternative record shop sells albums from bands like The Smiths, Siouxsie and the Banshees and other 1980s British icons as well as Björk's more recent remixes.

Elliott Bay Book Company
101 S. Main St.
☎ 624-6600
⇌ 343-9558
www.elliottbaybook.com
Founded in 1973 by Edgar Carr, the Elliott Bay Book Company is the Mecca of Seattle bookstores, offering a mishmash of all styles. This sublime bookshop, walled in by very warm and cozy exposed brick, is comprised of five rooms of books varying from fiction to religion to psychology to children's literature. Numerous book readings and autographing sessions by famous authors are held here as well. Bookworms can enjoy a coffee as they leaf through a chapter at the basement coffee shop, the Elliott Bay Café (see p 231).

Left Bank Books
92 Pike St.
☎ 622-0195
www.leftbankbooks.com
Seattle's very own left-wing bookshop, Left Bank Books stocks numerous books about different ethnic groups, gays and lesbians, left-wing politics, etc. Also

Shopping

to be found here are shirts emblazened with cutting feminist captions and names of blues bands. A good section is devoted to Beat literature, women's studies, fitness, nutrition and African Americans. Journalism, jazz, cinema, children's books and poetry are also a prominent feature of this unrivalled bookshop.

Marco Polo Travel Resource
713 Broadway E.
☎ *860-3736*
Those in search of maps can find their way to Marco Polo, which also sells travel guides. This concern serves as a travel agency, too.

Metsker Maps of Seattle
702 1st Ave.
☎ *623-8747*
Another travel bookshop, Metsker Maps of Seattle predictably offers a wide range of maps, as well as a few travel guides.

Sub Pop Records
1514 Pike Place, Suite 14
☎ *652-4356*
⇄ *441-8441*
www.subpop.com
Sub Pop Records is the production house that launched Nirvana, among other bands. Its small store exclusively stocks record-ings by the indie bands it represents and distributes: needless to say that here, nonconformity reigns su-preme. Adorned with a multitude of photographs of

musicians discovered by the company, this alternative music shop is the hangout of the Seattle music crowd.

Tooth & Nail
108 Occidental Ave. S.
☎ *624-4211*
⇄ *624-4207*
www.toothandnail.com/thestore
A mecca for Seattle counter-culture is the Tooth & Nail music shop, which prides itself on stocking the latest punk and contemporary releases as well as cult-vinyl offerings. This is the place to dig up records by bands such as Black & White World, Fluffy, Acoustic Shock, Windy Lyre, Slava Compilation, Wigtop or Breakfast With Amy, not to mention demos and CDs of myriad local bands.

Tower Books
every day 9am to midnight
20 Mercer St.
☎ *283-6333*
⇄ *285-2118*
Tower Books, a branch of the U.S. chain noted for the strategic location of its stores in major U.S. cities, boasts one of the best se-lections of books. History books, bestsellers, novels as well as the latest recorded hits, are offered at decent prices.

Tower Records/Videos
500 Mercer St.
☎ *283-4456*
Just northeast of Seattle Center is the Tower

Records[/Videos outlet, where the latest pop-chart and alternative underground hits make up the greater part of the selection offered. Tickets for Key Arena (see p 128) concerts are also available here.

University Bookstore
closed Sun
1225 4th Ave.
☎ *545-9230*
⇌ *224-9976*
4326 University Way NE
☎ *634-3400*
☎ *800-335-READ*
⇌ *634-0810*
www.bookstore.washington.edu
Though the University Bookstore carries the expected textbooks, novels and poetry anthologies can also be had at cut-rate prices.

University Bookstore Computers & Electronics
4300 University Way NE
☎ *656-4382*
Another outlet, University Bookstore Computers & Electronics specializes in computer manuals and software.

Wide World Books and Maps
1911 N. 45th St.
☎ *634-3453*
www.travelbooksandmaps.com
Founded in 1976, Wide World Books and Maps has the distinction of being the first travel bookshop in North America. With over 14,000 maps and travel guides in stock, this is a good place to purchase guides on the Seattle region or elsewhere. An on-line catalogue enables customers to buy the item of their choice via the Internet.

Watches

Jacob Laurent, SM
400 Pine St.
☎ *382-7259*
Located in Westlake Center (see p 224), the small Jacob Laurent, SM shop offers a wide selection of high quality watches for all budgets, the most popular brands being Kenneth Cole, ESQ, Roven Dino, Anne Klein and G-Shock.

Musical Instruments

Capitol Music Center
closed Sun
718 Virginia St.
☎ *622-0171*
☎ *800-426-9846*
⇌ *622-6983*
www.capitolmusiccenter.com
Music lovers will feel like kids in a candy store at the Capitol Music Center, where a good selection of guitars and keyboards await potential buyers. A good choice of karaoke and musical scores is also on hand.

Shopping

Snowboards

Snowboard Connection
604 Alaskan Way
☎ 467-8545
Though there are no ski resorts in the greater Seattle area, Snowboard Connection specializes in this popular local sport. The shop not only carries boots, clothing and boards, but also repairs and rents out equipment.

Hairdressing Salons

Vain
2222 2nd Ave.
☎ 441-3441
⇄ 441-3299
www.vain.com
For an unconventional haircut, scoot over to Vain, where you can also procure beauty products and wigs.

Souvenirs

Simply Seattle
1600 1st Ave.
☎ 448-2207
⇄ 448-9143
The Simply Seattle souvenir shop is the most interesting of its kind. The place sells a gaggle of books on the history of Seattle, in addition to standard shirts bearing the effigy of the Space Needle.

Sporting Goods

Seahawks EndZone Store
88 S. King St.
☎ 682-2900
⇄ 808-8314
Looking for shirts with the logo of the Seahawks, Seattle's pro football team? Then make a beeline for the Seahawks EndZone Store, located across from the now-defunct Kingdome, occupied by Safeco Field (see p 216) since July 1999.

Fairways & Greens Golf Center
1301 5th Ave.
☎ 341-9193
⇄ 341-9151
A must for golf aficionados, Fairways & Greens Golf Center is located on the pedestrian street in the Rainier Square Shopping Center (see p 119, 223). Sold here are a full range of golf clubs for all budgets as well as golf balls and the like. An on-site specialist, Kevin Wiggins, will help you find the equipment that best suits you.

Mariners Clubhouse
1800 4th Ave
☎ 346-4327
⇄ 346-4330
Looking for a Ken Griffey Jr. shirt? Then head to the Mariners Clubhouse, where shirts, pennants and even children's clothes emblazoned with the names of

the baseball team's players are sure to please both neophytes and die-hard fans of the American national sport.

Niketown
1500 6th Ave.
☎ 447-6453
⇄ 447-4725

Next to famed **Planet Hollywood**, Niketown peddles all the "swoosh"-laden sports gear Michael Jordan helped make (even more) famous worldwide. Conspicuous consumers can therefore stock up on the latest in pro sportswear, sneakers and caps here.

The North Face
1023 1st Ave.
☎ 622-4111

Lovers of the great outdoors will definitely want to check out the North Face store, which stocks an impressive array of backpacks, hiking gear, parkas, etc. These wares don't come cheap, however, so expect to part with quite a few greenbacks...

Patagonia
2100 1st Ave.
☎ 622-9700
☎ 800-336-9090
www.patagonia.com

The Patagonia store chain, which has outlets in Denver, New York City, Atlanta and other big U.S. cities, has long been synonymous with quality when it comes to outdoor gear. You'll find just about everything here,

be it shoes, sleeping bags or warm coats.

Children's Clothing

Lil' People
400 Pine St., Suite 324
☎ 623-4463
☎ 888-454-5736
⇄ 283-3753

If you're stumped as to what to bring back for your little tyke, pop round to Lil' People, which, according to many pundits, offers the best value for the money in town. You can purchase clothing for children up to eight years old, including overalls, brightly coloured skirts and hats in a wide variety of shapes and designs.

Women's Clothing

Talbots
413 Union St.
☎ 464-1456

Talbots will please women in search of chic, tasteful garments. The shop exclusively carries Seattle designer David Brooks' line of clothing, mainly beautiful corduroy pants, skirts and blouses.

Ann Taylor
1420 5th Ave.
☎ 623-4818

Located in the City Center shopping complex (see p 223), the Ann Taylor boutique exclusively sells the

Shopping

clothing line by the same name. The collection is essentially made up of very good-quality women's garments appreciated by both businesswomen and hip, city-dwelling gals.

BCBG
600 Pine St.
☎ *447-3400*
www.bcbg.com
The BCBG shop offers a beautiful range of women's apparel, as indicated by its French name (*Bon Chic, Bon Genre*).

Men's Clothing

Brooks Brothers
1335 5th Ave.
☎ *624-4400*
⇄ *233-9313*
Discerning businessmen in need of neck ties and power suits shop at Brooks Brothers. Founded in 1818, this landmark in business fashion also sells casual pants and shirts.

Europa for Men
1420 5th Ave., Suite 203
☎ *621-0350*
⇄ *587-0420*
Men concerned with their appearance may want to make a few purchases at the Europa for Men shop. Quality garments such as Coogi shirts and St. Croix woollens, as well as Torras & Spain leather togs, will satisfy the most demanding of consumers.

Unisex Clothing

Eddie Bauer
1330 5th Ave.
☎ *622-2766*
2720 University Village NE
☎ *527-2646*
www.eddiebauer.com
In business since 1920, the Eddie Bauer store has become an institution in America for women's and men's casual wear. Also available are household articles and walking shoes.

Burberrys
409 Pike St.
☎ *621-2000*
For classic clothing, nothing beats Burberrys' skirts and blouses or trench coats, for which the institution is famous.

Original Levi's Store
1500 6th Ave.
☎ *467-5152*
☎ *800-USA-LEVI*
⇄ *467-5154*
Those looking for a pair of jeans won't find better than at the Original Levi's Store, which - you guessed it - stocks nothing but the best-known brand of all.

Benetton
1420 5th Ave., Suite 210
☎ *382-9393*
⇄ *464-1166*
Hyped by its much-bally-hooed and decidedly striking ads, Benetton offers the customary range of baggy,

laid-back clothing in radiant or sobre colours.

Northwest Pendleton
closed Sun
1313 4th Ave.
☎ *682-4430*
The Northwest Pendleton chain of stores offers women's knits as well as pants and shirts for men. A store that caters to a forty-something clientele with an appreciation for quality casual clothing.

Nordstrom
1601 2nd Ave.
☎ *448-8522*
500 Pine St.
☎ *373-2111*
www.nordstrom.com
Shopping buffs are sure to find something at the Nordstrom store, which has clothing for women, men and children. There is no question as to the quality and quantity of the clothes here, and the very reasonable prices make this store a favourite with Seattleites.

Gap University Village
2730 University Village NE
☎ *525-1559*
The famous Gap store is strategically located in University Village (see p 224). Like its sister establishments, this outlet carries appealing, baggy or tight-fitting clothes appreciated by a rather young crowd.

Trendy Clothing

Experience
912 Alaskan Way
☎ *624-0960*
⇄ *624-0967*
www.experienceshoes.com
In the market for an ever-popular pair of Doc Martens? Then hotfoot it to Experience, where an incredible selection of shoes in tantalizing colours as well as just-short-of-outrageous clothing (perfect for ravers and dance-floor divas) are available at sometimes high, sometimes very affordable prices.

Retro Viva
1511 1st Ave.
☎ *624-2529*
After being greeted with a charming "Hello, Darling!", young fashion victims can browse through the second-hand goods on display here: sunglasses, shirts, T-shirts for ladies and gents as well as shoes. The ultra-cool service of the young, über-hip staff will please the most young at heart.

Banana Republic
500 Pike St.
☎ *622-2303*
⇄ *343-7080*
Housed in the former Coliseum Theater, now revamped from top to bottom, this Banana Republic outlet boasts fabulous-looking digs.

Shopping

The store features lovely garb for all occasions and there's always something on sale.

Wine and Spirits

Champion Wine Cellars
closed Sun
108 Denny Way
☎ *284-8306*
⇄ *483-6534*
Vintages from Washington State, France and Italy are skilfully displayed at Champion Wine Cellars, where the selection and prices are very enticing.

Pike and Western Wine Shop
☎ *441-1307*
⇄ *441-1308*
Established in the Pike Place Market area since 1975, the Pike and Western Wine Shop offers an assortment of wines and spirits from the Seattle area and beyond. Featured here, among other things, is a good choice of Merlot and Cabernet Sauvignon offerings.

Index

Index

Index

Travel Notes

Travel Notes

TRAVEL BETTER... TRAVEL THE NET

Visit our web site
to travel better...
to discover, to explore
and to enjoy more

www.ulysses.ca

ULYSSES
TRAVEL PUBLICATIONS
Travel better... enjoy more

Catalogue

Talk to us

Order

Distributors

History

Internet
Travel

_____

_____

_____

_____

_____

_____

_____

_____

_____

_____

_____

_____

_____

_____

_____

_____

_____

_____

_____

_____

_____

Travel Notes

Travel Notes

Other Ulysses Guides

US City Guides

Chicago
Home to a giant open-air museum of modern architecture and the
birthplace of electric blues: Chicago is all this and much more. This
guide leads you along its windy streets, through its lakefront parks
and into its ethnic neighbourhoods.
Claude Morneau
400 pages, 21 maps, 8 pages of colour photos
$19.95 CAN $14.95 US   £9.99
2-89464-058-7

Miami
With its fabulous Art Deco District, its futuristic downtown area
and its long beaches, Miami has become a great American city as
well as a Latin American centre. The full scoop on Miami's restaurants and nightlife. Excursions up the coast to Fort Lauderdale.
Alain Legault
336 pages, 20 maps, 8 pages of colour photos
$18.95 CAN $13.95 US   £9.99
2-89464-211-3

New Orleans
Complete coverage of this Louisianan city: its gastronomic delights,
its fascinating Mardi Gras festivities, its historic French Quarter, the
steam-boat cruises on the Mississippi and great jazz.
Richard Bizier, Roch Nadeau
256 pages, 14 maps
$17.95 CAN   £8.99
2-89464-074-9

New York City
An insightful cultural perspective with countless useful hints to
help vacationers and business travellers alike make the most of
their trip to the Big Apple. Walking tours of Manhattan, as well as
the surrounding boroughs.
François Rémillard
432 pages, 29 maps, 8 pages of colour photos
$19.95 CAN $14.95 US   £9.99
2-89464-088-9

Washington, Dc
Here is the Ulysses guide to the US capital, complete with tours of
the city's myriad museums and monuments. The city's ethnic
neighbourhoods and trendy nightspots are covered, as well as the
White House and Capitol Hill.
Lorette Pierson
336 pages, 17 maps, 8 pages of colour photos
$18.95 CAN $13.95 US   £9.99
2-89464-172-9

US State Guides

Louisiana
This guide reveals the rich history of Louisiana as it prepares
vacationers for a trip complete with delicious Cajun cuisine, grand
plantation-era mansions, Mardi Gras in New Orleans, the mysterious bayou and great jazz.
Richard Bizier
432 pages, 27 maps, 8 pages of colour photos, illustrations
$29.95 CAN   £14.99
2-89464-161-3

US Regions

The Beaches of Maine
Vacationers flock to the beaches and villages on the coast of Maine
each summer. With this pocket guide in your beach bag, the sandy
expanses around Ogunquit, Wells, Old Orchard, Kennebunk,
Portland and Freeport are at your fingertips.
Joël Pomerleau
128 pages, 6 maps
$12.95 CAN $9.95 US   £6.50
2-89464-066-8

Ulysses Green Escapes

Hiking in the Northeastern United States, 2 [nd] Edition
This practical guide covers the most beautiful hikes in the Northeastern US. With this one-of-a-kind book, the reader can choose
from a selection of more than 130 of the best hikes through Maine,
New Hampshire, Vermont and New York. Classification by degrees
of difficulty.
Yves Séguin
256 pages, 14 maps
$19.95 CAN $13.95 US   £8.99
2-89464-010-2

Western Canadian Guides

Calgary
Calgary is one of the fastest growing cities in North America. This
guide reveals the best of this dynamic Western city: museums,
parks, gardens, Olympic installations and the famous Stampede.
Jennifer McMorran
192 pages, 12 maps
$16.95 CAN $12.95 US   £8.99
2-89464-168-0
January 1999 (Canada); February 1999 (US & UK)

Vancouver, 2 nd Edition
This guide reveals the best of this young and vibrant metropolis.
Coverage of its multi-ethnic neighbourhoods, magnificent parks
and great restaurants is complemented by a detailed cultural
perspective.
Pierre Longnus, Éric Dumontier, Françcois Rémillard
208 pages, 15 maps
$17.95 CAN $12.95 US   £8.99
2-89464-120-6

Western Canada, 2 nd Edition
The only travel guide to cover both Alberta and British Columbia.
The Rocky Mountains, with their ski resorts and national parks, as
well as the metropolis of Vancouver, the burgeoning city of Calgary and a stop in Victoria, for a cup of tea!
Collective
496 pages, 45 maps, 8 pages of colour photos
$29.95 CAN $21.95 US   £14.99
2-89464-086-2

Order Form

ULYSSES TRAVEL GUIDES

☐ Atlantic Canada . . .	$24.95 CAN $17.95 US	☐ Lisbon	$18.95 CAN $13.95 US
☐ Bahamas	$24.95 CAN $17.95 US	☐ Louisiana	$29.95 CAN $21.95 US
☐ Beaches of Maine . .	$12.95 CAN $9.95 US	☐ Martinique	$24.95 CAN $17.95 US
☐ Bed & Breakfasts . . in Québec	$13.95 CAN $10.95 US	☐ Montréal	$19.95 CAN $14.95 US
☐ Belize	$16.95 CAN $12.95 US	☐ New Orleans	$17.95 CAN $12.95 US
☐ Calgary	$17.95 CAN $12.95 US	☐ New York City	$19.95 CAN $14.95 US
☐ Canada	$29.95 CAN $21.95 US	☐ Nicaragua	$24.95 CAN $16.95 US
☐ Chicago	$19.95 CAN $14.95 US	☐ Ontario	$27.95 CAN $19.95US
☐ Chile	$27.95 CAN $17.95 US	☐ Ottawa	$17.95 CAN $12.95 US
☐ Colombia	$29.95 CAN $21.95 US	☐ Panamá	$24.95 CAN $17.95 US
☐ Costa Rica	$27.95 CAN $19.95 US	☐ Peru	$27.95 CAN $19.95 US
☐ Cuba	$24.95 CAN $17.95 US	☐ Portugal	$24.95 CAN $16.95 US
☐ Dominican . . . . Republic	$24.95 CAN $17.95 US	☐ Provence - . . . . Côte d'Azur	$29.95 CAN $21.95US
☐ Ecuador and . . . . . . Galapagos Islands	$24.95 CAN $17.95 US	☐ Québec	$29.95 CAN $21.95 US
☐ El Salvador	$22.95 CAN $14.95 US	☐ Québec and Ontario with Via	$9.95 CAN $7.95 US
☐ Guadeloupe	$24.95 CAN $17.95 US	☐ Toronto	$18.95 CAN $13.95 US
☐ Guatemala	$24.95 CAN $17.95 US	☐ Vancouver	$17.95 CAN $12.95 US
☐ Honduras	$24.95 CAN $17.95 US	☐ Washington D.C. . .	$18.95 CAN $13.95 US
☐ Jamaica	$24.95 CAN $17.95 US	☐ Western Canada . .	$29.95 CAN $21.95 US

ULYSSES DUE SOUTH

☐ Acapulco	$14.95 CAN $9.95 US	☐ Cancun Cozumel . .	$17.95 CAN $12.95 US
☐ Belize	$16.95 CAN $12.95 US	☐ Puerto Vallarta	$14.95 CAN $9.95 US
☐ Cartagena . . . . (Colombia)	$12.95 CAN $9.95 US	☐ St. Martin and . . . . . St. Barts	$16.95 CAN $12.95 US

ULYSSES TRAVEL JOURNAL

☐ Ulysses Travel .... $9.95 CAN
   Journal $7.95 US
(Blue, Red, Green,
Yellow, Sextant)

☐ Ulysses Travel .... $14.95 CAN
   Journal 80 Days $9.95 US

ULYSSES GREEN ESCAPES

☐ Cycling in France .. $22.95 CAN
                 $16.95 US
☐ Cycling in Ontario . $22.95 CAN
                 $16.95 US

☐ Hiking in the ..... $19.95 CAN
   Northeastern U.S. $13.95 US
☐ Hiking in Québec .. $19.95 CAN
                 $13.95 US

Order Form

TITLE	QUANTITY	PRICE	TOTAL

Name _____

Address _____

_____

_____

Payment : ☐ Money Order ☐ Visa ☐ MasterCard

Card Number _____

Expiry date _____

Signature _____

Sub-total	
Postage & Handling	$8.00*
Sub-total	
G.S.T. in Canada 7%	
TOTAL	

ULYSSES TRAVEL
PUBLICATIONS
4176 St-Denis,
Montréal, Québec, H2W 2M5
(514) 843-9447 fax (514) 843-9448
www.ulysses.ca
*$15 for overseas orders

U.S. ORDERS:
GLOBE PEQUOT PRESS
P.O. Box 833,
6 Business Park Road,
Old Saybrook, CT 06475-0833
1-800-243-0495 fax 1-800-820-2329
www.globe-pequot.com